Jungian Film Studies

Jungian film studies is a fast-growing academic field, but Jungian and post-Jungian concepts are still new to many academics and film critics. Helena Bassil-Morozow and Luke Hockley present *Jungian Film Studies: The Essential Guide*, the first book to bring together all the different strands, issues and arguments in the discipline, and guide the reader through the various ways in which Jungian psychology can be applied to moving images.

Bassil-Morozow and Hockley cover a range of Jungian concepts including the collective unconscious, archetypes, the individuation process, alchemy, and signs and symbols, showing how they can be used to discuss the core cinematic issues such as narrative structure, gender, identity, genre, authorship and phenomenology. The authors argue that, as a place where the unconscious and conscious meet, cinema offers the potential for imagery that is psychologically potent, meaningful, and that plays a role in our personal psychological development.

This much-needed book, which bridges the space between Jungian concepts and traditional film theory, will be essential reading for scholars and students of Analytical Psychology, psychoanalysis, Jungian film studies, media, film and cultural studies, psycho-social psychology and clinical psychology. It will also appeal to analytical psychologists, psychotherapists and readers with an interest in film analysis.

Helena Bassil-Morozow, PhD, is a cultural philosopher, media and film scholar, and academic writer whose many publications include *Tim Burton: The Monster and the Crowd, The Trickster in Contemporary Film* and *The Trickster and the System: Identity and Agency in Contemporary Society* (all Routledge). She is currently working on several other Routledge projects. She is a Lecturer in Media and Communication at Glasgow Caledonian University, UK. www.hbassilmorozow.com.

Luke Hockley, PhD, is Research Professor of Media Analysis at the University of Bedfordshire, UK. He is a practising psychotherapist and is registered with the United Kingdom Council for Psychotherapy (UKCP). Luke is joint Editor in Chief of the *International Journal of Jungian Studies* (IJJS) and a member of the Advisory Board for the journal *Spring*. His publications include *Jung and Film 2*, *Somatic Cinema: The Relationship Between Body and Screen – a Jungian Perspective* and *The Happiness Illusion: How the Media Sold Us a Fairy Tale* (all Routledge). He lectures widely. www.lukehockley.com.

Jung: The Essential Guides
Series Editor: Luke Hockley
International Consultant: Susan Rowland

Accessing and understanding the work of C. G. Jung presents several challenges to readers who aren't formally trained in Analytical Psychology, from deciding which of his many volumes is most useful to them, to identifying and using the key concepts appropriately. The *Essential Guides* approach these challenges head-on. They offer those new to Jung an accessible and engaging introduction to the relevant theories and ideas in their discipline that are written by leaders in the field. The books also provide readers familiar with Jungian concepts with an insight into how his ideas can be applied outside the consulting room, to the arts, sciences and humanities.

www.routledge.com/mentalhealth/series/JEG

Jungian Film Studies
The essential guide
Luke Hockley and Helena Bassil-Morozow

Jungian Film Studies

The Essential Guide

Helena Bassil-Morozow and
Luke Hockley

Routledge
Taylor & Francis Group
LONDON AND NEW YORK

First published 2017
by Routledge
2 Park Square, Milton Park, Abingdon, Oxon OX14 4RN

and by Routledge
605 Third Avenue, New York, NY 10017

Routledge is an imprint of the Taylor & Francis Group, an informa business

British Library Cataloguing in Publication Data
A catalogue record for this book is available from the British Library

Library of Congress Cataloging in Publication Data
Names: Bassil-Morozow, Helena Victor, 1978- author. |
Hockley, Luke author.
Title: Jungian film studies : the essential guide /
Helena Bassil-Morozow and Luke Hockley.
Description: Milton Park, Abingdon, Oxon; New York, NY : Routledge, 2016. | Includes bibliographical references.
Identifiers: LCCN 2016027089| ISBN 9780415531443
(hardback : alk. paper) | ISBN 9780415531450 (pbk. : alk. paper) |
ISBN 9781315622231 (ebook)
Subjects: LCSH: Motion pictures—Psychologoical aspects. |
Jungian psychology.
Classification: LCC PN1995 .B2948 2016 | DDC 791.4301/9—dc23
LC record available at https://lccn.loc.gov/2016027089

ISBN: 978-0-415-53144-3 (hbk)
ISBN: 978-0-415-53145-0 (pbk)
ISBN: 978-1-315-62223-1 (ebk)

Typeset in Times New Roman
by Swales & Willis Ltd, Exeter, Devon, UK

This book is dedicated to the memory of Don Fredericksen – a pioneer and dear friend. 1946–2015.

Contents

Acknowledgements

There are many people we are grateful to and who have helped us in the preparation of this book. First a vote of thanks and gratitude go to Kate Hawes and Susannah Frearson at Routledge who have been unrelenting in their support of this project. As ever the unsung heroes of the publishing industry are owed a special thank you – our copyeditor Jonathan Hoare, our proofreader Julian Webb and our indexer Hilary Faulkner. To the designer of our amazing cover, Nigel Turner, we are truly grateful.

On a personal note Luke thanks Mary, his wife, for not grumbling over the missed weekends, and the sound of clattering computer keyboards late into the night resuming with the dawn chorus the following day.

Finally, our thanks go to the Research Institute of Media, Art and Performance (RIMAP) at the University of Bedfordshire, UK, who have so generously supported this research.

Acknowledgements

Introduction

Helena Bassil-Morozow and Luke Hockley

Jungian film studies is a fast-growing academic field. However, Jungian and post-Jungian concepts are still new to most academics and film critics. More often than not (and unsurprisingly) they neglect them in favour of the more familiar Freudian and Lacanian critical tools that they have been using for decades. Lacanian terminology in particular has become *de rigueur* in the academy as one of the primary frameworks that film theorists should know well (and employ systematically) despite its inherent and seemingly intentional lack of precision. Since the 1970s Lacanian film analysis has solidified into what amounts to an analytical establishment, while other psychoanalytic frameworks have been left relatively unexplored. This means that using the theories of C. G. Jung to analyse film narratives and the structures of cinema is the equivalent of thinking outside the academic box. It means to challenge the established norm of film theory. Throughout, this book will use the terms 'Jungian psychology' and 'Analytical Psychology' interchangeably. Jung coined the latter to distinguish his ideas from those of Freud's earlier psychoanalytic formulations. By finding points of correspondence and divergence with the established approaches, while at the same time emphasising the distinctive insights offered by Jungian approaches, this book will demonstrate the versatility and utility of Jungian theories as tools for the critical analysis of cinema.

Jungian film studies really took root at the start of the twenty-first century. Since 2001, the intervening years have seen the publication of numerous monographs that collectively have come to form the *corpus* of Jungian film theory. While hardly extensive, these volumes now exceed over thirty sole authored books and explore themes as diverse as directors, *auteur* theory, national identity, tricksters, phenomenology, production, textual analysis and reception theories. Indeed, we might say that Jungian film theory has dipped its toe into most of the areas that have been the concern of traditional film theory. The issue of diversity, coherence and the establishment of a definable body of knowledge with allied methodological approaches is one that will be returned to later in this introduction and repeatedly throughout the book. At this point it suffices to note that, as an expanding field, the volume of work in Jungian film studies is increasing, and the number of PhD theses concerned with Jung and cinema also continues to grow. As a subject, we are in a state of rude health.

Or are we? While not wishing to downplay the importance of this substantial body of work, in terms of sheer quantity it is dwarfed by the books that have been, and continue to be, concerned with psychoanalytic film theory in general, and in particular its Lacanian variation. Without doubt, in the academy the intricacies of Lacan, the striking parallels between his elaboration of *le stade du miroir* (the 'mirror phase') and the activity of watching a film continues to exert a fascination for the academic mind. This is not due to any hostility towards Jungian-orientated film theory; as noted above, it is more that Jungian concerns do not register on the intellectual radar of academic film studies. Here is not the place to assess why that is the case but psychoanalytic film theory has the advantage that it has a relatively well-defined set of terms and the objects of its study are reasonably well demarcated. It incorporates a series of theoretical approaches that, through Freudian and Lacanian lenses, sets out to understand and deconstruct the operations of the cinematic apparatus, the construction and encoding of films themselves, and their subsequent affective impact at the moment of reception. By contrast, Jungian film theory seems diffuse and unfocused – a miasma that floats alongside the more concrete and structural presence of psychoanalysis. It is enormously difficult to get any purchase on the subject and the answer to the dreadfully penetrating and simple question 'What *is* Jungian screen theory?' remains decidedly elusive.

Over the course of this book we will try to answer that question. We will do so in a decidedly Jungian manner, not by attempting a head-on definition but by circumambulating the question, by amplifying its themes and by gradually creating a web of interconnected meanings. As part of this undertaking we will also bring the different strands of Jungian film analysis together, and in so doing position it as a school of thought rather than a diffused set of ideas. Our intention is to allow new patterns to emerge, to offer fresh perspectives that provide useful and productive ways to understand films and our experiences of them.

Part I, 'Methods', contains chapters outlining the current state of Jungian film studies, and explains the importance of core Jungian concepts for cinema, television and media criticism, both popular and academic. Chapter 1, 'The context of Jungian film studies', deals with the history of the field, highlights its main issues and gives a brief overview of the career and research interests of several prominent Jungian film scholars.

Chapter 2, 'Using Jung to analyse visual narratives: tools and concepts', introduces key Jungian ideas and shows their significance for film studies: the individuation process, archetypes, alchemy, etc., which are invaluable concepts when dealing with the narrative aspect of films. The structuralist approaches of Joseph Campbell and Christopher Vogler are used to draw parallels between traditional narrative structures and Jung's theory of individuation – the process of becoming an individual in society. We will discuss the interpretive and symbolic value of such a structure, and show its positive qualities while also acknowledging its limitations. The chapter also includes a discussion of Jung's view of modernity and his assessment of the complexities of individuation in an age of mass communication. We argue that his writings on contemporary individuation (such as

'Modern Man in Search of a Soul') are indispensable for film studies, primarily because many cinematic narratives attempt to define the individual while at the same time providing a commentary on his or her relationship with society.

In addition, 'Tools and concepts' incorporates a Jungian angle on the ideas of the unconscious, projections and the nature and importance of images. With his emphasis on the psychological role of the image, Jung placed the visual above the linguistic. His 'Romantic' view of the unconscious throws light on the cinematic experience in general, and on the viewer's projective-introjective exchange with the moving image in particular. It shows how the fluid, ever-changing world of cinema and television is not unlike the fragmented, dissociated state of contemporary psychological life. This approach is also effective in explaining the affective power of cinema as a creative medium, as a 'collective experience' with powerful emotion-eliciting qualities.

Chapter 3, 'Jungian psychology: signs and symbols' explores Jung's understanding of signs and symbols and compares his views on this subject with those of Freud and the post-Freudians such as Jacques Lacan. We use James Hillman's interpretation of the symbolic, as well as Don Fredericksen's discussion (1979; 1980) of Jung's treatment of signs and symbols, to explain the difference between Jung's 'symbols' and Freud's metaphors/signs – a distinction that is ingrained in their respective psychologies. The symbol/metaphor dichotomy is the central point of discussion of the relationship between Jungian theories and semiotics. It is argued that this distinction can be used effectively to examine on-screen semiotic structures such as visual metonymies and synecdoches. In defining 'Jungian semiotics', we compare it to the ideas of several leading Western semioticians.

Part II, 'Applications', shows concrete ways of using Jungian theory to analyse moving images. In this part we take a Jungian look at the cornerstones of traditional film studies: genre, *auteur* theory, gender and stereotype, intertextuality, narrative structure, etc. and their interrelationships. Setting the scene, Chapter 4, 'Combining different methodologies in visual narrative analysis', endeavours to define the place of Analytical Psychology amongst other theories. Jungian concepts can be successfully applied to visual narratives in conjunction with anthropology, sociology, psychoanalytic theories, literary criticism and traditional film theory. We argue that Jungian film analysis neither replaces these methodologies nor directly competes with them, but can serve to fill the existing gaps and thus enrich the interpretive experience. For instance, while Jung and his early followers wrote extensively on the figure of the trickster, Victor Turner and Arnold Van Gennep's rites of passage concept takes the analysis of cinematic tricksters to an entirely new level. Both frameworks can be used to complement each other in the creation of a coherent and clear idea of the trickster figure as a psycho-anthropological driving force. Similarly, Jung's concepts of the individuation and collective unconscious provide an interesting angle on the so-called 'cinematic apparatus theory' (Jean-Louis Baudry, Christian Metz, etc.).

Chapter 5, 'The auteur theory: a Jungian view', focuses on the '*auteur*' and looks at the parallels between existing theories of authorship and Jungian approaches to film directors. It also reflects on the appeal of the *auteur* theory to a Jungian film critic. Importantly, it reveals Jungian film theory's profound interest in the personal vision of particular directors, despite its reputation as a body of theory that deals exclusively with popular narratives. We will explore the implications of using Jungian psychology to look at the work of individual directors, as in the Jungian studies of Nicolas Roeg (Izod, 1992), Howard Hawks (Branson, 1987) and Tim Burton (Bassil-Morozow, 2010).

In Chapter 6, 'Film genres and archetypes', we discuss the ways in which genre theory and archetype theory might usefully be used to interrogate each other. We also draw parallels between archetypes, symbols and film/television genres. Questions of intertextuality are reconceptualised using the idea of 'institutional amplification' in which the imagery and the themes of a film are regarded as 'amplified' in marketing material, movie posters, interviews and websites. In so doing, we show how these paratexts refer back to the source material and shape our understanding of the films.

Chapter 7, 'Jungians vs. Freudians: gender, identity and sexuality on screen', offers an opportunity to compare post-Freudian and non-psychoanalytic critiques of cinematic representations of gender, identity and sexuality (Laura Mulvey and other feminists, Mary Ann Doane, Kaja Silverman, etc.) with those offered by Jung and the post-Jungian camp. It is often thought that Jungian film analysis cannot offer an effective critique of the social because it is rooted in psycho-anthropological abstractions such as archetypes and the collective unconscious. We attempt to formulate a coherent framework of Jungian and post-Jungian concepts of the social and its influence on the individual. In doing so, we touch on questions of national, as well as personal, identity, and explore the dynamic between the social and the personal. The screenwriting industry is now significantly influenced by Christopher Vogler's *The Writer's Journey* (1998), which probably explains why more female protagonists in film and television than ever undertake journeys previously reserved for the male sex. We argue that Jungian theory is the right theoretical tool for the discussion of this new phenomenon.

Chapter 8, 'The body: phenomenology and cinema', looks at the human perception of moving images and the ways in which we assign meaning to cinematic narratives. The Jungian phenomenological approach concerns the ambiguity of the moving image and our 'layered' perceptions of it. This chapter examines the existing academic writing on phenomenology in film. Augmenting those established arguments, we argue that the intersubjective space – the distance between the screen and the viewer – is filled with 'the third image' that constitutes our own, unique and profoundly personal perception of the events happening on screen.

Why Jungian theory?

Psychoanalytic and psychological theories have occupied a significant place in film and media criticism almost from the beginning of the twentieth century, when both psychoanalysis and the moving image were becoming established.

Products of modernity, both have reflected the state of the modern psyche in their own unique ways. A rich and diverse vocabulary has been developed to describe various aspects of both the form and content of visual narratives. The Oedipus complex is Freud's biggest contribution to visual image analysis, but the subsequent work of Melanie Klein, Jacque Lacan, Wilfred Bion and others has also permeated film criticism for decades. Terms such as, 'the other', transference, repetition, sublimation, the gaze, the mirror stage and so forth have been divorced from their therapeutic contexts and used to discuss narratives, visuals and the socio-political aspect of films and cinema. Film criticism has employed Freudian terminology alongside definitions and concepts borrowed from semiotics and linguistics, to cover some of the gaps in the professional jargon that was still under construction, still lacking confidence and precision of expression. Psychoanalytic and linguistic terms made film studies sound more serious and 'scientific' and they gave it a credibility that was important for the budding discipline.

In addition, filmmakers themselves have been actively employing psychoanalytic findings to inform their practice from the 1920s onwards. For instance, when devising their courageous and shocking project, *Un Chien Andalou* (1929), the young Luis Buñuel and Salvador Dalí kept in mind Freud's definitions of sexuality and aggression. Besides, psychoanalysis allowed them to discuss the political aspect of all these issues, and the ways in which the repression of instincts is rooted in capitalist ideology and is carefully managed by it. Human passions are dangerous and difficult to control once they escape, which means that political systems needs to deal with them before any trouble starts. The merger of Marxism with Freudian philosophy proved particularly attractive to the creative class in the first half of the twentieth century because it showed the socio-political roots of repression. This perspective revealed how limitations to personal freedom started early in the individual's life and continued into adulthood, affecting all areas of existence: family life, workplace, gender relations, social conditions and political participation. In short, it revealed how repression dominated the individual's life. As a tool of analysis, Freudian psychology has therefore been proved of value for examining various aspects of film: from technical issues to narrative structure and content. Theorists like Christian Metz and Laura Mulvey used it to discuss, amongst other issues, the attraction of the imaginary and the exploitation of this attraction by the capitalist machine, and sexism and obsessions on screen. In Freudian film studies, the unconscious is politicised. Far from being a personal issue, it becomes a wider problem, a communal issue, shaped and directed by social forces.

Psychoanalytic film theory has historically been grounded in Freud and Lacan, and more recently British Object Relations has also found new favour. Of course, neither of these two founding fathers wrote much about film. Moreover, Freud was openly hostile towards Hollywood, and in particular its representation of the work of clinical psychoanalysis. Really, what we are referring to here as psychoanalytically informed film theories are the post-1970s structuralist and semiotic reworkings of psychoanalytic concepts in ways which honed them and which also rendered productive tools for the interpretation of media texts. These tools were used in the breaking of cultural codes and deconstructing ideologies, and they aimed to show that what appeared natural and unproblematic, in fact, was cultural and troubling.

However, by the early 1980s psychoanalytic cultural criticism was running out of steam despite the fact that there remain cadres of scholars who continue to wave the psychoanalytic flag. There began to emerge some early signs that a renaissance in Freudian and Lacanian thinking was beginning. It was also in that period that Jungian film studies began to take shape. Don Fredericksen published 'Jung/Sign/Symbol/Film' in the *Quarterly Review of Film Studies* (1979; 1980). Early in the 1990s, John Izod wrote a Jungian analysis of the films of Nicolas Roeg, and as his research student at that time, Luke Hockley was working on one of the first PhDs that used Jungian film theory, revised and published much later as the book *Cinematic Projections* (2001b). At that time the field was coming to terms with the complexities of Jung's writing. The task of unpicking his thinking was, and remains, quite an undertaking, never mind the question of how it might be applied productively to analyse films and to think about the institution of cinema.

Today, Jungian-orientated film and media theories are infused with a range of psychoanalytic concepts, and in particular they embody a number of central ideas that have been derived directly from Analytical Psychology. Specifically, there is a rhizome of interconnectedness between the psychological and clinical, and the ways in which that is coming to inform film theory is rich and productive. In understanding what lies beneath the surface of films, Jungian film theory relies on the deep mycological transmission of psychological ideas and concepts to permeate the work at an almost chemical and subterranean manner, and in so doing to suffuse the soil and earth of our film theory: psychoanalytic ideas (including Jung's) are central to the 'ground' of understanding.

Yet, there is a parallel process and what many do not know is that for nearly twenty years (since the publication of Christopher Vogler's book, *The Writer's Journey: Mythic Structure for Writers* [1998]), the film industry has been steadily absorbing Jungian ideas and related ways of approaching symbols and narratives. Vogler's text aimed to teach a commercial approach towards narratives using a highly structured outline. Today we can even speak of 'the Vogler effect' when filmmakers and screenwriters refer to films using a particular mix of Jung, Campbell and Freud (Vogler occasionally mentions elements of Freudian psychology too).

In distinction to psychoanalytic film theory instead of the power of the word and the rhetoric of language mobilised in the act of structural deconstruction, what Jungian-orientated film and media analysis offers is a set of conceptual modes of engagement whose roots are in the dynamic and developmental ideas of Jungian Analytical Psychology. As will become clear throughout this book, one of the issues with Vogler's approach is that, like psychoanalytical film theory itself, it is too structural and too conscious. In promoting an alternative approach, we are suggesting that we avoid the all too neat and easy solution of taking a Jungian concept and then applying it to a film, a television programme, a computer game or whatever might be our current interests.

Here are a few pitfalls to avoid. Jung pioneered the idea of archetypes, so let's go and find archetypes in films, for example the shadow, the anima and the wise old man. Jung wrote about dreams as depicting the current situation in the unconscious, so let's analyse films as dreams that depict the current situation in the unconscious of society. Jung thought that symbols had a 'third not logically given' – let's take images from films and make interpretations that don't appear to stem logically from the films themselves. Jung wrote about alchemy and change, let's treat films as alchemical elements and look at personal and cultural change. It is important not to oversimplify Jung's ideas, and not to use them as tools for the reductive analysis of film texts which could otherwise be amplified – i.e. examined in a 'respectful' manner taking into consideration the complexity and independence of unconscious processes behind both filmmaking and film viewing.

If we are to eschew such an overly literal and structural approach then what comes in its place? Analytical Psychology provides a number of vantage points that offer a fresh look at the media landscape and which can offer some new insights into the psychological aspects of mediation. On the way to these viewpoints, it is worth noticing how individual Jungian ideas exist in something of a field and operate as a hermeneutic matrix of understanding. Here it is helpful to note that in the consulting room the meaning of the client's psychological material is not something that is fixed. Instead the depth psychological perspective regards meaning as arising from the relationship between client and therapist, between analyst and patient. Importantly, it is co-created, unstable, partly conceptual and partly felt. It is not that this concept or that concept pins down the elusive meaning of a dream, for example. It is more that the transient and shifting meaning of a dream itself is something that needs to be held; a dream that had one meaning at the start of therapy comes to mean something rather different after several years. Put simply, the meaning of an image is not fixed. The Jungian approach to images, and films in particular, seeks to preserve such unstable and shifting qualities – it is polysemic in orientation and regards meaning as a process in which the film itself, its viewers and film theorists are together engaged in a hermeneutic activity through which meaning is constellated and brought into being.

It might appear that following this, Jungian film studies a priori cannot be political or discuss social issues, for Jungian psychology lacks the tools for analysing 'the wider issues'. Perhaps the best it can do is provide a framework for constructing, categorising, labelling and analysing narratives: the hero myth consisting of multiple steps, in which the hero invariably undergoes a transformation and gets resurrected in one way or another. However, as a tool of analysis the hero myth is indeed itself shallow and reductionist. Once the characters are categorised as 'shadows', 'animas', 'animuses', 'old wise men' and 'representations of the self', it becomes difficult to see the bigger picture beyond this reductionist description. All meaning in such a structure centres on the vague heroic achievements of the protagonist and his or her encounters with various parts of the self. All the while, the social aspect of the hero's journey merely frames the narrative: at the start of his journey the protagonist leaves his community, and then re-joins it as a 'changed' man after his adventures. This is a general, fairy tale structure, which apparently cannot accommodate the complexities of the modern world. Seemingly, it therefore cannot be used to analyse narratives beyond Disney creations or Hollywood blockbusters. However as will be discussed in Chapter 1, this is an erroneous view. Despite the 'general' character of the structure, it is possible to use it to analyse socio-political issues – because the hero's journey is never fully his or her own, but is also a part of the social process. Further, the psychological worth of an image does not necessarily stem from its aesthetic and intellectual qualities – it is quite possible, even normal, to find something of psychological worth in images that lack cultural sophistication.

Unlike Freudian psychology, Jungian thought never looked like it could be used to solve social problems. To this day it is all too frequently viewed as a mystical philosophy, medievally apolitical, dealing with the deeper problems of existence, but almost totally uninterested in anything beyond UFOs, alchemy, poltergeists and the vague multi-step process called individuation. Moreover, individuation, with its shadows, old wise people, and animas and animuses, is regularly illustrated with the dreams and visions of medieval monks, and with tales about witches, wizards, magical animals and so on and so forth. Surely, so the argument runs, nothing could be further from our social and psychological reality than the analysis of mermaids and the examination of the philosopher's stone. At a time of armed conflict, mass murders, cataclysmic social change, political upheavals and ecological concerns such arcane imagery is the last problem on people's minds. Therefore, most film theorists seem to conclude, Jungian psychology is only suitable for discussing the hero's mythological journey into a world of princesses, towers, talking fish, magic swords and so forth. From such a perspective it appears that Jungian psychology is only suitable for encoding personal change into symbolic terms as a means to make it look more attractive in ways that are escapist and delusional.

However, what is not often taken into consideration is that Jung *was* in fact interested in politics, and apart from supernatural events and magical mandalas, he did write about the problems of society at some length. Yes, he often omitted the details and wrote about politics in general terms, but he was in reality deeply concerned with what was happening around him. He was concerned with the individual's relationship with those in power, and was particularly interested in ways in which people form an unthinking mass and so can become a destructive crowd.

Moreover, it turns out that Jung's interest in arcane and esoteric ideas such as synchronicity, alchemy, UFO sightings and magic were also geared up towards an analysis of the psychological relationship between the individual and society. For Jung, these curious and unusual phenomena were all linked to what he termed individuation – the process of becoming oneself and finding one's place in society. He regarded individuation as a life-long teleological process in which personal identity is bound up with a coming to terms with life's difficulties and frustrations. While inexplicable events and poltergeists may not be the most effective ways of explaining complex social and political problems, and are certainly different from the apparently scientific ones employed by the post-Freudian camp or encoded in the Lacanian framework, such psychological fantasies, events and experiences can still be seen as effective and colourful metaphors of personal and collective change. In short, such phenomena can be usefully interpreted and understood in psychological terms.

Further, such creative fantasies are kindred spirits of the cinema whose origins are partly in the magic lantern shows of the seventeenth century and the nineteenth-century optical entertainment of the phantasmagoria. There is something 'otherworldly' about watching a film in the cinema for we enter a world of ethereal images that, while lacking in physical substance, have the capacity to evoke powerful physical and emotional responses. In this sense, the cinema is one way that contemporary society keeps the symbolic life and mythological world alive. As a place where the unconscious and conscious meet, cinema offers the potential for imagery that is psychologically potent, meaningful and that plays a role in our personal psychological development. It is not at all unusual for people to have strong attachments to individual films, or for films to crop up in personal therapy to good psychological effect. In short, cinema can be part of the process of individuation.

However, individuation is not only a personal process, it is also very much about society. Importantly, in Jung's view, individuation is not about narcissistic impulses, and is not about always doing what you want regardless of what others think. Every individual has to strike a certain balance between personal interests and the interests of his or her family, community and society. Only then are they able to function, and to be creative. Personalities cannot develop by themselves, without any outside influences: they form themselves in relation to, and in conflict with, their environment. The task of the individual, on the one hand, is not to get engrossed into the collective and, on the other, not to become so narcissistically individualistic that life will stop making sense. Only by interacting with others does the individual see the difference between self and environment, and only by building oneself into the social structure does one become fully human. As Jung puts it:

> In general, [individuation] is the process by which individual beings are formed and differentiated; in particular, it is the development of the psychological *individual* as a being distinct from the general, collective psychology. Individuation, therefore, is a process of *differentiation*, having for its goal the development of the individual personality.
>
> (CW6: 757 – emphasis as original)

Obviously, this balance is very difficult to find. Jung doubted the modern individual's ability to control his own unconscious impulses. In fact, he had two concerns:

that modern people were not as independent-thinking as they thought; secondly that they were quickly becoming individualistic (in other words, un-individuated) and too removed from their communal roots. On the surface of it, these two issues contradict each other. Yet, deep down they concern the same phenomenon – the modern human's ability to maintain independent thinking in the face of societal pressures without detaching from society completely. Jung saw this as one of the key problems of modernity and the times in which the communal mostly takes the form of the bureaucratic and the systemic. We are still unable to tell the difference between the group and ourselves; the individual and the crowd.

The dichotomy between the social and the personal is also one of the key issues of film studies – for example, how does one derive personal (and profound) meanings from what essentially is a mass form of entertainment? How does one distinguish between one's own feelings, affects and desires, and those encoded into the film by the producer, director or writer? Equally, what of the feelings of the people watching this film with you and discussing it afterwards? How do we know that these emotions are 'ours' and not programmed into us by someone else, or that you are crying when watching a sad or sentimental movie scene because you feel like it, and not because the person in the seat next to you started crying?

Jung had a lot to say about the individual's relationship with society. As social creatures, we feel pressurised into being like everyone else; into behaving 'in accordance with', into complying with rules and regulations which replaced the rituals binding together pre-industrial communities. He comments:

> we see every day how people use, or rather, abuse the mechanism of imitation for the purpose of personal differentiation: they are content to ape some eminent personality, some striking characteristic or mode of behaviour, thereby achieving an outward distinction from the circle in which they move. We could almost say that as a punishment for this the uniformity of their minds with those of their neighbours, already real enough, is intensified into an unconscious, compulsive bondage to the environment.
>
> (CW7: 242)

As the twentieth century progressed, Jung famously wrote about the ways in which the State was being transformed in the minds of its subjects into a kind of idol: it is invoked, made responsible, grumbled at and perceived as 'the inexhaustible giver of all good' (CW10: 554). Many critics, in particular Christian Metz and Jean-Louis Baudry, emphasised the dangers of blindly following the Hollywood machine, which is not only capable of, but relies on the manipulation of human emotions for the sake of making a financial profit and ideological purposes. While systems offer ready-made solutions, and this can be attractive for someone who struggles with genuine intellectual and emotional independence, they also constrain, while apparently helping us to make the right decisions.

In his writings, Jung kept warning about the dangers of solutions offered by systems in which society is elevated to the rank of a supreme ethical principle

(CW10: 554). Although human beings lost some of their contact with ritual at the onset of modernity, they still look for structures and systems through which to provide the emotional and ideological backbone for their lives. As humans we are still ritual animals, and knowingly or not we look for someone to organise our lives and thoughts for us. Far from being independent individuals and happy with this state of affairs, modern humans are unhappy. In fact, we are in despair without a supporting structure, and consider ourselves fortunate when we are allowed to join one. Thus, bureaucratic and corporate structures replaced what used to be communal ties, and now provide us with 'meaning' and 'direction'. Such is the power of the impersonal forces in the human psyche – we want to belong, to be part of a social group, even if the social group takes artificial and superficial forms. Moreover, not only do we happily merge with the mass and the structural, we are also blissfully unaware of it:

> There is indeed reason enough for man to be afraid of the impersonal forces lurking in his unconscious. We are blissfully unconscious of these forces because they never, or almost never, appear in our personal relations or under ordinary circumstances. But if people crowd together and form a mob, then the dynamisms of the collective man are let loose – beasts or demons that lie dormant in every person until he is part of a mob. Man in the mass sinks unconsciously to an inferior moral and intellectual level, to that level which is always there, below the threshold of consciousness, ready to break forth as soon as it is activated by the formation of a mass.
>
> (CW11: 23)

Individuation, Jung implied, was the means though which it was possible to counteract this pernicious, alluring influence of undifferentiated social behaviours and attitudes. In distinction to Freud, he thought that, apart from the personal layer of the conscious existed another, collective layer, and it is this collective layer that made the call of the crowd so irresistible, even for the most enlightened individuals. It is not that Jung did not have hope for the modern man – he did; but he was also aware that the words 'freedom', 'independence' and 'democracy' were often unable to rebuff the magic of collective thinking. Paradoxically, cinema is both an alluring collective apparatus and a solution for the individuation problem, offering us collective (and often 'standardised') narratives which we can use to individuate and to illuminate our own, sometimes complex and convoluted, emotional life.

To conclude, despite going almost unnoticed by mainstream film studies, the birth of a Jungian way of approaching film and media theory is of necessity proving a rather bloody one that involves the murky business of dispatching Freud and Lacan. To draw on an image that is enjoying something of a renaissance, such patricide is a bloody delight and our particular richness is that we have three fathers that, vampire-like, we can feed on.

We have characterised the role of the central ideas of a Jungian informed screen studies as rhizomic and mentioned some of the ones that Jungian film and media scholars have sought to work with: individuation, complex, archetype, affect, the teleological understanding of the psyche, the tension between the individual and the social, intersubjectivity, projection, symbol and so forth. Implicit in these is the inheritance from Freud and Lacan, as we cannot escape the idea of the look, the scopic regime, the cinematic apparatus and the Oedipal. Nor should we leave these founding ideas behind as they retain a use and a utility. Likewise, the mirror phase and its relation to cinematic structures and cultural ideology remains an important part of the picture.

A Jungian-informed approach to cinema does not offer a prescription. Nor is it a set of tools for analysis. Rather, it is a set of sensitivities that offers a different framework within which to go about the work of understanding how it is that meaning is made in, by and, crucially, with media artefacts. The complexity and sophistication of this framework will emerge over the course of this book. In this introduction we have not presented the details of the paradigm that is the Jungian orientation to the screen. This is not out of perversity; it is more that no such paradigm exists. Indeed it is questionable whether such a model can, or should, ever exist. It is sometimes remarked in Jungian analytic circles that there is no such thing as Jungian analysis as its practice varies so much from analyst to analyst. What Jungian analysts share is not technique but an ethos. So too as Jungian film studies begins to come of age it meanders in and around more established film theory and in so doing serves generally to enrich the land in which our theoretical endeavours are rooted.

Part I

Methods

Chapter 1

The context of Jungian film studies

Helena Bassil-Morozow and Luke Hockley

Jungian film studies is a relatively young field, and many of its postulates have been borrowed from Jungian literary criticism (briefly discussed later in this chapter). It has primarily taken two main directions: narrative analysis (John Izod, John Beebe, Terrie Waddell, Helena Bassil-Morozow, Catriona Miller, Andrew McWhirter) and phenomenological criticism (Luke Hockley, Greg Singh). Christopher Hauke explores both how films are made and their effect on the audience, both their narrative and phenomenological aspects. Of course, there is considerable overlap between the two areas. With Hockley offering detailed textual readings and Izod seeking to understand the attributes of the cinematic experience, for example, it follows that the distinction offered here is one of degrees.

The group exploring the application of Jungian ideas to screen media has primarily focused on the narrative structure, individuation, archetypes, symbols and signs while the phenomenological circle has explored the issue of meaning in moving narratives and the therapeutic properties of images. Yet, as alluded to above, both the angles are complementary and draw inspiration from Jung's concepts of individuation, archetypes and the 'dual unconscious' consisting of the personal and collective parts. In other ways, both the groups examine the impossibility of completely separating conscious and unconscious experiences, and telling the definite difference between the personal and the collective in the individual's life. Cinema, which acts as a mass mirror, offers fantastic opportunities for reflecting on the fluid border between the individual and the collective, the personal and the social. Its structures, as well as their meanings, reflect the difficulty of drawing a clear line between individuals and their unconscious, between individuals and their society. A highly visual medium, cinema questions the very idea of an independent individual.

Don Fredericksen was one of the first academics to explore the applicability of Jungian theory to screen media. In his article 'Jung/Sign/Symbol/Film' (2001), Fredericksen compares the Freudian and Jungian takes on signs and symbols. He argues that Freud's analysis of works of art is essentially semiotic (and, as such, reductive), while Jung's treatment of creativity and its products is symbolic (i.e. allowing interpretive freedom). A sign has only one possible meaning while a symbol can have a whole hierarchy of interpretations. Fredericksen demonstrates 'our need and our capacity to be open to meaning – filmic and otherwise – of a kind and in places where semiotic attitudes have not previously found it' (2001: 17). He also points out that, by attaching ourselves to particular critical opinions, 'we are denying ourselves a sense of meaning – and a wisdom – at once very old and very alive in the contemporary world, including the world of film' (2001: 17).

Fredericksen criticises the existing – and predominant – semiotic approaches in film studies (influenced and shaped by linguistics, literary criticism, psychoanalysis and Marxism), including works by Peter Wollen (*Signs and Meaning in the Cinema*), Christian Metz (*Film Language: A Semiotics of the Cinema*) and Jurij Lotman's *Semiotics of Cinema*. He also rejects Metz for using a range of pseudo-scientific concepts such as 'code', 'message', 'system', etc. (Fredericksen, 2001: 24). Jung, Fredericksen argues, did not emphasise the systemic in interpretation. This goes against the normal instincts of a Western thinker which are to make a rational construction allowing one to explain things in an ordered and clear way. For Jung, such an approach seemed reductive. He did not shy away from the inexplicable, the irrational and the mysterious, which, on the one hand, negatively influenced his reputation, and, on the other, allowed him to create a fluid description of human development. Like many other Jungian theorists, Fredericksen traces the roots of this 'loose', democratic attitude towards imagery and narrative to the concept of the collective unconscious as an unfathomable, pre-human entity which needs to be respected. No human mind should aspire to uncover the mystery of its symbols. As symbolism is a more powerful tool in film than it is in a printed text, it is important to 'amplify' rather than interpret film images (Fredericksen, 2001: 34). This is a point that will be explored further in Chapter 3, 'Jungian psychology: signs and symbols'.

In this book we will argue that the semiotic approach, even though only partially compatible with the Jungian critical angle, is nevertheless a useful tool that can be used in conjunction with the Jungian approach. Moreover, together with psychoanalysis, it can be employed to fill the gaps in Jungian film theory – the gaps that are detrimental and that make it difficult for it to receive a wider dissemination. In the academic world Jung has the reputation of a 'mystic' and a 'shaman', for which the notion of the collective unconscious with its irrational unfathomability is mostly often the cause. One of the main ideas of this book is to show that Jungian thinking is not only compatible with the 'normal' Western 'semiotic approach', but that it can also have a fruitful and mutually enriching dialogue with it. Even though 'the semiotic vs. the symbolic', generally speaking, was the main reason for the split between Jung and Freud back in 1913, the two approaches do not necessarily exclude each other.

Fredericksen also warns Jungian film studies against becoming a reductive approach only interested in decoding archetypal structures and individuation patterns instead of regarding moving images from a variety of perspectives. He is worried by the tendency of Jungian film scholars to write about popular and schematic narratives, thinking that it might lead to 'archetypal literalism': 'Jungian criticism can feed off a kind of *archetypal literalism* when it abstracts any archetypal register from the concrete peculiarities of a film' (Fredericksen, 2011: 102). The way out of this would be close textual analysis of cinematic narratives while curbing the instinct to generalise and to look for 'archetypes' in every single film or television series.

Instead, Fredericksen suggests, Jungian film analysis should focus on therapeutic goals: to combat 'the corruption of consciousness' and to 'nurture psychological life' (2011: 102–105). The first task entails challenging the audience rather than pleasing it; and the second enlightening the viewers, helping them understand themselves. Ultimately, Fredericksen argues, '*we are at the service of something deeper than the popular*, something deeper than the semiotic register of living, something beyond the literal' (2011: 107). In other words, Jungian film studies should concentrate on the conscious elaboration of symbols, thus promoting their deeper understanding and enhancing their educational and therapeutic value.

John Beebe is a Jungian analyst who has had a long-standing interest in films, and in how to approach them with integrity and depth. Perhaps he is best known for the ways in which he has used Jungian typology (Jung's theory of personality type) to analyse characters in films. His article '*The Wizard of Oz*: A Vision of Development in the American Political Psyche' (2011) set out to do just that but also succeeded in placing that analysis in a broader political landscape. Beebe is also particularly interested in Jung's concept of the *anima*, which, in broad terms, is the culturally ascribed 'feminine' aspects of largely unconscious behaviour that occur in men. (The equivalent trait for women is termed the *animus*.) His most extensive work on the subject is *The Presence of the Feminine in Film* which is co-written with Virginia Apperson (2008). Ranging over films as diverse as *Notorious* (1946) and *The Lives of Others* (2006), the book charts what the 'feminine' means as it is experienced in the cinematic context. As such, the authors assert that film gives body to Jung's conception of the feminine.

The line of succession is perhaps closer between Fredericksen and John Izod, than Beebe. Izod is another of the founding fathers of Jungian film studies. His more recent publications include *Myth, Mind and the Screen: Understanding the Heroes of Our Time* (2001), *Screen, Culture, Psyche: A Post-Jungian Approach to Working with the Audience* (2006) and *Cinema as Therapy* (2015; co-authored with Joanna Dovalis). Izod has offered a range of in-depth interpretations of films, tracing individuation, archetypes and the hero myth in moving image narratives. For instance, in *Screen, Culture, Psyche* he explores the protagonists' quest for self-understating throughout Stanley Kubrick's *Eyes Wide Shut* (1999), Bernardo Bertolucci's *Stealing Beauty* (1996), *The Dreamers* (2003) and *Besieged* (1998), and Andrew Niccol's *S1MONE* (2002). He also examines old myths and the use of archetypes in Westerns as a genre and discusses the therapeutic value of screen media.

Izod draws on Jung's idea that the psyche of the individual is inseparable from the psyche of his or her society, and that the process of individuation and spiritual progress are only as successful as society allows them to be. In other words, we are back to the central problem of Jungian psychology: the psychological state of the individual directly depends on the state of society. Films directly reflect this interdependence and render the struggle of the contemporary urban dweller to individuate. Cinema is nothing more than just another cultural form, and for the purpose of psychosocial dynamics it is as good as any other. It links the collective unconscious, with its symbolic language, to the outward world – to society and culture. Izod writes:

> In common with all cultural forms, films are vehicles for symbolic energy charged not only with collective consciousness but also with shared, irrational material that has its source in the unconscious. . . . symbols found in screen texts (like other cultural forms) must indeed, to conform to Jung's meaning of the word, have a dimension that received energy from the unconscious.
>
> (Izod, 2006: 18)

He also notes that the concept of individuation is particularly applicable to Western cinema because it is based 'on the exaltation of the individual' and is aimed at solving the problems of personal development. The individual is the focus and the centre of Western culture (Izod, 2006: 11).

Moreover, individuation suits the type of narrative adopted by mainstream cinema: linear, realistic, plausible, with a clear personal history and a traceable psychological development of the protagonist. Characters

> should have not only an outer life of words and deeds, but also an inner one to which audience members give their assent. That assent is commonly won by an interplay between outer and inner life governed by narrative cause and effect. Typically, something that happens in the story world affects a protagonist. The character's inner response to that occurrence changes his or her mental state and causes a reaction that motivates the way he or she reacts.
>
> (Izod, 2006: 11)

This is the type of narrative to which most audience members can relate – the story of challenge, struggle and victory – the story of personal development, the story which gives hope for the ordinary person living in a complex and unpredictable modern world. This focus on the individual and his or her path in life is exactly what Christopher Vogler capitalised on in his book *The Writer's Journey: Mythic Structure for Writers* (1998), which will be discussed in detail in the chapters that follow.

Terrie Waddell too is interested in the role of the individual and society and is a prominent representative of the 'narrative' school. She has published numerous monographs and edited collections in which she explored archetypes and gender in screen media. Her most notable works include *Mis/takes: Archetype, Myth and Identity in Screen Fiction* (2006) and *Wild/Lives: Trickster, Place and Liminality on Screen* (2009). For instance, in *Mis/takes* Waddell examines the connection between Analytical Psychology and myth. She is primarily interested in the trickster archetype, and the state of liminality in which it exists.

She traces liminality to a number of moving image narratives, including *The X-Files* (1993–2002; 2016–), *The Sopranos* (1999–2007) and the BBC sitcom *Absolutely Fabulous* (1992–2012). She claims that 'to examine the way that identity is disrupted and developed in contemporary film and television involves drawing on the core archetypal patterns central to [Jung's] understanding of the psyche and mythology' (Waddell, 2006: 1).

Waddell argues that Analytical Psychology offers a good set of tools for the analysis of visual images:

> The three major concepts integral to Jung's 'analytical psychology' provide an obvious framework for analysing the visual media: first, images common in dreams, myth and creative art are often projections of unconscious archetypal patterns; second, there is a 'collective unconscious' where these patterns are constellated; and third, the gradual conscious unravelling of these structures promotes the development of a more aware sense of self.
>
> (Waddell, 2006: 1)

In her books she examines the way archetypes (primarily the trickster and the child) are manifested in films and television programmes. For instance, in *Mis/takes* she discusses the psychopomp incarnation of the trickster in Alejandro Amenabar's *The Others* (2001) and the female trickster spirit in the BBC sitcom *Absolutely Fabulous* (1992–2012).

In *Wild/Lives: Trickster, Place and Liminality on Screen* Waddell further explores the various incarnations the trickster takes on screen, using as examples (amongst others) the television series *Deadwood* (2004–2006) and *Lost* (2004–2010), Steven Soderbergh's *Solaris* (2002), Werner Herzog's documentary *Grizzly Man* (2005) and a US reality show *The Biggest Loser* (2004–). She astutely concentrates on television series and reality shows rather than traditional film because, although fleeting and perishable, TV programmes and media items reflect the collective unconscious more fully as they are often made in direct response to consumer preferences.

Like Waddell, Helena Bassil-Morozow concentrates on the role individuation and archetypes play in moving image narratives. Her publications include the monographs *Tim Burton: The Monster and the Crowd* (2010), *The Trickster in Contemporary Film* (2012) and *The Trickster and the System: Identity and Agency in Contemporary Society* (2014). The overarching theme of her research is the relationship between the individual and society, and particularly the ways in which individual identity is formed. She uses screen media narratives as metaphors to explore and examine this relationship.

Bassil-Morozow's first book, *Tim Burton: The Monster and the Crowd* organises the films of Tim Burton around the concept of the child archetype, and traces its various incarnations in his films. She argues that his male (and some of his female) characters are variants of the *puer aeternus*. The child in Burton's films never stays the same and takes a range of forms: the monster, the superhero, the maniac and the genius. These guises overlap and amalgamate as the cultural manifestations of the archetype are never solid but always fluid. Burton's protagonists often combine a range of roles: Edward Scissorhands (*Edward Scissorhands*, 1993) and Willy Wonka (*Charlie and the Chocolate Factory*, 2005) are childish geniuses and Bruce Wayne (*Batman*, 1989; *Batman Returns*, 1992) is a superhero who feels like a monster. In fact, his 'monster' side, the Joker – the shadow of the modern individual – is split off and keeps haunting him in the streets of Gotham City.

Bassil-Morozow's second book, *The Trickster in Contemporary Film*, also focuses on a single archetype – this time the trickster. In her monograph she regards the trickster as a psycho-anthropological figure, a metaphor of change, and groups the qualities demonstrated by tricksters in myths and fairy tales – shape-shifting, licentiousness, control issues, scatology and association with the animal world. She then shows how these motifs manifest themselves in contemporary comedy film – and particularly movies featuring Jim Carrey, including *Dumb and Dumber* (Peter and Bobby Farrelly, 1994), Chuck Russell's *The Mask* (1994) and Peyton Reed's *Yes Man* (2008). Interestingly enough, both Waddell and Bassil-Morozow concentrate in their works on the trickster figure as it reflects the spirit of the post-industrial times and shows the changes in the collective psyche more faithfully than any other image. The trickster is pure change, pure movement, which makes him a suitable metaphor for the description of the fast-paced environments and lifestyles of Western societies.

More recently, Bassil-Morozow has been extending the trickster metaphor to the analysis of the relationship between the individual and society. In *The Trickster and the System: Identity and Agency in Contemporary Society* she focuses on the dynamics between the individual and civilising structures, and on the ways in which human identity is formed and managed. The book traces the trickster's machinations to a number of political and social phenomena, including the capitalist economy, mass media and the creative impulse. The trickster and the social forces controlling and shaping the individual's behaviour exist in a kind of symbiosis which allows the system to renew itself by using the trickster's energy and inventiveness. Thus, every successful social structure should have an in-built trickster whose vitality and thirst for change keep it alive, and ensure progress and improvement. By contrast, the stifling and silencing of the trickster (any dissenting voices) means solidification of structural elements of society. This inevitably leads to oppression, stagnation and eventual dissolution of the system.

Christopher Hauke, too, is interested in the question of structure and system but primarily in relation to the production and reception of films. Hauke's professions inform his vision of moving image narratives: he is an academic author and lecturer, a game developer, an enthusiastic filmmaker and a Jungian analyst. The two collections he co-edited with his colleagues, Ian Alister and Luke Hockley, are, respectively, *Jung and Film: Post-Jungian Takes on the Moving Image* (2001) and *Jung and Film II: The Return* (2011). Hauke's general view on cinema and its interpretation are quite in line with the rest of the Jungian film coterie: symbols should be left be, and not over interpreted. Looking for a definitive meaning in a film is not a mature attitude because it gives an illusion of safety and control. True meaning is unpredictable, exciting or even dangerous, and is linked to that moment in space and time when the film is being watched by this particular audience. There is nothing clear or universal about the meaning of film texts. Hauke writes:

> In any psychological analysis of film it is all too tempting to become reductive and to look for the 'meaning' of movies and their narratives in a psychobiography of the directors and writers concerned. Too many film critics follow this type of analysis when a psychological perspective is not otherwise to the fore . . . I think this only goes to demonstrate how the culture of psychoanalysis and the cultural fantasy of the aetiology of childhood have taken such a grip throughout the twentieth century – one which shows no sign of abating.
> (Hauke, 2001: 160)

Hauke's book *Jung and the Postmodern: The Interpretation of Realities* (2000) outlined a whole range of issues that post-Jungians have been trying to solve for decades: the role of Jungian psychology in our time, its place among other psychologies, the pluralism of Jung's theory, the semiotic versus the symbolic, mass media and identity, postmodern gender from a Jungian perspective, etc. Ultimately, Hauke argues, Jungian psychology is a response to modernity which 'brings it in line with many aspects of the postmodern critique of contemporary culture' (Hauke, 2000: 1). In this sense, Jung is a theorist of culture as a whole who still retains the psychotherapeutic aim of healing (Hauke, 2000: 1).

In his most recent book, *Visible Mind: Movies, Modernity and the Unconscious* (2014), Hauke discusses films in terms of their mythological value for the contemporary individual. Today's heroes, when lost on their spiritual journeys in the coldness and sterility of soulless urban landscapes, inevitably turn for help to stories that spring from the collective layer of the psyche. Atomised modern individuals still share the collective psychological ground that 'makes itself known largely in projection' (Hauke, 2014: 5). Cinema becomes the mirror that brings together the various elements of the broken psyche; it is a voice-giving device for making sense of the individual's experiences. As such, it is deeply therapeutic.

In Chapter 8 of his book – titled 'Unusual Suspects' – Hauke examines the therapeutic value of films. For him, movies are as useful a material in a psychotherapy session as any other (photographs, dreams, drawings). Films take to the surface everything that is hidden; they make visible the workings of the mind, for images are more eloquent and easily processed than words. A client may come in searching for words to describe her problem with her husband, or looking for a pattern to describe his behaviour, and end up comparing him to Bill Murray's character in *Groundhog Day* (1993). Another client may feel dissociated from his anger, and then find its realisation on screen, in *Fight Club* (1999) – Brad Pitt's portrayal of the brutal and tricksterish rebel Tyler Durden living on the margins of the capitalist society (Hauke, 2014: 155). Movies speak to us, Hauke shows, in ways that are simultaneously universal and personal, individual and communal. We encounter similar issues in the hope of mending our psychological brokenness and lack of self-understanding. It is this common archetypal base that allows us to empathise with each other. It is also this base that ensures a film's popularity and commercial success, for it makes a narrative understandable to a wide range of people all around the world. The magic of the film lies in its ability to bring the fragments of the psyche together, to unite the audience – but also to make each member of it feel 'whole' – the process that Jung referred to as 'individuation'.

In an attempt to discover where the magic originates, Hauke visits the other camp and interviews people who give us movies: an actor, a cinematographer, a director, a set designer, an editor and a screenwriter. Contemporary films tend to be unwieldy creations made by many different people, none of whom has the final say. All of the interviewees describe filmmaking as a mysterious, almost alchemical process, which is not to be explained rationally. At the same time, they do their best to make sense of the creative activity behind filmmaking. For instance, the British writer and director Paul Morrison (famous for his 1969 footage of John Lennon at home with Yoko Ono and the white piano) admits that he is still 'fighting to allow space for something that you don't know in advance – for the unexpected to happen' (Hauke, 2014: 147). You can only make creativity work for you if you fight for it, if you leave gaps in the filmmaking process through which the unconscious can enter it (Hauke, 2014: 147).

Another Jungian film theorist, Catriona Miller, identifies a different type of gap, or fissure in the text and is particularly interested in gender in moving image narratives analysed from a Jungian point of view. She has published a range of articles challenging gender representations in contemporary television and cinema. Her publications include, among others, 'Dracula Was a Woman' (2009; in *Treat or Trick?*, edited by Hugh O'Donnell and Malcolm Foley), '"I Feel Like a Failure": In-House Feminism' (2011a, in *House: The Wounded Healer on Television*, edited by Leslie Gardner and Luke Hockley) and '*Twilight*: Discourse Theory and Jung' (2011b, in *Jung and Film II: The Return*, edited by Christopher Hauke and Luke Hockley). In her texts, Miller focuses on the potential of Jungian theory for film studies as well as on the applicability of Jung's ideas to the analysis of gender in screen media.

Miller is particularly interested in the ways in which the distribution of power between genders is presented in cinema and television narratives. In 'Dracula Was a Woman' she discusses the ways in which female power is presented in vampire narratives. In '"I Feel Like a Failure": In-House Feminism' she analyses how the 'heroic, white, male doctor' (2011a: 189) myth is both challenged and perpetuated in contemporary medical dramas, especially in the popular television series *House* (2004–2012). In many ways, Dr Gregory House (Hugh Laurie) is a difficult yet brilliant man bent on overcoming numerous difficulties set out before him during the narrative, and he expects the female characters to remain on the side-lines of this myth or serve to endorse it. Yet, there are several female characters in the series that challenge his status or doubt his intellectual supremacy. They belong to the 'foxy, professional female' type and demonstrate leadership qualities (Miller, 2011a: 189–199).

Yet, as Miller notes, the *problem* of female leadership in screen media narratives is structurally *problematic*. While 'the hero's journey . . . is a familiar cultural trope', the feminine one 'is far less well described' (Miller, 2011a: 199). Moreover 'the real problem with applying the monomyth to a female hero's journey is that her "return" is particularly problematic. There is no leadership role for her to step into. There is no kingdom (queendom) for her to rule over' (Miller, 2011a: 199).

Traditional individuation narratives, abundant in Hollywood, lend themselves particularly well to Jungian film criticism. For instance, the British media scholar Andrew McWhirter outlines the individuation narrative in *The Matrix* trilogy (The Wachowskis, 1999–2003). He argues that,

> with any basic knowledge of Jung one could draw parallels with archetypal figures and motifs, from the circular narrative beginning and ending with the spiritual 'Heart of the City' hotel to a cast running order: Neo as Hero's Journey, Trinity as Anima, Morpheus or Oracle as Old Wise Man, Agent Smith as Shadow, or the Trickster as shape-shifting agents.
>
> (McWhirter, 2014: 271)

The entire trilogy can be seen as the individuation process 'whereby Neo successfully integrates the unconscious and the conscious realms of the psyche' (McWhirter, 2014: 272). Importantly, McWhirter shows the importance of Jungian theory for the narratives reflecting the ordeal of the individual having to negotiate his or her individuality in capitalist modernity. Chapter 2 discusses in more detail the 'contemporary hero' narratives that express the anguish of the postmodern individual.

Shifting to the more phenomenologically orientated aspects of Jungian film theory, Luke Hockley and Greg Singh both explore the ways in which screen media influence the audience, and the formation of meaning in the moving image narratives. In their texts they discuss cinema as a form of therapy, how viewers negotiate meanings with films, the role of active imagination in the consumption and enjoyment of images, cinephilia, bodily manifestations of the viewer–screen relationship, among other topics.

Hockley is a psychotherapist as well as a film scholar, which means that he incorporates his knowledge of psychotherapeutic processes into his analysis of screen media and vice versa. In his books he explores the therapeutic potential of moving image narratives. In *Frames of Mind: A Post-Jungian Look at Cinema, Television and Technology* (2007) Hockley draws attention to the fact that traditional film theory surprisingly paid little attention to viewers' emotional relationship with the moving image (Hockley, 2007: 35). In *Somatic Cinema* (2014) he investigates the limitations of Lacanian film theory for film analysis and regards 'the pleasure of looking' from a Jungian point of view. He argues (in line with Jung's view of symbols) that any meaning produced by on-screen imagery is both powerful and personal:

> Cinema audiences have a relationship with films in which meanings are not just transmitted from the screen to the viewer. Rather, individuals negotiate

> meanings with films. Sometimes this happens consciously when, for example, we work hard at interpreting a film, at being sensitive to its cinematic and aesthetic qualities and at becoming attuned to its use of metaphor, symbol and subtleties of its narrative. However, this negotiation of meaning can also take place at an unconscious level. In such cases a personal complex is activated, and our cultural and aesthetic sensibilities are overwhelmed by the strength of the affect. When this happens the meaning and values that are found and placed in a film can be a mystery to others. . . . We can find powerful meanings in the most unlikely of places.
>
> (Hockley, 2014: 39)

Hockley also transposes one of the central issues of Jungian psychology – the contrast between the collective nature of symbols and their personal meaning – onto film viewing. When an individual encounters a collective fantasy material, the effect is unpredictable and fleeting (Hockley, 2014: 47). This process 'is analogous to the manner in which individual analysis can allow for an encounter with the collective as a means for the individual to become more fully the person he or she is' (Hockley, 2014: 37).

Hockley notes that if we pause for a moment to think about those most fundamental of psychological images – dreams – then a therapist does not discriminate between a client's dream on aesthetic grounds (though clients often do – it's not a very interesting dream they say, only to discover that despite the initial resistance, their dream turns out to be more fascinating than had been anticipated). Nor do therapists say to clients: 'Go away and have a more beautiful dream, have a more sophisticated dream, have a more complicated dream for us to work on'. Instead in therapy we work with what the unconscious produces, and the reality is that the unconscious lives in the everyday stuff of life that is human experience.

For Hockley, these statements about the everyday qualities of psychological experience and insight have the effect of shifting the locus of attention away from the conceptual sophistication of the filmmaking itself to refocus on the appeal of films themselves. Of course films are popular for a variety of reasons. Yet, it is the underlying psychological attraction of mainstream films that is of interest to many film scholars interested in Jung. The intrinsic value, or otherwise, of the film itself is not the main object of concern. In *Somatic Cinema* Hockley explores the ways in which the psychological meaning that viewers find in films is a result of an individual relationship in which personal psychological responses intermingle with the images and sounds of the film to create a new meaning that is not part of the narrative of the film. He refers to this as the 'third image' – not the image on the screen, nor the image that arises from the work of interpretative activity, but a third image that exists in the space between viewer and screen – analogous to the intersubjective space between client and therapist.

Hockley examines how, from the perspective of textual analysis, the shifting meaning of media products is a curious idea. Of course textual studies too assert the unstable meaning of texts whose literary or film structures break down under the weight of close textual analysis and in so doing reveal either new meanings, or alternatively the lack of meanings. But what film and media studies does not embrace so readily is the sheer complexity of the psychological relationships we have with media artefacts. For Hockley the interwoven form of these matrices of meaning is enmeshed to the point where it is almost impossible to conceive of a film, television programme, computer game as single artefact – such artefacts exist *only* in relation to other artefacts – so too, while meaning is bound into the text it is at the same time outside it. Meaning is both inside the text and outside it; it arises from our personal relationship with the text and is also in the cultural consumption of the text; it is conscious and unconscious, historical and contemporary, material and immaterial – all at the same time.

Hockley notes how from the clinical perspective this is altogether less remarkable. Illustrating the point, he notes how a dream that is recounted to two therapists will result in two different meanings as the fabric of the interaction between client and therapist has the effect of altering the material of the lived experience. So too it follows that a range of meanings will emerge as the product of different relationships in different settings. So too a dream might very well have one meaning at the start of therapy yet years later it comes to mean something quite different. One of the challenges which Jungian-informed screen studies offers to the clinical perspective is to accept the deep psychological value that arises from the cultural consumption of contemporary media. This requires the therapist to suspend their desire to pin down meaning and to put on hold the desire to 'understand' what the client is saying. This, of course, is impossible, but what is manageable is to hold the interpretative imperative with the knowledge that insight is relative – to acknowledge our desire to master the material of our clients, while knowing that it needs to be resisted. Just as with media artefacts, meaning is inside and out, personal and cultural, historical and contemporary, material and immaterial, conscious and unconscious, thought and felt, all at the same time.

For Hockley, the issue of felt meaning as one part of the matrix of meaning relations is one of the distinctive qualities that a Jungian orientation to such experiences affords the emphasis it has on affect and the feeling-tone of the image. In other words, in making and finding meaning in films viewers bring themselves, their psyches, their personal preoccupations and concerns, and in doing so forge a unique and personal relationship with the film. This is one of the deep rhizomatic patterns that Hockley thinks infuses our understanding of media artefacts. Interestingly, he notes that psychoanalytic film studies have not been overly concerned with the experience and phenomena of affect. It does get the occasional mention but it is an area that is under-theorised, at least in terms of screen criticism. Instead, psychoanalytic approaches have tended to be more structural in their orientation and are concerned with examining the apparatus of the text, the physical conditions of reception in the cinema and the ways they encode cultural values and ideologies. The role of psychoanalysis in that setting is to decode the images. Much as Freud used psychoanalysis to burrow underneath the defences of consciousness, to unearth early sexual trauma, so too psychoanalytic film theory attempts to expose the workings of patriarchal ideology and demonstrate how something apparently neutral is actually heavily cultural and often repressive.

Greg Singh also focuses on the emotional and affective nature of film viewing, and particularly on the role of affect produced by screen media on both identity formation and collective discourse. For instance, in *Feeling Film: Affect and Authenticity in Popular Cinema* (2014b), Singh argues that cinema is an ideal candidate 'for thinking through the expressive potential of cultural production from a psychological perspective' because, being 'psychomimetic', it reflects the relationship human beings have with the outside world (Singh, 2014b: 11). Singh carefully dissects the process of watching (or, rather, experiencing), a film by analysing both its 'noticeable' and 'incidental' aspects, and by carefully considering the

> discrepancy between individual instances of viewing, collective discourse in the popular imagination, and how the narrative image of the film . . . tends to be composed of more general ideas of spectacle and emotional impact gathered from ephemera such as marketing materials, poster art, trailers and the popular review system.
>
> (Singh, 2014b: 34)

In their works Singh and Hockley both focus on more than the text. This decentring of the text in theory is important for a Jungian-informed approach. Of course, Jungian approaches to texts can and do help with the interpretation of a text. It is possible and profitable to look at the formal elements of film (or other artefact) in which a Jungian sensibility helps to make sense of material in ways that other approaches might not. But it is also the case that increasingly there is an attempt to see films as part of a matrix of meaning, in a relational manner with viewers, films and culture more generally. The intention is to preserve the fluidity of meaning within a film, regarding it as a site of change, contestation and as in flux. By contrast, the work of textual interpretation sometimes attempts to 'fix' meanings by offering ever more compressive and convincing insights into the narrative, its imagery, its characters and themes.

The recent work by Hockley and Fadina (2015) *The Happiness Illusion: How the Media Sold Us a Fairytale* illustrates the direction of this more free-flowing type of approach. Arguing against fixed certainty in text and in psychological life more generally the psychological concept of happiness is interwoven with a variety of approaches – some Jungian, others post-Jungian, still others from age studies, feminism, film theory – as a means to explore how media texts are complicated sites of meaning. As a whole, the book attempts to maintain its fluidity, using the motif of the fairy tale to contain changing meanings and conceptual concerns.

As we can see, Jungian film theorists are generally concerned with the same issues as Jungian literary critics: the semiotic/symbolic division, the dichotomy between the universality of the symbol and the personal meanings it generates, the fleeting nature of meaning and affect, the psychological value of the hero myth, the relationship between the social and the personal in cinematic narratives, and the nature of the creative process – be it the process of *making* a film or the process of *watching* one.

Chapter 2

Using Jung to analyse visual narratives

Tools and concepts

Helena Bassil-Morozow

This chapter explores the ways in which Jungian psychology can be employed to analyse visual narratives. It shows the usefulness of the key concepts of Jung's Analytical Psychology (individuation, archetypes, the hero myth, collective unconscious, etc.) for film and television criticism. It also deals with Jungian and post-Jungian psychology's assessment of modernity and postmodernity, and explain how these views can be applied to the analysis of screen media. Finally, it presents a Jungian angle on the unconscious and the projective-introjective processes in communication, and links these processes to the human perception of cinematic images.

Human beings tend to organise information about the world and themselves into accessible and continuous information sequences called narratives. We make meaning of the events and happenings in our lives by reconstructing them into stories. Such a reconstruction implies transformation and change. We become someone else, we create our own doubles, and we have more control over their lives than we have over our own. As Fireman *et al.* argue, 'personal narration gives continuity to self and meaning to action as it locates and values present activity in the context of past experiences and projected outcomes' (Fireman *et al.*, 2003: 5).

Moreover, through narratives (both personal and external), we connect ourselves to our society, and find our place in our community and culture. One overarching theme of myths and fairy tales, for instance, is the boundary between the individual and his or her community; between the acquired cultural values, and personal desires and decisions. The protagonist 'goes to seek his fortune' when he wants to find his own path in life, to separate himself from his surroundings. In other words, when he wants to become an individual.

Narratives feature prominently in Analytical Psychology. In fact, individuation and the archetypes – the core concepts of Jungian psychology – are none other than a flexible narrative framework and its changeable contents. In this sense, Jung's Analytical Psychology is more suitable for analysing narratives than any other psychotherapy theory. Unlike Lacan, Jung did not think that the unconscious is structured like a language. Its language is visual – it consists of images, of pictures, of archetypes. The unconscious is pre-civilised, pre-cultural and pre-linguistic. Only its 'personal' layer is affected by culture, but its deepest layer and its collective one is shared by all, regardless of their backgrounds.

Jungian psychology is also progressive and forward-looking as it is geared up for the creation of meaning in human narrative instead of being obsessed with the past roots of present problems.

Thanks to its emphasis on collective, vague, general experiences, Jungian psychology is particularly (but not exclusively, as is often mistakenly thought!) suitable for the analysis of narratives belonging to the fantastic genres. In this sense, there has never been a better time in the history of film criticism for Jungian Analytical Psychology. The emergence of technology-dependent genres in the past twenty years including CGI, 3D and IMAX has led to the proliferation of fantasy, sci-fi, epic and high-powered action films. All these can be called 'individuation genres'. This in its turn generally led to the emphasis of structure and action over psychological detail or relationship intricacies between characters. Jungian psychology is often criticised for its acute interest in the supernatural over the real, and in the spiritual, abstract meaning of life over everyday situations and events. By contrast, Freudian and post-Freudian ideas are traditionally regarded as practically applicable and referring to concrete events in the individual's past and present. Similarly, popular, 'low brow', genres such as action films are traditionally criticised for being escapist and simplistic, not reflecting the complexity and richness of the human experience, and gliding over and/or barely touching upon childhood problems and relationship issues.

Every time has its heroes; and heroes tend to mirror the psychology and realities of their time. The superhero narrative is the myth of our time – no less psychological or important than mythological gods and heroes of the past such as Prometheus and Achilles. One cannot dismiss popular films as meaningless and empty just because they are loved and watched by the masses. Popular entertainment has the same psychological depth as 'elite' narratives. In fact, non-realistic genres follow the hero myth schema in its purest form. At their base are progression and transformation, however unrealistically and schematically presented. They become mirrors in which viewers see themselves – often idealised and distorted by the magic of cinema. Yet, no self-analysis and self-reflection are possible without a mirror, without an externalisation of some sort; and cinema, being a visual and therefore an immediately accessible medium, offers a route to such self-analysis.

Jung writes about the tendency of human beings to learn about themselves and the outside world by looking in the mirror, via all kinds of projections. Without an external object reflecting your inner self and reiterating your psychological contents, no such learning is possible:

> All the mythologized processes of nature, such as summer and winter, the phases of the moon, the rainy seasons, and so forth, are in no sense allegories of these objective occurrences; rather they are symbolic expressions of the inner, unconscious drama of the psyche which becomes accessible to men's consciousness by way of projection – that is, mirrored in the events of nature. The projection is so fundamental that it has taken several thousand years of civilization to detach in it some measures from its outer object.
>
> (CW9, I: 7)

In fact, cinema is based on the mechanism of projection. It is also a mass event because projection, despite its personal aspects, also tends to be both a social phenomenon and a social event. A stream of moving images gives viewers the opportunity to reflect upon themselves as individuals as well as participants in their society; as actors and agents of social forces. Individuals (and this is a very Jungian idea) only feel alive when participating in communal life.

The personal and the collective unconscious

Jung hypothesised that archetypes, the building structures of personal and collective narratives, reside in the collective unconscious. Jung defines the collective unconscious as a suprapersonal yet objective system, unknowable in its vastness. Even so, one should attempt to know oneself as fully as possible precisely because the biggest regions of one's psyche are submerged below the conscious level and it is beneficial for them to be made as conscious as possible. As Jung comments:

> the collective unconscious is anything but an encapsulated personal system; it is sheer objectivity, as wide as the world and open to all the world. There I am the object of every subject, in complete reversal of my ordinary consciousness, where I am always the subject that has an object. There I am utterly one with the world; so much a part of it that I forget all too easily who I really am. 'Lost in oneself' is a good way of describing this state. But this self is the world, if only a consciousness could see it. That is why we must know who we are.
>
> (CW9, I: 46)

The collective unconscious is therefore always there as a semi-forgotten but omnipresent layer of the psyche. It manifests itself in dreams and fantasies, and through projections and in therapy in the transference between therapist and client. Consciousness and civilisation often neglect its manifestations. Hence, Jung writes, all man's strivings 'have been directed towards the consolidation of consciousness. This was the purpose of rite and dogma; they were dams and walls to keep back the dangers of the unconscious; the "perils of the soul"' (CW9, I: 47). Importantly, collectivity is both internal and external: on the one hand, one is connected with the whole of humankind via the collective unconscious, and on the other the individual is influenced and shaped by his or her environment. In this sense, individual consciousness is sandwiched between the two types of collectivity. This makes for a precarious position in which one has constantly to assert one's intellectual and emotional independence.

Unlike the collective unconscious, which is the 'historical soul' of humankind, its personal counterpart contains concrete information about human beings, from uniquely personal attributes (such as tastes and temperament) to his or her social and familial background. It also harbours childhood complexes (to which

Freudian psychology attaches such a major importance). By contrast, for Jung the personal unconscious, with its individual issues, is a small part of a much larger unconscious structure.

Jungian theory emphasises the importance of the collective as both impersonal and interpersonal in the life of the individual. Consciousness, Jung reminds us, is only the tip of the iceberg, and it is no match for the unconscious which, in spite all our efforts to re-associate repressed contents with consciousness, 'calmly goes on producing dreams and fantasies' (CW7: 205). These dreams and fantasies also tend to throw themselves onto external objects in order to solve the conflict and unite the psychic opposites outside the conflict zone, so to say. When real people (for instance, psychotherapists) become such objects, they often end up carrying heavy projections on their shoulders, yet 'one would have to be a demigod at least to sustain such a role without a break, for all the time one would have to be the giver' (CW7: 206). A successful resolution of the conflict would thus involve someone (or something) becoming a sort of container handling the transference and enabling the 'alchemical' transformation of another's unconscious contents to happen. A successful transference, Jung continues, can cause (if temporarily) the whole neurosis to disappear, 'and for this reason it has been rightly recognised by Freud as a healing factor of first-rate importance, but, at the same time, as a provisional state only, for although it holds out the possibility of a cure, it is far from being the cure itself' (CW7: 206).

Transference (the transposition of one's feelings onto another, often infantile in origin) and projection (relocating one's own difficulties onto another person or object) ease human suffering by emptying the problematic corners of the unconscious of its brooding contents. Surely, there should be other ways of dealing with such psychological concerns. And there are. Cinema offers vast therapeutic possibilities and opportunities for self-reflection for those in need of mediating their problems, or filtering them through a third party. These problems and feelings can be projected or transferred onto on-screen characters, which, due to the mechanical nature of the moving image (it is infinitely replicable, and the actors as human beings are distanced from the final project), provides safe, disposable vessels for containing and possibly transforming any festering psychological problems.

Screen media are mass phenomena, and a vehicle by which the individual can get access to the collective unconscious and its symbols. During the projective-introjective exchange which is part of the experience of film watching, the individual's unconscious is activated – that is, both its personal and collective aspects. It is this dual structure of the unconscious that makes it possible for human beings to transpose their personal issues onto films, and to recognise their personal lives in rather generalised narratives made for mass consumption. Yet, despite their blatantly collective nature, moving image narratives touch each individual in a unique way, and allow projections (and introjections) to take a variety of forms reflecting particular moments and aspects of the individual's life. This universality, reflected – paradoxically – as a unique set of feelings, thoughts and emotions in each viewing experience, is due to the fact that universal patterns in narratives in general and, in cinematic ones in particular, get coloured by distinctive individual experiences.

Like the Jungian vision of the psyche, cinema is a medium based on relativist principles. Nothing is ever set in stone in cinema. From its emergence at the end of the nineteenth century, it has questioned and negated the notions of truth and reality by its very existence, and by the fact that it is a form of mass entertainment. Cinema does not deal with 'facts' – arguably, even documentary cinema is less interested in truth than in the entertainment potential of the story. Documentary narratives are (more often than not) about human nature, about how it manifests itself in a narrative; they concern the story, not the fact. Like the psyche, cinema is a distorted, approximate depiction of reality rather than its faithful representation. Moreover, even though physically being a barrier, the screen also represents the absence of all barriers between fantasy and reality as it 'becomes' the site of projection; it 'comes to life', so to say.

The overarching theme of screen media is the blurring of all boundaries (a typical postmodern ploy); these include the boundaries between fantasy and reality, between the audience and the film, between genres, between cinematic codes and sub-codes, and between the different aspects of the narrative. This blurring of boundaries further leads to the loss of the 'actual' reality. Closer to us than the stage, which physically separates the fictional event from the public, the screen is subtler in its enticing flicker. A relativist phenomenon capable of creating and erasing realities, the moving image is the ultimate medium of impermanence; the ultimate proof of the non-existence of ultimate proofs. Everything shown on screen can be questioned and nothing is purely and ultimately factual. It may be argued that moving image narratives are anti-authoritarian as (despite the claims of *auteur* theory) they do not support the idea of the author, the concept of 'high' and 'low' forms. All cinema, even in its most 'highbrow' *auteur* versions, is ultimately a form of entertainment that is made to be enjoyed and which aims to cause emotional affect in the audience.

Similarly, there are no 'high' and 'low' brow archetypes. Indeed, popular screen media cannot be 'highbrow' because it is by definition a mass-aimed phenomenon. It lacks the foundations of exclusivity and specialness that characterise the arts made by hand; those arts are more 'material', and although replicable, still boast the 'original' from which all the copies are made. Cinema does not have such an original; it is infinitely replicable – particularly today, in the age of multiple platforms and digital marketing. It links individuals to each other, ensuring collectivity and consensus where they seemingly do not exist.

Whatever one's unique path in life, it is next to impossible for the individual to circumvent the collective. After all, all human beings go through the same life experiences and phases: separation from parents, initiation, maturation, finding a partner, dealing with one's negative traits, establishing relationships with others, finding one's true vocation, dealing with the mid-life crisis and growing old. This explains the attractiveness of familiar and repeating patterns in narratives, both literary and cinematic, for specific details embellishing the narrative skeleton do not obscure its commonplace, ritualistic and enduring base. Self-reflection is only possible when it bounces off another object that acts as a mirror for the contents of our psyche. In this sense narratives become like mirrors as we learn about ourselves in a safe and indirect way.

In the moment of film watching, the emic (internal participant) and the etic (external observer) positions merge on the basis of the universality of human experiences, thus blurring boundaries between the internal and the external, and creating a fluid vision of the situation being experienced. Seeing oneself on screen, being transformed into someone else, being transposed into another's body, losing the sense of self, brings about self-awareness as it drags the individual out of her, often stale, vision of herself. Importantly, because of cinema's multiple focalisation practices, the moving image acquires a certain psychological three-dimensionality as we are allowed to see the same problem from different perspectives. The narratologists Vera Nünning and Jan Rupp argue that when the same motif is taken up on several levels of narration, these levels become 'related to each other in multiple ways through mirroring and confirmation as well as through contrast and subversion' (Nünning *et al.*, 2013: 14). Moreover, such mirroring and confirmation amount to a projective–introjective exchange that happens in a safe environment, by proxy, via the characters. This means the viewers do not have to go directly through the pain and suffering experienced by the protagonist.

Another issue associated with the seductiveness of the collective unconscious and over-identification with its primordial contents in relation to the moving image is the sheer addictiveness of cinematic narratives. Jung theorised that transference and projection are temporary solutions to the problem of individuation, and cannot replace 'thinking for yourself'. They cannot become a sort of external brain. While narratives offer the possibility of illuminating one's psychological condition, they cannot become an individual's fantasy second life – some kind of externalised individuation.

The process of becoming an individual involves making independent decisions rather than being a copy-and-paste existence whereby one uses segments of someone else's narrative, real or fictional, instead of thinking for oneself. Indeed, watching a film can induce in the individual a false sense of accomplishment because of the sheer powerfulness of the feeling of identification with the characters. This kind of identification is a lazy path to self-understanding as it dupes the individual into thinking that he or she has achieved something without actually attaining it. Addiction to this process comes as a result of the lack of emotional and intellectual satisfaction when the illusory nature of cine-individuation process becomes apparent as one needs more when the previous instalment of cinematic narratives comes to an end. Cinematic and television narratives are only useful when they are treated as guides, not as complete substitutes for the actual individuation process. They are not solutions or ideal recipes.

The hero of our time

We perceive superheroes on many levels because, even sharing the same basic human experiences (growing up, initiation, finding a partner, establishing a family, discovering our identity and our path in life) and the same environment (urban landscapes, an office job, mass media and the social networks), we nevertheless regard the world in unique ways shaped by the relationships with our parents and siblings, our genetic predisposition, our childhood experiences, etc. In this way, a film is simultaneously seen on both the personal and collective levels, the superficial and archetypal. For example, if one narrows down Batman as a hero rooted in his time, one gets the image of the modern individual trying to deal with a whole hierarchy of issues: personal, social and collective.

Yet, on the basic universal level, Batman is the protagonist of a traditional hero myth. In this sense, he is no different from the stock mythological heroes with superhuman abilities and unusual birth such as Achilles, Aeneas or Beowulf. Like them, he kills evil creatures, fights for justice, tries to define his identity in relation to society, protects his community and seeks eternal glory. Any hero of this scale symbolises the universally recognisable themes of power and control, achievement and failure, maintaining the balance between individualism and socialisation, and between narcissism and adaptation. Myths of modernity reproducing specific problems of industrialised Western societies such as environmental concerns and the ruthlessness of the capitalist system, superhero narratives nevertheless follow traditional narrative structures and act as mirrors aiding the viewers in self-reflection and better understanding of their environment.

Any image, figure or symbol permeates different levels of the psyche, the collective (universally understood individuation quest), the contemporary collective (Batman as a fighter with the dark side of modernity – urban crime, mass media influence, loneliness and psychological fragmentation) and the personal (you want to be a superman in order to impress the girl of your dreams, or to prove something to your friends or your parents). As individuals are inseparable from their background and cannot be regarded in isolation from the specific concerns of their community, the universal, the culturally specific and the uniquely individual in superhero narratives form the three layers that outline the complex psychosocial existence of an ordinary person in a fast-changing society. They are ways in which contemporary individuals make sense of the world – and themselves.

At the same time, the democratisation of the hero myth, exemplified in superhero narratives, has another side to it: the precarious boundary between fantasy and reality, the dangerous moment of withdrawal of projections, the ability to balance one's narcissistic ambition with one's everyday persona. Not surprisingly, in a bout of self-reflection, the superhero industry has spawned a number of dark parodies such as *Kick-Ass* (directed by Matthew Vaughn, 2010) and *Birdman* (Alejandro González Iñárritu, 2015), exploring the threshold between the invincible persona of the hero and the ordinary person adopting it and attempting to live in it.

This new trend points at a deep-seated cultural unease about the loss of realistic perspective in favour of mythologisation of one's life. One of the reasons narratives exist is in order to make us think about our place in society, not to submerge us into the fantasy life forever. The 'superhero complex' comes out of the danger of identification with the collective psyche. It is far too easy to lose oneself in the collective unconscious, and to start thinking that one's human frame is only a representative of some kind of divine force on Earth – it is too easy to start thinking that one is superhuman. An ordinary man always wants to be something bigger than a small insignificant person. Yet, he possesses a fair share of 'ambition, vanity and misplaced naiveté' and is tempted by 'prophetic inspiration and desire for martyrdom' that is a form of 'regressive longing' (CW7: 260). This often leads to inflation by identification with the primordial images from the collective psyche – the hero being one of the most common ones. This is a special case of persona identification, where the ego becomes wedded to the outer mask of the persona, and seemingly cannot shake it off. Here the key role of the persona in assisting in social adaptation is lost and the individual becomes stuck in the outer world and is consequently unable to gain further access to the unconscious – at least until the persona identification is dissolved.

Kick-Ass (2010) is an initiation narrative that follows the adventures of Dave Lizewski (Aaron Johnson), a high school student who buys a superhero costume and attempts to develop superhuman abilities, but has to deal with the limitations of his physical frame when assorted villains repeatedly remind him that he is only human – and therefore mortal. *Birdman* (2010) harbours an even darker message: the superhero myth is a narcissistic project, a malaise of our time, and a very temporary solution for otherwise realistic problems. Not surprisingly, the protagonist is an ageing Hollywood actor Riggan Thomson, who used to play the superhero Birdman, and is portrayed by Michael Keaton, famous for playing Batman in Tim Burton's *Batman* (1999) and *Batman Returns* (1992). Thomson is given a chance to revive his career by writing and directing a Broadway play. Yet, Birdman the hero stubbornly refuses to leave as Thomson hallucinates that he is levitating, hears Birdman's voice telling him about the good old days when they used to be 'superheroes', and daydreams about setting cars aflame with a snap of his fingers. The battle between fantasy and reality reaches its apogee in the last scenes of the film when Thomson apparently forgets about his mortality and humanness altogether, and imagines that he can fly.

Conceiving the collective unconscious as an ocean 'thinking' in images is a powerful idea, and some directors familiar with Jung and Campbell admit 'fishing' universal patterns out of it and fleshing them out in accordance with the culture of their time. For instance, the author of the *Mad Max* franchise, George Miller (Bravin, 2015), insists that the figure of the lone warrior – a universal archetype that changes shape in line with the culture into which he is born (thus becoming an archetypal image) – came to him from the collective unconscious. The culture in question is the dark, inhuman side of the post-industrial society that in the films has destroyed itself by its greed and reckless use of the planet's resources.

Moreover, Miller sees himself as a vehicle for the symbols coming from the collective unconscious, and says that he listens to its images carefully – 'makes a sincere effort' to realise its vision. According to Jung, the unconscious thinks in symbols – not in words. Not surprisingly for a director drawing his inspiration directly from the unconscious, the *Mad Max* films (1979–2015) are highly visual with limited dialogue and precision storyboarding. As alluded to in Jess Bravin's interview (2015), Miller was careful to preserve the unconscious imagery and he did not want to obscure it by dialogue. The image, he says, exists all around the world in different incarnations: 'In Japan they said Max is a samurai, in Europe, they said it's a western on wheels, in Scandinavia they said he's a lone Viking warrior and so on' (Bravin, 2015). Eventually Miller realised that he 'tapped into a kind of Joseph Campbell collective unconsciousness . . . and made a very sincere effort, unconsciously, to tell that kind of story' (Bravin, 2015).

The imagery used by Miller as a unique pattern (archetypal images) on his universal narrative canvas (archetypes) is that of a post-apocalyptic barbarism, with people dressed in rags and battered leather fighting for meagre resources in dusty, relentless desert. The main resource is gasoline, and people driving rusty cars, rigs and motorcycles will fight to the death for a drop of it. Throughout the tetralogy, Miller's vision of survival and loss of humanity is fleshed out in similar images and colours: fiery hot desert sun, blood mixed with dirt and dust, basic, 'steampunk' vehicles that crafty humans fashioned out of what remained of their science and technology, dog food instead of proper food, burning tyres and exploding cars, contaminated water instead of rivers, etc. By the fourth film (*Mad Max: Fury Road*, 2015) this vision became so magnificent that it reached the proportions of a large-scale post-apocalyptic ballet, orchestrated with admirable precision.

Yet, despite their visual originality, the stories told in the tetralogy are universal (the hero myth), as well as raise awareness of global ecological issues. They are simultaneously contemporary and historical, and aim to prompt the discussion of what it means to be human in the contemporary industrialised world.

Individuation and archetypes

Film critics traditionally see Jungian psychology as a source of structural devices such as the individuation/hero myth and the archetypes that are its contents. Imperfect as it is, Christopher Vogler's book *The Writer's Journey* clearly showed the applicability of Jungian ideas for both screenwriting and film criticism. The individuation process is essentially an optimistic concept that presupposes a certain degree of balance, progressivity, maturation and hope in an individual's life. We have this hope for ourselves, and we also find it appealing when it is reflected in cinematic narratives. This too is what we want to see in films – a story, a development, a progression, a tale of transformation. Individuation – the hero myth – is an ideal metaphor for the description of psychological transformation in a person's life.

Unlike Freudian psychology, which is backward-looking and searching for answers to present problems in the individual's past, Jungian theory is more about the future: it is about evaluating one's present position in life and trying to plan the future with this knowledge. The past is important, but not decisive. One learns about oneself as one goes along the path of life, and this process is progressive and aimed at the attainment of psychological wholeness. Although this wholeness can never be fully achieved, one could – in theory – approach some kind of peace with oneself, a pact with one's psyche by appeasing the inner demons. If not peace, then individuation offers the potential for a state of equanimity with ourselves, how we are in the world and the ability to cope with the challenges and difficulties of everyday life.

There is nothing wrong with having inner demons, though – indeed, they are unavoidable. Everyone individuates, and, since human beings share the collective unconscious, we all have similar individuation milestones. These milestones are expressed in metaphors and metaphorical situations – or archetypes and archetypal situations, as Jung preferred to call them. All human beings have issues with parents or parental figures, initiate, struggle with their undesirable character traits such as envy, greed and aggression, deal with instincts and sexuality, try to find their path and place in life, look for love and acceptance, and try to achieve something significant before death. In other words, individuation is the basic skeleton which is then filled out with personal details: all parents (and the issues associated with them) are different; and the ways in which human beings experience sexual feelings are also very individual. Cinematic narratives provide frameworks for reflecting on a variety of individuation moments, and, as the interaction with the screen is one-way, they are also pliable canvasses for one's fantasies and projections. They are ideal providers of objects for one's individuation narrative.

Although individuation is analysable, it is mostly a creative, spontaneous process, a 'natural process within the psyche' that is 'potentially present in every man, although most men are unaware of it' (Jacobi, 1973: 107). It is driven by what Jung called the centre of personality – the Self which stands for psychological wholeness (not perfection) and a freedom from all worldly conflicts and peace with oneself. This centre is more of a guideline and a phantom rather than something that can be really achieved. One can dream of achieving wholeness, but this might never happen. There is nothing tragic in this state of things, however. Having inner conflicts is only human, and while it is possible to integrate some of these issues, it is not possible to get rid of them completely. Arguably, nor is it entirely desirable as the resolution of psychological conflict is one of the spurs to creativity. Meanwhile, narratives show us our unique problems while, at the same time, making us realise that we do not suffer alone, and that our problems are as personal as they are universal.

Whereas the Self is the unattainable personality centre uniting the different parts of the psyche, the ego is responsible for our conscious being. It contains one's unique personality traits and defines who one is as an individual. As such, it is the centre of consciousness. Jung writes:

> The ego is, by definition, subordinate to the Self and is related to it like a part to the whole. Inside the field of consciousness it has, as we say, free will. . . . it finds its limits outside the field of consciousness in the subjective inner world, where it comes into conflict with the facts of the Self.
>
> (CW9, II: 9)

The Self is connected with the collective while the ego distinguishes the individual from collectivity, both internal and external.

Jung writes in 'Psychological Types':

> In general [individuation] is the process by which individual beings are formed and differentiated; in particular, it is the development of the psychological *individual* as a being distinct from the general, collective psychology. Individuation, therefore, is a process of *differentiation*, having for its goal the development of the individual personality.
>
> (CW6: 757, emphasis as original)

In this sense, the individuation process truly joins together the individual and the collective, the personal and the social. It emphasises the fact that there is no individual without society, and no singularity without culture. Every human being is a product of his or her environment; or, as the anthropologist Clifford Geertz puts it, men have a psychological necessity to belong to a collective identity – 'Dobuan or Javanese, Hopi and Italian, upper-class and lower-class, academic and commercial' (1973: 49). Only through their culture can individuals attain completion because culture is there to fill the 'information gap' between 'what our body tells us and what we have to know in order to function' (1973: 49).

Archetypes, as Jung envisaged them, are the constituents (as well as stages) in the individuation process. Because they represent different human experiences, they more or less define what it means to be human. Jung singled out a range of archetypes, all corresponding to particular psychological issues in the life of the individual: the shadow, the anima, the animus, the child, the trickster, the old wise man, the old wise woman and the self. There are many others, and indeed it is a point of some debate as to the extent to which the number of archetypes is fixed – certainly, the variation in the images assumed by archetypes seems at the same time to be endless and yet they are immediately familiar.

Archetypes are essentially clusters of unconscious content and are 'invisible' for consciousness. In this way, Jung distinguishes between the 'original' archetypes and their concrete realisations, archetypal images – the shapes and forms they take in particular cultures and in individual minds. He writes:

> there is a considerable difference between the archetype and the historical formula that has evolved. . . . Their immediate manifestation, as we encounter it in dreams and visions, is much more individual, less understandable and more naïve than in myths, for example. The archetype is essentially an unconscious content that is altered by becoming conscious and by being perceived, and it takes its colour from the individual consciousness in which it happens to appear.
>
> (CW9, I: 6)

Unlike complexes that inhabit the personal level of the unconscious, archetypes reside in its collective part. Jolande Jacobi explains that they:

> make up the actual content of the collective unconscious; their number is relatively limited for it corresponds to 'the number of typical and fundamental experiences' incurred by man since primordial times. Their meaning for us lies precisely in the 'primordial experience' which is based on them and which they represent and communicate. . . . We find them recurring in all mythologies, fairy tales, religious traditions and mysteries. . . . Prometheus the stealer of fire, Heracles the dragon slayer, the countless creation myths, the fall from paradise, the mysteries of creation, the virgin birth, the treacherous betrayal of the hero, the dismembering of Osiris, and many other myths and fairy tales represent psychic processes in symbolic images. Similarly, the figures of the snake, the fish, the sphinx, the helpful animals, the Tree of the World, the Great Mother, the enchanted prince, the *puer aeternus*, the Mage, the Wise Man, Paradise, etc., stand for certain motifs and contents of the collective unconscious.
>
> (Jacobi, 1973: 47)

The archetype, according to Jung, has a numinous effect – i.e. it is emotionally powerful and overwhelming for the one who is experiencing it. In fact, it is so powerful that it is almost out of human control – 'the subject is gripped by it as though by an instinct'. It is even more potent than an instinct as 'instinct itself can be restrained and even overcome by this power' (CW5: 225).

Not surprisingly, the term 'archetype' has been appropriated by popular culture and used to describe the idea of an object or phenomenon being a typical representative of its class; a sort of golden standard. Today 'archetypal' and 'the archetype' are used as umbrella terms to describe a range of cultural commonplaces – something that is recognised by all consumers of popular culture as a 'typical' representative of its group. Thus, there are archetypal cowboys, archetypal princesses, archetypal villains and even archetypal journalists. In fact, this popular definition of archetype is now used in place of 'stereotype'. Anything or anyone fitting into a particular cultural role can be described as being 'archetypal' or 'archetypical'.

This popular vision of the archetype as a recognisable representative of a particular culture is what Jung would call 'archetypal image'. Archetypes themselves are ideas or structures that are unrelated to any concrete or specific culture. Archetypal images, by contrast are more concrete realisations of archetypes. Unlike archetypes, which exist in the collective unconscious and represent general ideas and situations: the great mother, the shadow, the child, the trickster, etc., archetypal images belong to a particular culture. For instance, Cruella de Vil is a pop culture version of the great mother archetype (its negative aspect), Harry Potter is a version of the child archetype, and the Joker from the Batman myth is usually presented as a shadow (sometimes with the elements of the trickster). Archetypal situations are universal patterns, which in myth, dreams and the life of the individual take slightly personalised forms. For instance, birth, initiation, falling in love, fighting with evil and searching for truth are all archetypal situations.

The shadow

According to the classical Jungian scheme, archetypes are encountered during the individuation process in a particular order. More contemporary Jungian thinking sees archetypes working in clusters, and in a more unpredictable manner. Jolande Jacobi upholds the classical order in her book about the basics of Jungian psychology. The shadow, according to this sequence, is the first figure that the emerging individual encounters on her or his individuation path.

The primary position of the shadow in the individuation process, in fact, echoes Freudian and post-Freudian theory's preoccupation with narcissism and the ways in which the child deals with its own selfish impulses and instincts before it can be accepted as an individual into the social order. Although Jung never compared the shadow with narcissism (and his psychology did not inherit Freud's interest in it), in many ways this archetype can be seen as a 'mythological' equivalent of it.

Jung defined the shadow as primarily 'a moral problem that challenges the whole ego-personality, for no one can become conscious of the shadow without considerable moral effort. To become conscious of it involves recognising the dark aspects of the personality as present and real' (CW9, II: 14). As such, the shadow is the 'dark brother' in whom all the negative aspects of human nature are stored. It is home to greed, aggression, envy, jealousy, fear and hatred.

Humans' relationship with the shadow has always been a key *leitmotif* of art and literature. Human struggle with it is brilliantly described, for instance, in Stevenson's *The Strange Case of Dr. Jekyll and Mr. Hyde* (1886) and Oscar Wilde's *Picture of Dorian Gray* (1890). Morality and civilisation fight with the shadow, and human beings usually try to forget about its existence because its qualities are shameful and unacceptable in a civilised society. These qualities are not conducive to peaceful human interaction and coexistence, and certainly go against the Kantian categorical imperative. Jung uses colourful metaphors to describe this archetype: it is 'a tight passage, a narrow door, whose painful constriction no one is spared who goes down to the deep well' (CW9, I: 45). The doppelganger is the mirror of our 'good selves', and, as such, it is always inside us:

> Whoever looks into the mirror of the water will see first of all his own face. Whoever goes to himself risks a confrontation with himself. The mirror does not flatter, it faithfully shows whatever looks into it; namely, the face we never show to the world because we cover it with the persona, the mask of the actor. But the mirror lies behind the mask and shows the true face.
>
> (CW9, I: 43)

The shadow, Jung theorised, comes in two versions: the personal and the collective. The collective version is particularly terrifying because it emerges when personal negative feelings become multiplied and transform into collective negative feelings, when hatred, envy and rage express themselves on a mass scale.

This is why it is important to recognise and deal with one's own personal shadow lest it becomes seduced by the power of the mass:

> It is a frightening thought that man also has a shadow side to him, consisting not just of little weaknesses and foibles, but of a positively demonic dynamism. The individual seldom knows anything of this; to him, as an individual, it is incredible that he should ever in any circumstances go beyond himself. But let these harmless creatures form a mass, and there emerges a raging monster; and each individual is only one tiny cell in the monster's body, so that for better or worse he must accompany it on its bloody rampages and even assist it to the utmost. Having a dark suspicion of these grim possibilities, man turns a blind eye to the shadow-side of human nature. Blindly he strives against the salutary dogma of original sin, which is yet so prodigiously true. Yes, he even hesitates to admit the conflict of which he is so painfully aware.
>
> (CW7: 35)

One cannot get rid of the shadow entirely, but one can learn to manage it. As such, it is an important part of the individuation process. As Christopher Hauke notes in *Jung and the Postmodern*, for Jung, individuation means integrating neglected parts of the psyche in the hope to become 'fully oneself':

> nothing more or less than being fully oneself. This means including parts of oneself that have been lost or neglected not only due to circumstances or personal history – parents, upbringing and so on – but have also been lost or neglected due to the collective conditions of the era and culture . . . . However, the personal and the collective, as well as the past and the present, are difficult to differentiate and separate in any final way.
>
> (Hauke, 2000: 109)

Cinematic narratives often employ the shadow to show the split personality of the modern individual. For instance, Tyler Durden (Brad Pitt) in *Fight Club* (1999, directed by David Fincher) is the nameless protagonist's doppelganger who represents his repressed, split-off personality traits. Tyler is a social terrorist who professes his disdain towards society, and who does everything the narrator does not dare to do: urinates in the food at restaurants where he works as a waiter; makes soap out of liposuction fat and sells it to posh perfumeries; destroys an Apple store; and has outrageous sex with the protagonist's girlfriend Marla (Helena Bonham Carter). As the film progresses, the double gets madder and more dangerous in his plans to destroy the global financial system while the spineless protagonist makes half-hearted attempts to control his runaway 'second nature'. Like many doppelganger narratives, the film ends with the protagonist killing his double, nearly dying himself as a result (because the shadow is an inseparable part of human nature; one cannot just 'kill it off'), and redeeming the world by releasing it from the grip of capitalist greed and globalisation.

The anima and the animus

In the classical model of individuation after the encounter with the shadow, the individual has to deal with the anima or the animus – the contrasexual 'soul image' residing in the person's psyche and defining his or her relationships with the opposite sex. In myths and fairy tales these archetypal images can be presented in both their positive (helping, kindly, useful) and negative (demonic) incarnations. As a rule, men have to deal with two types of the anima: the domestic (passive) angel, and the sexual or intellectual (proactive) whore. Women are endowed with more than one animus: in fact, some are possessed by a chorus of animuses, all so loud that they make the women in question impossible to manage. It is clear from this outline of Jungian theory that Jung's view, and that of the early Jungian analysts, on the animus and the anima were quite inflexible, for they only wrote about heterosexual people, and theorised about the 'treacherous' anima that lures men into trouble, and the 'loud' animus that turns women into impossible, uncontrollable creatures (both are discussed in more detail in Chapter 6). Notwithstanding these descriptions none of the archetypes can be completely integrated into consciousness, or made 'safe' and innocuous. The best an individual can do is to try and illuminate the archetypes, who come to us in the more personalised and anthropomorphic form of archetypal images, thus allowing them to speak via various narratives: dreams, fantasies, literature, cinema and television.

The old wise man and the old wise woman

Parental issues (and beyond) are reflected in the figures of the old wise man and the old wise woman. Like any archetypes, they can be 'good' or 'bad'. The old wise man, who often materialises in fairy tales in the form of magicians, father figures or helpful (or evil) elves, stands for meaning, and often brings to the ailing or confused hero some calcification about his or her desperate situation. This archetype, Jung writes, represents 'knowledge, reflection, insight, wisdom, cleverness, and intuition on the one hand, and on the other, moral qualities such as goodwill and readiness to help, which make his "spiritual" character sufficiently plain' (CW9, I: 406). Yet, in its negative incarnation it may appear as a wicked villain who 'does evil for evil's sake': a ruthless king, a concocter of poisons or a horrid water spirit. This ambivalence reflects the dynamic character of the psyche in which nothing is ever set in stone, all views are relative and should be balanced out by the opposite. 'Too much of a good thing' can also be bad.

Similarly, the wise old woman (who has a certain affinity with the great mother archetype, discussed in more detail in Chapter 6) can appear to the protagonist as a helpful motherly figure or a wicked witch, and can symbolise now 'wisdom and spiritual exaltation' and 'helpful instinct and impulse that . . . cherishes and sustains', and now 'anything secret, hidden, dark; the abyss, the world of the dead, anything that devours, seduces and poisons' (CW9, I: 158). The mother is ambivalent as she is both 'the loving and the terrible mother' (CW9, I: 158).

Both the old wise man and the old wise woman go way beyond the figures of the individual's actual parents, and symbolise more universal issues: primarily, growing up, establishing a balance between consciousness and the unconscious; getting in trouble and looking for help during this process. These 'wise' archetypes, despite the possibility of them turning into evil figures, represent the ability of the psyche to self-direct, self-train and self-heal. For instance, Luke Skywalker in *Star Wars* (1977, directed by George Lucas) is advised by Obi-Wan Kenobi, but also externally motivated by Darth Vader, the two father figures illuminating the two sides of the protagonist's own nature and guiding him towards better self-understanding and self-reflection.

The child

According to Jung, in fairy tales and myths the child archetype is linked to the archetype of the self. The child is a future hero, and many mythological saviours are child gods. In the individuation process, the wonder-child 'paves the way for a future change of personality' and 'anticipates the figure that comes from the synthesis of conscious and unconscious elements in the personality. It is therefore a symbol which unites the opposites; a mediator, bringer of healing, that is, one who makes whole' (CW9, I: 278). In myths, the (usually male) child prodigy possesses miraculous abilities: he can casually kill dangerous snakes as he lays in his cot (Heracles), survive numerous assassination attempts like Dionysus, or, like Harry Potter, play a trick or two on the evil members of his adopted family.

As a rule, his birth is unusual. He is a child of a god or a goddess, and in many cases his high status parents prefer to remain anonymous. This element of the motif implies that a godlike infant cannot be produced by ordinary parents; surely his unusual abilities come from very special people. Yet, despite his special abilities and influential parents, the child's life is fraught with danger. He has merciless and ruthless enemies: for instance, the goddess Hera who tried to destroy the unborn Dionysos out of jealousy because he was the child of Zeus and a mortal woman, Semele, or King Herod who according to the Gospel of Matthew ordered the murder of all the infants in Bethlehem hoping that the baby Jesus would be among them.

Jung theorised that the child motif corresponded to the birth of the personality and its development and eventual survival in the world. It represents the 'infancy' of the individuation process, its fragile, humble beginnings. Growing out of the unconscious, and into an unsafe world, is a heroic process. The hero-ego, the conscious psyche 'emerges' from the primordial darkness, and tries to establish itself in its surroundings and to gain a unique identity. Attainment of a recognisable personality marks the birth of the individual as someone separate from the crowd, as well as someone relatively independent from the unconscious, from 'mother nature':

> The Hero's main feat is to overcome the monster of darkness: it is the long-hoped-for and expected triumph of consciousness over the unconscious. . . . The

> coming of consciousness was probably the most tremendous experience of primeval times, for with it a world came into being whose existence no one had suspected before. 'And God said: "Let there be light!"' is the projection of that immemorial separation of the conscious from the unconscious. . . . Hence the 'child' distinguishes itself by deeds which point to the conquest of the dark.
>
> (CW9, I: 284)

The abandonment motif is an integral aspect of the child myth because, translated back into the language of individual development, it symbolises personal independence, even when it has been achieved through isolation and hardship. Abandonment, Jung writes, is necessary because it triggers the birth of the individual as a separate entity (CW9, I: 285). Moreover, the child

> is all that is abandoned and exposed and at the same time divinely powerful; the insignificant, dubious beginning, and the triumphant end. The 'eternal child' in man is an indescribable experience, an incongruity, a handicap, and a divine prerogative; an imponderable that determines the ultimate worth or worthlessness of a personality.
>
> (CW9, I: 300)

The child is a future hero, a future individual, and becoming an individual is a difficult task.

Many directors utilise the child archetype in their films. For instance, Tim Burton's outcast protagonists are all versions of the child archetype. This 'misfit' image can appear in various forms in Burton's movies: the persecuted monster, the mad genius, the maniac, the dishevelled teenager living in his own Gothic castle on a hill, and the disturbed superhero who fights his horrible shadow. These guises often overlap ('the child' is also 'the genius' and 'the maniac', etc.), creating a complex picture of the typical Burtonian male character – a weird, isolated little boy who grows up to be a lonely artist. The childish protagonist invariably has a dark imagination and is never accepted by the ordinary people who often hate him or even want him dead (Batman, Edward Scissorhands, Willy Wonka). More recently, Burton has been making narratives with female protagonists in them, notably *Alice in Wonderland* (2010) and *Big Eyes* (2015). Both the female protagonists – Alice (Mia Wasikowska) and the painter Margaret from *Big Eyes* (Amy Adams) fit into the 'dark child' pattern characteristic of Burtonian individuation: both are creative, different, oppressed, battling against societal prejudice and defending their right to be individuals amongst 'normal people'.

Although Burton's protagonist is in conflict with his or her environment – the notorious crowd of commoners who fail to understand him or her – he or she still attempts to give something back to society, and is keen to transform it to the best of his or her abilities. Despite the split personality and the 'monstrous' darkness they harbour, Bruce Wayne, the assorted Edwards, Victor, Vincent and Alice still function as human beings; they are able to empathise with others; they are able to relate (albeit badly and in their own way). Edward Scissorhands epitomises the Burtonian protagonist as he used to be – creative, dishevelled, immature, funny and lovingly mad. This kind of protagonist is eclectic yet harmonious. He can transform his anguish and pain into tree sculptures (Edward Scissorhands), funny mechanical contraptions (Pee Wee), crime-fighting devices (Batman), innovative chocolates (Willy Wonka), science (Ichabod) and silly B-movies (Ed Wood). The conflicting sides of his personality work well together because his creativity keeps him afloat and allows him to connect with others.

The trickster

In his essay 'On the Psychology of the Trickster Figure', Jung gives this archetype a whole range of contradictory definitions. To a large extent, this contradictoriness is inevitable because the trickster's role in social structure can be regarded as either, or both, positive or negative depending on whether you see it from the point of view of society or from the position of the freedom-seeking individual. The trickster is both 'subhuman and superhuman, a bestial and divine being, whose chief and most alarming characteristic is his unconsciousness' (CW9, I: 472). The trickster, Jung writes, is a creature of the unconscious, the wise fool, the clown and the delight-maker. He has a dual nature: half-animal, half divine. Tricksters reverse the hierarchic order, are shapeshifters and are famous for their malicious tricks and pranks. Jung also mentions the strong link between the trickster figure and the tradition of carnival, where the Devil appeared as *simia dei* – the ape of God (CW9, I: 465–472). It is also 'a faithful reflection of an absolutely undifferentiated human consciousness, corresponding to a psyche that has hardly left the animal level' (CW9, I: 465). This archetype will be discussed in more detail in Chapter 4.

The self

The archetype of the self stands for the never-achievable psychological wholeness. Jung writes that 'wholeness can be realised for one moment only – the moment that Faust was seeking all his life' (CW12: 321). The self encompasses all the elements of the psyche, both 'reachable' and 'unreachable'; it comprises 'consciousness first of all, then the personal unconscious, and finally an indefinitely large segment of the collective unconscious whose archetypes are common to all mankind' (CW9, I: 634). Unlike the other archetypes, which can become personalised and 'are permanently or temporarily included within the scope of the personality', the self is both simple and extremely composite, and largely impersonal.

The idea of a hero's journey is to bring the quester nearer to this unity, the psychic perfection which eliminates all conflicts and problems. Although the achievement of this inner peace and absolute perfection is impossible, the hero during the journey attempts to solve at least some of the problems (such as dealing with the shadow, for instance – or coming to terms with the great mother). In narratives, the self is the driving force of the story, and the protagonist's main motivation vehicle.

The archetype of the alien

The alien is one of the most popular characters in contemporary film and television – so popular, in fact, that it has almost become a new archetype. Its biggest competitor and antagonist is the urban superhero, and both are linked to the spiritual crisis of the technologically advanced civilisation. Extra-terrestrial invaders have dominated science fiction and horror genres even since Georges Méliès *Trip to the Moon* (1902), and their firm presence in moving image narratives was mirrored in the UFO obsession and invasion fantasies that proved enduring in popular imagination throughout the twentieth century.

Alien invasion is a good umbrella metaphor that covers a whole set of contemporary anxieties. The alien figure possesses distinct characteristics: it is highly intelligent, mysterious, omniscient, confident and can read minds. These features render themselves particularly well to the stock sci-fi themes of mind control, conspiracy and paranoia – the traditional sublimation of political fears of such a diverse scope as totalitarian communist governments, capitalist mind-manipulation, colonialist occupation, the hidden power of the media, secret service conspiracies and other forms of 'big brother' control and surveillance. Not surpassingly, the theme of alien invasion is closely linked to conspiracy theories and to rumours that governments are hiding information about extra-terrestrial visitors. Such conspiracy theories and their accompanied paranoid and persecutory affects are also commonplace fantasies for people with borderline personalities. In turn this suggests the proximity of these fantasies to the collective unconscious.

Some cinematic aliens invade from the inside by stealing human minds and invading their bodies; others arrive on Earth openly and destroy its cities by fire. Monsters from the *Alien* franchise (1979–1997, directed by Ridley Scott, James Cameron, David Fincher and Jean-Pierre Jeunet) would belong to the first group; and mass invaders from *Independence Day* (1996), directed by Roland Emmerich, Tim Burton's *Mars Attacks!* (1996), Steven Spielberg's *The War of the Worlds* (2005) or *Edge of Tomorrow* (2014, Doug Liman) would belong to the second. In both the narrative types, human beings lose control over themselves and their habitat while a more powerful force takes over.

In the middle of the twentieth century, at the height of the Cold War and after the horrors of the Second World War, alien obsession was a big part of the cultural climate. In his book *The Monster Show: A Cultural History of Horror* (1993), David Skal demonstrates how the threat of physical annihilation shaped horror entertainment in the US:

> Most Americans found it easier not to face the invasion/annihilation anxieties directly; they found indirect expression in McCarthyism, UFO hysteria,

> and perhaps, most pointedly, in the popular medium of lurid and sensational comic books that had been growing steadily since the end of World War II.
> (Skal, 1993: 230)

Thus, the war gave creative industries new imagery, themes and symbolism because it 'had introduced two radical new forms of mechanized death – the atomic bomb and the extermination camp' (Skal, 1993: 229). In this sense, the alien is an 'estranged' version of a human being; it is the ultimate other, the doppelganger, the shadow who serves as a mirror for reflecting conflicting human qualities back to the audience. Patrick Luciano explores these themes in detail in his 1987 book *Them or Us: Archetypal Interpretation of Fifties Alien Invasion Films.*

Jung had his own explanation of the alien obsession phenomenon. In his essay, 'Flying Saucers: A Modern Myth of Things Seen in the Sky' (1958), he explores a number of UFO sightings, and compares them to similar psycho-spiritual experiences that took place in the Middle Ages. The collective unconscious, as we remember, looks for suitable symbols to express itself. These symbols (archetypal images) are culturally determined, unlike their core contents (archetypes). Jung suggests that the image of the spaceship is the contemporary version of the archetype of the Self – the psychological unity, the image of godlike perfection which we aim to become but will never achieve. The UFOs became a powerful mass dream image partly because, in Jung's words, 'anything that looks technological goes down without difficulty with modern man' (CW10: 624).

Jung explains the round shape of flying saucers in terms of universal religious symbolism; in his view,

> the circular symbols have played an important role in every age . . . . There is an old saying that 'God is a circle whose centre is everywhere and circumference nowhere'. God in his omniscience, omnipotence, and omnipresence is a totality symbol *par excellence*, something round, complete, and perfect. . . . On the antique level, therefore, the UFOs could easily be conceived as 'gods'.
> (CW10: 622)

By the 1950s alien invasion had already become a collective dream theme, with people reporting cases of spotting shiny globes in the sky, being abducted by aliens, of extra-terrestrials carving out patterns on crops or aliens sharing wisdom with their 'less intelligent brothers'. In fact, the figure's ambiguity – its unpredictability and aggression offset by advanced intellect and superhuman abilities – make it an ambivalent projection of humanity's battle with its own shadow.

Even after the two world wars, Jung argues, there was still a belief in the people's intrinsic goodness and the power of human consciousness to control its animal impulses. This belief 'thrust itself to the forefront in the form of a symbolic rumour, accompanied and reinforced by the appropriate visions' and therefore activated an archetype 'that has always expressed order, deliverance, salvation and wholeness' (CW10: 624). In contemporary Western society, Jung writes somewhat optimistically, 'consciously rationalistic enlightenment predominates' and that 'belief in this world and in the power of man has, despite assurances to the contrary, become an . . . irrefragable truth' (CW10: 623). Every age has its symbols reflecting the same eternal conflicts and universal problems. The UFO thus becomes a saviour, a Christ-like visitor coming to planet Earth to redeem its inhabitants from themselves, or, alternatively, in the form of the angry God from the Old Testament, punishing human beings for their sins and wrongdoings.

In the past fifty years, the alien has become such a stock feature in television and cinema that it has transcended its 'alienness'. Comedies about visitors from outer space, such as *Mars Attacks!* (2000), the *Men in Black* (1997–2012) franchise, *My Stepmother Is an Alien* (1988; Richard Benjamin), *Spaceballs* (1987; Mel Brooks) and *Paul* (2011; Greg Mottola), prove that we are prepared to laugh at ourselves, our incompleteness and our dreams of godlike 'perfection'. The alien has almost been recognised as a projection, as a vessel onto which humans project their fears of themselves, and their hope that the higher nature in them prevails over the dark impulses and traits.

Christopher Vogler's *The Writer's Journey* and Joseph Campbell's monomyth

The screenwriter and development executive Christopher Vogler particularly capitalised on the founding concepts of Jungian psychology: the individuation process and archetypes. In his book, *The Writer's Journey: Mythic Structure for Writers* (1998) Vogler transforms the ideas of Joseph Campbell and Carl Jung into a sort of Hollywood cookbook aimed at helping screenwriters create commercial yet spiritually meaningful narratives. *The Writer's Journey* is an interesting phenomenon in the world of writing guides and psychoanalytic criticism. It blatantly defies the prevalence of Freudian thinking in the cinematic arena, both in its style and content, and asserts the usefulness and supremacy of the Jungian approach to screen narratives.

It is not just the structure that Vogler borrows from Jung and Campbell. In the introduction to the book, he is very particular about infusing visual images with meaning and spirituality – he firmly believes that the goldmine, the structure he discovered, is not only commercial, but also capable of making people think and improve their lives. The motivation behind the book was to create a template for personally meaningful stories. His working as a story analyst for Fox 2000 taught him that good films were affecting the organs of his body 'in various ways, and really good ones were stimulating more than one organ' (Vogler, 2007: x). Even his writing style has elements of 'new age' thinking in it:

> A book goes out like a wave rolling over the surface of the sea. Ideas radiate from the author's mind and collide with other minds, triggering new waves that

> return to the author. These generate further thoughts and emanations, and so it goes. The concepts described in *The Writer's Journey* have radiated and are now echoing back interesting challenges and criticisms as well as sympathetic vibrations. This is my report on the waves that have washed back over me from publication of the book, and on the new waves I send back in response.
>
> (2007: xiii)

Having imbibed the Jungian idea of the collective unconscious – which has also become a significant part of the book's philosophy – Vogler also claims that his cookbook is not an artificial invention, that he was not trying to judge the unconscious by rational means, but instead listened to its waves and eventually elicited from it *The Writer's Journey*.

Vogler takes different archetypes – the hero, the trickster, the shadow, the mentor (wise old man or woman), etc. – and analyses each of them with examples from (mostly popular Hollywood) films. He also separates the hero's journey into phases or steps (call to adventure, refusal of the call, meeting with the mentor, the ordeal reward, the road back, etc.), and discusses each of them in detail. Curiously, Vogler mixes Jung's and Freud's ideas in an attempt to create his own analytical language, for instance: 'In psychological terms, the archetype of the Hero represents what Freud called the ego – that part of the personality that separates from the mother, that considers itself distinct from the human race' (2007: 29).

Vogler's proposed narrative structure follows that outlined by Campbell in *A Hero with a Thousand Faces* rather faithfully. Underlying Campbell's *monomyth* (the common pattern found in most narratives all around the world) is the anthropological concept of the rites of passage: *separation – initiation – return* (Campbell, 2008: 23). The only trait that unites all monomyth heroes is 'being different' from the rest of their community. In other words, they attract extreme reactions from the people in their surroundings. In everything else they are completely different: they can be very stupid or very intelligent; complete failures or very successful; very handsome or, by contrast, not at all attractive. Yet, the protagonist remains unfulfilled because he or she does not comply with the norms of his or her community. The composite hero of the monomyth, Campbell argues:

> is a personage of exceptional gifts. Frequently he is honoured by his society, frequently unrecognised or disdained. He and/or the world in which he finds himself suffers from a symbolical deficiency. In fairy tales this may be as slight as the lack of a certain golden ring, whereas in apocalyptic vision the physical and spiritual life of the whole earth can be represented as fallen, or on the point of falling into ruin.
>
> . . .
>
> Whether the hero be ridiculous or sublime, Greek or barbarian, gentile or Jew, his journey varies little in essential plan.
>
> (2008: 29–30)

According to Campbell, narrative is a way of organising the often confusing signals coming from the unconscious. Without structure (and narrative provides a firm structure for often subliminal life experiences) we would drown in impressions, fears, choices and instinctive reactions. Narratives hold together the experience of being human. Echoing Jung, Campbell writes:

> The unconscious sends all sorts of vapours, odd beings, terrors and deluding images up into the mind – whether in dream, broad daylight, or insanity; for the human kingdom, beneath the floor of the comparatively neat little dwelling that we call our consciousness, goes down into unsuspected Aladdin caves.
>
> (2008: 5)

Narratives also save us from insanity by collecting, arranging and managing the unconscious urges. At the same time, in the Aladdin caves not only jewels but also a dangerous jinn abides:

> the inconvenient or resisted psychological powers that we have not thought or dared integrate into our lives. And they may remain unsuspected, on the other hand, some chance word, the smell of a landscape, the taste of a cup of tea, or the glance of an eye may touch a magic spring, and then dangerous messengers may appear in the brain. They are dangerous because they threaten the fabric of security into which we have built ourselves and our family. But they are fiendishly fascinating too, for they carry keys that open the whole realm of the desired and feared adventure of the discovery of the self.
>
> (2008: 5)

In other words, we like stories and find them fascinating because they bring us meaning and self-discovery despite that a journey into the depths of oneself can be both dangerous and threatening to the existing psychological layout of our lives. Interestingly enough, and despite the overall Jungian hue of his writings, Campbell argues that Freudian concepts are more suitable for examining the first part of the individual's life whereas Jung's ideas are better for dealing with what happens after the mid-life crisis. In fact, Campbell is astute in his observations and in his assessment of the overall directions of these two schools of psychological thought: he notices that Freudians are more interested in personal psychology, and Jungian writing tends to be more general and vague, and concerns larger issues: life and death, the meaning of life, spirituality and social processes. He writes:

> Sigmund Freud stresses in his writings the passages and difficulties of the first half of the human cycle of life – those of our infancy and adolescence, when our sun is mounting towards its zenith. C.G Jung, on the other hand, has emphasised the crises of the second portion – when, in order to advance, the shining sphere must submit to descend and disappear, at last, into the night-womb of the grave.
>
> (2008: 8)

Narratives also provide a safe way of dealing with unconscious contents and urges. Not everyone is born a hero, and not everyone is capable of belonging to one of the two 'hero extremes' – different and accepted or different and rejected. For millennia, fairy tales, myths and rituals have been providing 'normal people' (the ones who do not wish to be different, to become 'heroes' and to forge their own path) with meaning and ways of organising their experiences and instincts:

> The multitude of men and women choose the less adventurous way of the comparatively unconscious civic and tribal routines. But these seekers, too, are saved – by virtue of the inherited symbolic aids of society, the rites of passage, the grace-yielding sacraments, given to mankind of old by the redeemers or handed down through millennia.
>
> (Campbell, 2008: 17)

Interestingly, Campbell distinguishes between the heroic 'inner call' and the external call of a 'doctrine' – a communal, religious, social or political structure provided to the individual by the governors of the community. He does not give preference to either because, in his view, both are equally valid ways of using narratives to organise and manage one's life experiences. Much more perilous is the condition of the modern man who is left without myths and therefore without guidance; spiritually hanging 'in mid air':

> It is only those who know neither an inner call nor an outer doctrine whose plight is truly desperate; that is to say, most of us today, in this labyrinth without and within the heart. Alas, where is the guide, that fond virgin, Ariadne, to supply the simple clue that will give courage to face the Minotaur, and the means then to find our way to freedom when the monster has been met and slain?
>
> (2008: 17)

Ultimately, Campbell claims that the man or woman we call modern is a lonely creature plucked from his or her culture and left exposed to a changing and fast-paced lifestyle. Neither Jung nor Campbell had any idea what kind of psychological change would occur in the minds of individuals at the beginning of the twenty-first century, but the first half of the twentieth century already looked 'too much' to them. Without myths, Campbell writes, the modern man follows the narratives left to him – the personal narratives called dreams. Psychoanalysis is there to help him analyse these dreams. In this sense, psychoanalysis is a replacement of the old communal structures which played the role of providing the individual with meaning via myth and ritual:

> Freud, Jung and their followers have demonstrated irrefutably that the logic, and the deeds of myth survive into modern times. In the absence of an effective general mythology, each of us has his private, unrecognised, rudimentary, yet secretly potent pantheon of dream.
>
> (2008: 2)

Campbell writes about personal mythology via dream work, but he does not make the obvious connection between cinema and dreams. The result of this omission is that it misses the collective element of contemporary mythology. It transpires that Campbell insists on the personal and intimate aspects of modern narratives, but seems to forget that radio and cinema had been producing immediately accessible narratives for at least fifty years. Campbell's individual is torn from his roots and his psychological survival depends on the ability of psychoanalysis to interpret his private dreams. The public, easily accessible forms of dreams – such as films – are not mentioned.

Vogler who proceeds to fill in the obvious gap picks up this connection. The hero's journey embeds both our general life principles and guidelines for screenwriters and Hollywood executives. This means that films become our dreams, aimed at fulfilling our psychological needs and acting as our mirrors without any mediators – no need for psychoanalysis or philosophy. It is possible to manipulate the audience's emotions, Vogler argues in the 'Ordeal' section, by making the hero's path thorny and unpredictable, by making them empathise with the hero throughout his or her numerous ordeals, by giving them the opportunity to experience extreme emotions in the safety of their homes or movie theatre:

> People pay good money for a taste of death. Bungee-jumping, skydiving and terrifying amusement park rides give the jolt that awakens fuller appreciation of life. Adventure films and stories are always popular because they offer a less risky way to experience death and rebirth, through heroes we can identify with.
>
> (Vogler, 2007: 160)

Cinema is individuation personified. More so than fiction thanks to its visuality, it has always been a sort of condensed and accelerated individuation process, a kind of commercial version of the hero myth. Jung's writings on contemporary individuation are indispensable for film studies, primarily because most cinematic narratives attempt to define the individual and to provide commentary on his or her relationship with society. In fact, cinema is a form of mass individuation, a form of self-reflection for large groups of people. In cinema, cultural, social and political problems become apparent as it provides a platform fortheir discussion.

There is a shadow side to all this and as a result of Vogler's further commercialisation of the individuation structure, cinema and television have become machines generating individuation narratives for busy viewers who are no longer aware of their psychological processes, their place in the environment or ways of connecting with other human beings. This kind of viewer does not have time for musing over things or thinking about 'life, the universe and everything'. In this way, individuation becomes externalised and is presented in a processed form, rather like nicely packaged supermarket products.

The symbol: between the personal and the collective

The symbol is one of the central concepts of Jungian narrative criticism, for symbols are the language in which the otherwise 'mute' collective unconscious speaks (see Chapter 3, 'Jungian psychology: signs and symbols'). They help this vast ocean express itself, turning the collective into the personal, providing ways for human beings to deal with the complexity of internal life as well as with the necessity to be part of society. Importantly, symbols should be respected and not over-interpreted; they are not signs with a fixed meaning, but have multiple meanings. This view is rooted in Jung's theoretical conception of the symbol. It lacks Freud's pseudo-scientism in that is does not attempt to sound like a finished system of thought, complete with precise definitions and rational explanations of psychological phenomena.

Jung stressed the supremacy and independence of symbols, which differ from both metaphors and signs. Symbols, Jung implies in his writing, should be respected in that they are not subject to precise analysis or exact definitions. In order to function and exist, they need breathing space, and this precludes the application of the scientific approach to them. The products of the collective unconscious, symbols defy interpretation. They demand to be respected and not dismantled, deciphered or 'explained away'.

The ultimately unknowable meaning of a symbol and the way it fits an individual's situation are the main points of difference between Freudian and Jungian approaches. Freud's 'semiotic' attitude requires an exact interpretation while Jung's approach of amplification (or deferred interpretation) adopts a more creative and tentative approach to the meaning of creative and dream-imagery. Jung does not see the unconscious as being linguistically structured, hence his rejection of semiosis in favour of amplification. He writes in 'Psychological Types':

> The concept of symbol should in my view be strictly distinguished from that of sign. Symbolic and semiotic meanings are entirely different things . . . . A symbol always presupposes that the chosen expression is the best possible description or formulation of a relatively unknown fact, which is none the less known to exist or is postulated as existing . . . . Every view which interprets the symbolic expression as an analogue or an abbreviated designation for a *known* thing is *semiotic*. . . . The symbol is alive only so long as it is pregnant with meaning. But once its meaning has been born out of it, once that expression is found that formulated the thing sought, expected, or divined even better than the hitherto accepted symbol, then the symbol is *dead*, i.e., it possesses only an historical significance . . . . An expression that stands for a known thing remains a mere sign and is never a symbol. It is, therefore, quite impossible to create a living symbol, i.e., one that is pregnant with meaning, from known associations.
>
> (CW6: 814–817, emphasis as original)

The symbol in the Jungian world is everything; it is the biggest piece of the cultural puzzle as well as the most important element in works of art and dreams. As Steven Walker observes, 'By emphasising the image over the word, Jungian psychology differentiates itself radically from Freudian, Lacanian and other psychologies that stress the task of interpreting the *language* of the unconscious' (Walker, 2002: 3). Thus, a symbol is a relative and 'immediate' thing, rather than a permanent, ready-made set of meanings. In a symbol, the relationship between the signifier and the signified is, indeed, highly arbitrary. The symbolic, from the point of view of Jungian psychology, constitutes the base of all meaning-making in the life of the individual.

Here then is one of the rhizomatic structures mentioned in the Introduction to this book. Psychoanalytic interpretation is predicated on the oedipal sexual aetiology of neurosis. In order for an image to be understood a stripping back of layers of psychic and cultural encoding is required to reveal what happened in childhood. This is a type of psychological archaeology in which the 'truth' behind a psychological symptom has to be unearthed, even in the face of resistance and the conscious defences of the patient. By contrast, a Jungian orientation sees meaning as something that is much less certain, as subject to change, as something that is as much made by society and through our individual responses as it is inscribed and intrinsic to the image itself.

One of the reasons for the relatively unfixed meaning of images (and by extension media products) is that the Jungian model of the psyche is teleological, which is to say it is both forward looking and possesses purpose or intent. Whether this should be understood in a literal or metaphorical manner is outside the scope of this discussion but what is significant is that this offers a somewhat different approach to that offered by the Freudian models of the psyche, which tend to see the current state of the psyche as the result of historically accruing events. In Freudian models, the task of analysis, personal and cultural, is to decode the workings of the psyche, working through its defence mechanisms to bring the original trauma(s) into the light of day. Of course Jungian thinking is not without such developmental aspects, particularly where British Object Relations and the work of Melanie Klein have played an important role and Helena Bassil-Morozow has started to incorporate these ideas into her work on the state of modernity.

Because Jung divided the unconscious into the personal and the collective, his vision of 'what it is made of' was radically different from the linguistic approach of the Freudian and post-Freudian school. The collective unconscious is an ocean of impulses and instincts, and by definition it cannot be structured like a language. Rather, it is a floating sea of experiences. In a way, Jung argues, it is similar to a film – a series of moving images inhabiting the human frame, realising itself and, essentially, making itself visible in projection. As he comments:

> The psyche consists essentially of images. It is a series of images in the truest sense, not an accidental juxtaposition or sequence, but a structure that is throughout full of meaning and purpose; it is a 'picturing' of vital

> activities. And just as the material of the body that is ready for life has need of the psyche in order to be capable of life, so the psyche presupposes the living body in order that its images may live.
>
> (CW8: 618)

By 'images' Jung means both symbols and archetypes – and in his writings he often does not distinguish between the two. Moreover 'images' for Jung can be further subdivided into those that are 'personalised' concrete realisations and those that are 'collective' abstract ideas. An archetype is an irrepresentable idea, whereas archetypal images are concrete realisations of archetypes in dreams, fantasies, myths, etc. In Jung's own words, 'the perceptible archetypal image is not identical with the inherited form [i.e. archetype], which allows an indefinite number of empirical expressions (Jung, *Letters*, quoted in Walker, 2002: 12). For instance, 'dying-and-rising god' is an archetype, but Osiris, Dionysus and Jesus are archetypal images. Similarly, female initiation of sexual contact is an archetype, whereas stories of the beauty and the beast, Little Red Riding Hood and Bluebeard's castle are archetypal situations.

By itself, the collective unconscious is speechless. It is dark, passionate and confused, and needs a language to make itself clear and understood. Its free-floating impulses can be turned into narratives with the help of symbols. Being human – having to deal with the mind-body dichotomy – means processing complex emotional experiences As Christopher Hauke puts it in his book, *Visible Mind: Movies, Modernity and the Unconscious* (2013),

> popular forms such as cinema can provide holding necessary for intense experiences, making them more accessible and more bearable. When an intensity of emotions is mixed with the less intense it becomes more bearable, bringing with it the possibility for psychological and emotional repair and growth.
>
> (Hauke, 2014: 4)

These more bearable experiences take root in the personal unconscious – the place where the vague experiences of the collective unconscious acquire shapes and narrative lines. The personal layer of the unconscious is structured by culture and by language. The amorphous contents of the collective unconscious transform into 'words' and 'phrases' of particular cultural constructs. As Oliver Davies puts it, 'Whereas the Lacanian unconscious is composed of potentially word-forming linguistic structures, the Jungian (collective) unconscious is made up of structures with a potential for image formation' (Davies, 2004: 66–67). It is images, not words, that hold the primary importance for Jung.

Symbols are the building bricks of all narratives whether they are in the dreams of psychic life, myths and fairy tales or fiction, and films. We need symbols to deal with the otherwise confusing depth of pre-civilised emotions experienced by all people. Thus people, to help the unconscious express itself and to make the experience of existing and relating more bearable, create symbolic images. Such images make us aware of ourselves and others and assist in creating a meaningful narrative out of our lives. Symbols make us human; they are part of being human. Importantly they stand at the threshold between the unconscious and consciousness and are the language of creativity – an unconscious and often unpredictable force which helps people deal with everyday experiences.

Symbols differ from both signs and metaphors in that they are capable of holding multiple – and often opposing – meanings. In a symbol, the relationship between the signifier and the signified is, indeed, highly arbitrary. Drawing upon Jung's democratic position of 'anti-exactness', Don Fredericksen argues:

> We must understand that Jung's distinction between sign and symbol ultimately elaborates two distinct modes of apprehending and explaining the psyche and its products – not just two distinct psychologies but two distinct ontologies and philosophies of value.
>
> This point is succinctly illustrated by Jung and Freud's differing explanations of, and attitudes toward, incest fantasy and symbolism. Freud interpreted the incest fantasy concretely. . . . Freud labels the distorted or disguised expressions of the incest wish 'symbols', incorrectly so according to Jung. For the latter, Freud's 'symbols' are in fact signs, standing for the putatively known, albeit repressed, desire of the patient to have physical intimacy with a parent. Their meaning can be completely explained by Freudian analytic procedures that reduce them to their underlying cause.
>
> (Fredericksen, 2001: 19)

For Jung, the symbol is always bigger than the sum of the dreamer's (or the author's) biographical details, and significantly deeper than any literal or pre-existed meaning. The unconscious, Jungian psychology implies, would not want to be interpreted in any other way – and especially given a fixed explanation. Leonardo's childhood dream of being visited in his cradle by a vulture which opened his mouth with its tail demonstrates the difference between the literalness of Freudian interpretations and the Jungian symbolic approach. In the essay 'Leonardo Da Vinci and a Memory of His Childhood', Freud famously interprets the dream in sexual terms – as a metaphor for fellatio – and expresses his amazement that 'phantasy is so completely passive in character' (2001: 86). By contrast the Jungian Erich Neumann criticises Freud's personalistic treatment of Leonardo's bird fantasy. For Neumann, even though Freud's interpretation makes sense and is partially correct, it is still too narrow and does not take into account many other aspects of Leonardo's creative life:

> In connection with the infant lying in his cradle, the bird's tail is primarily a symbol of the maternal breast; but at the same time, Freud correctly interpreted it as the male genital organ. From this basic constellation emerging in the childhood memory, he attempted to derive both the personal mother

> complex of the fatherless Leonardo and a passively homosexual tendency in his love life. Both derivations are false and require a correction, since the 'vulture fantasy' is a transpersonal, archetypal constellation, and not one that may be derived personalistically from Leonardo's family romance.
>
> (Neumann, 1974: 8–9)

His treatment of the symbols in Leonardo's dream is more respectful than Freud's – both towards the artist and his creativity. In his interpretation, Neumann opens up the depth of the symbol by arguing that the nature of the dream is suprapersonal – it is the great man fed by the unconscious, by mother nature, by the spirit:

> The mother represents also the uroboric, i.e., male-female, greatness of the mother in relation to the child she bears, nourishes and protects. In this function, her life-giving breasts . . . often become phallic symbols, in relation to which the child takes the attitude of receiving and conceiving.
>
> (1974: 9)

In Neumann's analysis, the bird symbol acquires a wide spectrum of meanings: it is a breast, a penis, a mother, a father, the uroboric world of the child, the unconscious, creativity and renewal. It is a symbol of empowerment rather than rape (which was implied in Freud's interpretation). Leonardo was given a sign that he was going to be special; that he was going to be led and fed by the forces of creativity welling up from the unconscious and seeking expression.

Man, Neumann says, creates symbols because they help him make meaning out of the messy, unpredictable, impulsive, dark whirlwind of unconscious forces:

> The psychic undercurrents which determine man's feeling and image of the world are manifested through colours and forms, tones and words, which crystallize into symbolic spiritual figures expressing man's relation both to the archetypal world and to the world in which he lives.
>
> (Neumann, 1974: 84)

Moreover, man is the co-creator of his narratives: he helps the unconscious shape them:

> In the original situation man's emotion in the presence of the numinosum leads to expression, for the unconscious, as part of its creative function, carries with it its own expression. But the emotional drives which move the group and the individual within it must not be conceived a dynamic without content. For every symbol, like every archetype, has a specific content, and when the whole of a man is seized by the collective unconscious, this means his consciousness too. Consequently we find from the very start that the creative function of the psyche is accompanied by a reaction of consciousness, which seeks, at first in slight degree but then increasingly, to understand, to

> interpret, and to assimilate the thing by which it was at first overwhelmed. Thus at a very early stage there is a relative fixation of expression and style, and so definite traditions arise.
>
> (Neumann, 1974: 85)

The symbol is the soul of the narrative, and is linked to the archetype. Symbols are transpersonal, and the transpersonal is the archetypal, Neumann argues (1974: 15). Although we cannot really understand the vastness of symbols, to grasp the whole scope of what, say, the archetypal feminine means to mankind, we can at least gain some general idea of it (1974: 15). Any creative man 'travels the archetypally determined way', expressing the unconscious in symbols and weaving narratives out of them as he goes along (1974: 21).

Jungian individuation and the modern age

Cinema is one of the most prominent creations of modernity. Its birth coincided with the acceleration of modern life. In a way, it symbolised the devaluation of reality at the expense of all things unconscious – dreams and fantasy. Cinema provided an escape from the strains and fast pace of modern life; its narratives brought meaning and structure to the hectic metropolitan world. The moving image became the mirror of modernity that reflected the individual's life back to him- or herself, thus helping him or her to bring together the fragments.

Narratives have been providing individuals with meaning since time immemorial. In this sense, cinema was simultaneously different and similar to previous media forms. Similar because it still worked with the linguistic code, and different because the presence of other codes – movement, lighting, sound, acting – made it ever more powerful and influential. It became an all-enveloping experience, capable of drawing the individual in, emotionally influencing her – and even changing her as a person. More than just a form of entertainment, it became a tool, an instrument, an emotional and ideological weapon. Since its birth at the beginning of the twentieth century it has existed on the border between personal experience and social life.

Christopher Hauke notes that modernity – the age of psychoanalysis and improved ways of self-reflection – also 'developed the technology that could reflect their lives back to themselves, framed on the cinema screen'. Cinema and psychoanalysis, both providing people with tools for analysing their subjectivities, have always walked hand in hand:

> The first films were screened publicly in 1895, the same year that Freud was delivering his initial findings and Jung was turning his reading of Nietzsche into what would become his psycho-social theories of analytical psychology . . . . Judging by its huge popularity, the invention of film came at exactly the right moment. The arrival of moving pictures seems to coincide with a general need for self-reflexivity and self-knowledge already being generated elsewhere in the culture.
>
> (Hauke, 2014: 7)

Thus, moving images give the contemporary individual plenty of opportunities to make up for the hectic lifestyle of the modern world and the lack of spirituality and ritual. They also serve as an outlet for passions that are capable of absorbing a range of projections, which otherwise would have remained unconscious and dangerously repressed or hidden. Hauke writes:

> In ancient, medieval and pre-Enlightenment times, human beings bridged their inner and outer worlds by the use of symbols. . . . cinema now constitutes both a site and a vehicle for our projections, especially the projection of archetypes of the collective unconscious. The making and viewing of films is vital in an age that has, in Jung's words, abandoned the gods of Olympus.
> (2014: 5–6)

Many contemporary films that on the surface are schematic and have no value beyond basic entertainment in fact turn out to reflect the psyche of society as much as – if not better than – their high-brow, serious and psychologically detailed counterparts. Take, for instance, 'end of the world' blockbusters, in which a superhuman protagonist (or a group of them) saves the human race from extinction: the *Matrix* trilogy (1999–2003); Spielberg's *War of the Worlds* (2005), films based on Marvel superheroes, the *Resident Evil* films (2010; 2012), *The Avengers* (2012), *Interstellar* (2014), etc.. These movies, with their apocalyptic visions and impressive visuals, express a deep-seated anxiety in the individual surrounded by technology and alienated from his fellow human beings. In the anxiety-driven world of the city, in which relationships are unavoidably subjected to objectification, and emotional closeness is a temporary or even unattainable state, fantasies of destruction and annihilation replace the hopefulness that comes with normal human connection. Modernity (and the acceleration of the speed of life) had been associated with technogenic and natural catastrophes as a punishment for breaking the laws of nature *à la* Victor Frankenstein. These films betray a deep-seated doubt in humankind's rationality and objectivity, as well in its ability to control the collective shadow in the form of envy, greed, aggression and other basic survival impulses that are triggered by the necessity to fight for resources. Many of these films – including *Interstellar* (2014) and *Mad Max: Fury Road* (2015) – emphasise the 'fighting for resources' motif while, at the same time, showing that human beings are also social creatures, and that they are capable of thinking about others alongside protecting their own interests.

The new type of superhero – a hero who redeems the psychological fragmentation and the loneliness of the contemporary individual – saves his species from extinction by saving himself from his own shadow and by attempting (but not always succeeding) to relate to others and to overcome his loneliness. Importantly, Neo, Batman, Spiderman, Superman and the Iron Man are prepared to sacrifice themselves for their society. The contemporary hero is as much about redemption of primarily social ills and sins as his or her classical and religious predecessors. The way he or she seeks for personal glory is inseparable from his or her desire to save the world, and to redeem it from 'common humanity' and from his or her own selfishness and greed, the character traits which in a group of individuals become the collective shadow.

Temenos

The concept of *temenos*, which Jung used extensively in his writings to denote a transformational place and an atmosphere in which change can happen, can be applied to cinema as both a physical space in which people share an experience, and as an emotional process. For Jung, *temenos* is a place that *contains*. It holds, nurtures and transforms various psychological experiences. Importantly, any psychological transformation of this kind in which segments of individuation take place is a sort of ritual enclosure, and has an aura of magic and unpredictability around it. For instance, Jung writes in *Psychology and Alchemy* that *temenos* is 'a taboo area where [the man] will be able to meet the unconscious' (CW12: 63) and where a drama, a ceremonial takes place (CW12: 170). It is what the anthropologist Victor Turner calls a liminal space, a transitional spatial and temporal enclosure, a psychological arena where boundaries are crossed, and the trickster is released, which means that this space should be particularly guarded and controlled lest it become a vortex of uncontrollable experiences instead of being a useful experience which can be integrated into the individuation process.

Cinematic narratives are contemporary versions of eternal myths. People have always used tales as meaning-making devices, and moving images are particularly good for this purpose. Cinema as *temenos* has the possibility 'of becoming an imaginal space' and film watching offers 'a special place where psyche can come alive, be experienced and be commented upon' (Hauke, 2014: 4). Cinema provides containment for what would have otherwise been clouds of experiences, dumb, unexpressed clusters of unconscious contents. Movies give them a voice and a language:

> by engaging with films a version of active imagination is stimulated which can then engage the unconscious – potentially in as successful a fashion as our conscious attention to dream imagery and other fantasies. . . . Often the experience sought and encountered in therapy can be both intense and painful, and for this reason they are often defended against and avoided in daily life. Popular cultural forms such as cinema can provide the holding necessary for such experiences, making them more accessible and more bearable. When an intensity of emotion is mixed with the less intense it becomes bearable, bringing with it the possibility of psychological and emotional repair and growth. As in therapy, the raw material offered by cinema is made available in a form that the psyche can work upon more consciously.
>
> (Hauke, 2014: 4)

'Containment' also hints at maternal behaviour, at unconditional acceptance and love, at the good version of the great mother (the 'good mother' of Object

Relations) whose affection can transform and transcend any issues and problems an individual might have. The moving image as a mother, as a kind of containing vessel and a womb, as a transitional object which absorbs, holds, and keeps projections, offers space for maturation and transformation just by the virtue of it being displayed on 'a silent screen', of not engaging in a dialogue; by the virtue of being a copy, a highly reproducible medium, a form of mass entertainment. For, originals speak loudly and copies remain silent.

Being *temenos*, cinema as both a darkened movie theatre and a form of mass entertainment is thus capable of accepting individual projections, which then become personal fantasies and individuation templates. It is a true merger of the personal and the collective, of multiplied narratives, collectively experienced, and individual perception of them, which then becomes therapeutic, and absorbs and transforms the painful and complex experience of being human.

Alchemy

Jung often used intricate, multi-layered metaphors to describe a whole range of psychic processes. These metaphors include individuation, alchemy, the uroboros, archetypes, syzygy, mandala, etc. These are vague and somewhat indeterminate concepts that contrast sharply with those of other Western theorists (and particularly his psychoanalytic rivals) who have chosen instead to create apparently scientific networks that are held together by seemingly precise terms and coherent theory. Jung's approach was deliberate and intentional, and he avoided precise terminology because it has the effect of diminishing the autonomy of the unconscious and in so doing creating an illusion of control over it.

Alchemy is one such metaphor, and he used it to describe many things from therapy to relationships to creativity. As a metaphor, alchemy loosely outlines any process involving transformational change and the birth of something new out of raw materials, be they physical or psychological. For Jung, alchemy, which in actuality was a pseudo-science preoccupied with creating an idealised, unrealistic substance (the philosopher's stone or an elixir of life), was the ultimate expression of the transformative powers of the human psyche. Any process can thus become alchemical: dreams (and their analysis), psychotherapy, relationships, self-discovery, writing and painting, or even more mundane activities such as gardening or masonry.

James Hillman writes in *Re-Visioning Psychology* (1975) that alchemy was 'depth psychology of an earlier age' (Hillman, 1975: 90). Moreover:

> The materials, vessels, and operations of the alchemical laboratory are personified metaphors of psychological complexes, attitudes, and processes. Every one of the alchemist's operations upon things like salt, sulphur, and lead were also upon his own bitterness, his sulphuric combustion, his depressive slowness. The fire he tended and regulated with careful exactitude was the intensity of his own spirit, his failing or burning interest.

> By means of concretely physical fantasies, the alchemical psychologists worked at the same time on both the soul in his materials and the soul in himself. In the depth of the soul there was also psychopathology, and in fact the substances and processes themselves were conceived in pathologized language, so that in alchemy we find pathologizing as an integral, necessary aspect of soul-making.
>
> (Hillman, 1975: 90)

Alchemy is essentially a metaphor for transformation. Interestingly, Jung describes the symbolic process that is personal change as experienced through archetypes of transformation almost as though it were a cinematic narrative. The process resembles pictures found in alchemy that are full of obscure and complex, yet significant images containing encoded meaning. As Jung notes, the symbolic process 'is an experience *in images and of images*' and is permeated by

> a rhythm of negative and positive, loss and gain, dark and light. Its beginning is almost invariably characterised by one's getting stuck in a blind alley or in some impossible situation; and its goal is, broadly speaking, illumination or higher consciousness, by means of which the initial situation is overcome on a higher level.
>
> (CW9, I: 82)

Like a film, it can span months or even years – or come in a flash of illumination.

This magic is not accidental. The analytical process, which involves the discussion between the conscious and the unconscious parts of the psyche, has a goal as it advances towards some meaning, however perplexing this process (or the resultant meaning) may be (CW12: 3). Moreover, this process seeks its own goal independently of external factors (CW12: 4). The way to finding this meaning 'seems chaotic and indeterminable at first, and only gradually do the signs increase that it is leading anywhere' (CW12: 34). As Terrie Waddell writes in *Mis/takes: Archetype, Myth and Identity in Screen Fiction*, 'like the metaphors the alchemists set up to explain the process of individuation, . . . films and television programmes . . . also contain images that suggest a reworking of the same desire for integration, utopian "wholeness", or genial inner dialogue' (Waddell, 2006: 18). Characters strive

> to come to terms with uneasy 'truths' about their lives and in the process begin to either realise (or fail to realise) that only by recognising and accepting these unnerving aspects of themselves, are they able to discover an identity beyond misplaced/mistaken façades.
>
> (Waddell, 2006: 18)

The alchemical change happening on screen, in characters' lives, reflects the transformation in each individual member of the audience. The reason why we seek narratives (and visual narratives are particularly good for the purpose of triggering the process of alchemical transformation in us) is because we have an instinct to move on as we weave meaning out of psychological chaos and look for signposts that would eventually take us to our goal. Alchemy is a practice of hope aimed at generating solutions and meaning. Moving images, too, have the potential to transform and to give meaning.

Filmmaking itself can be seen as an alchemical process. In a way, it should feel like magic to those creating movies, for it entails the emergence of a picture seemingly out of nowhere, out of the darkness of the camera box, be it the traditional film camera, or its digital version. Nothing is as easy in the process of creating a movie as it looks to the audience: for instance, cinematography involves a range of rough, physical manipulations including heavy cameras, lenses and lighting equipment, to say nothing of the precise knowledge involved in writing, planning, arranging, lighting and filming a scene. When all this precision, all this knowledge comes together live on screen, the result is unbelievable – has this perfection come out of nowhere? Cinema is the kind of magic that creates life out of crude or lifeless matter.

Chapter 3

Jungian psychology

Signs and symbols

Luke Hockley

Introduction

This chapter develops some of the concerns of the previous one by focusing on the basic distinctions between signs and symbols as they are understood in the context of film theory. It does so as a means of highlighting some of the distinctive qualities of the Jungian approach to films and also to underscore some of the pitfalls inherent in it. In the early part of the chapter there are some basic definitions of sign and symbol, signifier and signified. Subsequently, the argument contextualises and fractures those seemingly clear distinctions. Toward the middle and end, this chapter presents a more nuanced argument as a means to locate the distinctive qualities of a Jungian conception of the symbolic. In so doing it mounts a critique of Lacanian and Deleuzian ideas.

The last chapter introduced a Jungian view of symbols. Developing that understanding and reflecting the polyvalent character of the terms sign and symbol, this chapter is deliberately wide-ranging and more media focused. It encompasses semiotic elements and psychoanalytic concepts alongside post-Freudian and Jungian interpretations. The hope is that these terms become sites of contestation and in so doing they resist fixed secure meanings and usage. It would be a mistake to assume that the Jungian orientation towards films offers certitude, or that it provides interpretations that are always superior to other theoretical approaches. Indeed we maintain that to approach films accepting the Jungian lens distorts as much as it clarifies is profoundly Jungian for, as Jung repeatedly states, the unconscious evades definition and interpretation – it is as much experienced as it is understood. As he puts it, 'The unconscious is not this thing or that; it is the Unknown as it immediately affects us' (Prefatory Note to the 1958 revision of *The Transcendent Function* CW8: 1916/1958: p. 68).

With this in mind, on first appearances at least, it might seem the meeting of semiotics with Jungian psychology is akin to introducing matter to antimatter – the end result is predictable and explosive. Semiotics is the 'scientific' study of signs and how they convey meaning. With its origins in the work of the American philosopher C. S. Pierce and the structural linguistics of Ferdinand Saussure, semiotics sets out to provide a logical approach to understanding how language and images convey meaning. It was Saussure who first introduced the distinction between signifier and signified in the sign. His conceptualisation revealed how the meaning of a sign (in our case an image, but for Saussure a linguistic sign – or word) is more than it depicts. (Of which more in a moment.) That idea was taken up by Roland Barthes and developed into the cultural side of semiotics, most notably in his book *Mythologies* (1957). By contrast, Jungian psychology values the non-rational and the intuitive as a means to gain an insight into how images function as purveyors of psychological meaning. This chapter will not reconcile such differences, as this would be a foolhardy and impossible undertaking. Instead, it is going to use some of the insights of a structural and broadly semiotic approach as a way to elucidate some of the strengths of the Jungian position. In so doing, it will show the limitations of both.

At its most basic, semiotics makes a distinction between the signifier and signified. For example, the word apple (signifier) while looking nothing like an actual apple, nonetheless refers to the signified – apple. There is therefore a closed system of relationships between signifier and signified in which the signifier refers to the signified. Such a relationship is based on a code that, once learnt, ensures a stable association between the different elements in the linguistic system. This idea of a closed system of stable meanings whose significance has to be learnt can be transferred from the linguistic realm to other channels of communication. At a meta-level, images (as a medium) can be analysed in terms of signifier and signified, and burrowing down so too can individual images, or films, or television programmes, as can other media such as plays and so forth. Each 'text' offers a closed world (play, film, image) in which the differing elements can be analysed. The problem with this approach perversely rests in its strength, namely that the system of meaning is self-referential, and so it is impossible to locate the meaning of the images as part of a historical discourse. Thus diachronic analysis is out of the question in this type of textual criticism, while synchronic analysis is its strength. It is by deconstructing the synchronic chains of meaning that it is possible to reveal the current cultural meaning of the image. While images might well rely on our knowledge of similar images for their meaning, semiotic analysis focuses on the internal construction of the image, and how the different elements relate to each other to create meaning. Such detailed textual readings break an image down (or deconstruct a text) into signifying elements for example colour, text, typography, spatial relationships, in order to identify which elements convey what meaning. For example in an image of an apple, is it red or green? Small or large; whole or with a bite taken out of it; positioned where in the image? And so forth. A semiotic analysis is much less likely to look at the image of the apple in mythology – though it might, if other elements of the images suggest that – a snake, or fig leaf or naked body picking an apple from a tree in a garden, for example.

The whole set of signifying elements is referred to in semiotic terminology as the paradigmatic set and the individual signifying units into which the elements are combined are termed syntagms. As an illustration, a wardrobe is a paradigmatic set, which combines the individual elements (garments) that can be worn (combined) according to certain rules into a syntagm (socks go on feet not hands). It follows that films are composed at a meta level of shots that are combined to form meaningful sequences. It is also possible to think of the conventions of a genre as a type of paradigmatic set from which each individual film chooses certain elements, which are subsequently combined according to genre specific rules or codes and conventions.

Another way of approaching this distinction between signifier and signified is to approach the image in terms of denotation and connotation. The denotive aspect to the image is assessed in terms of its accurate representation of an object. Connotation refers to the meaning that is bought to the denotive image. For example, the flag of Scotland, the Saltire, does not look like Scotland but it connotes Scotland. Even more importantly it also invokes a notion of Scottishness – a series of myths of Scotland, and what it means to be Scottish.

Jungian psychology has its codes and conventions too. For example, water stands as a symbol for the unconscious, as do forests. Up tends to be spiritual while down suggests descent into the unconscious. The search for lost treasure of some sort evokes the search for the individuated self. Thus the link between the denotation and connotation is highly codified. There is a strong argument for resisting these rather mechanistic and reductionist interpretations, and many Jungians will do just that. However it is rather difficult to find examples of Jungian textual criticism that propose alternative connotative meanings. While the Jungian view of images appears to be flexible, intuitive and non-rational, in fact it is highly codified, constrained and structured. Jungian psychology has its own paradigmatic set and its own rules and conventions about how the different elements may be combined syntagmatically. In this respect, Freudian and Jungian views of the image and symbol are actually much closer than they first appear, and much closer than Jung himself allows for.

Freud and the symbolic

From a psychoanalytic perspective it is possible to argue that while Freud's theory of symbols emerged in his mature writing, these ideas were already latent in the early stages of his thinking. (Laplanche and Pontalis [1988] provide a concise summary of the evolution of Freud's views about symbols.) Irrespective of whether symbols appear in culture or in dreams, Freud is rather cautious about their psychological role and function. On the one hand he warns against the ancient methods of dream interpretation while at the same time he notes in those practices some similarities to his own method. In particular, he comments on the way in which an image stands for something else – in other words, while the image is denotative he notes how its meaning lies in its connotations.

Freud also stresses the mediating role that language plays between the unconscious and consciousness. Here language has a symbolic function – not in the semiotic sense of symbol, but in the way that it can symbolise an unintended meaning. This is the theory that underpins the famous Freudian Slip, otherwise referred to as parapraxis, in which an unconscious wish, or repressed desire, slips through the defences of consciousness, despite our best attempts to repress it. The basic idea that language has a proximity to the unconscious is something that is crucial to the ideas of Jacques Lacan, and here we have an early inkling of this connection.

Freud was particularly interested in the occurrence of symbols in dreams. He thought that typically dreams express a fantasy or conflict that in a disguised way give voice to forbidden sexual desires and/or, wishes. Freud posits two layers to the dream: manifest content and latent content, to which he adds a process he terms 'dream work' in which latent content is turned into manifest content. In essence, the dream work takes sexual desire, often connected to the impossibility of the Oedipal situation, and through a series of mechanisms renders the fantasy in a more culturally and personally acceptable manner. Freud identified three distinct parts of the process of dream work: visualisation (in which a thought becomes an image), condensation (in which two ideas become conflated in a single object) and displacement (an idea or thought is attached to an iconically different object, thereby avoiding the defences of consciousness and the desire to censor our unacceptable fantasies – this is the root of sexual perversion.) The work of dream interpretation is to elicit the patient's associations to the dream image. Alternatively the analyst might apply an 'objective' interpretation to the dream by utilising skills in deconstructing the dream work, to reveal the latent sexual meaning of the dream's imagery.

One of the curious aspects of 'psychoanalytic symbols' is that there is a considerable range of objects that can take on symbolic form. Freud came to the realisation that latent sexual content could be 'worked' into manifest content, in a way that rendered the sexual dimension in a seemingly non-sexual manner. In order for this to happen he thought there needed to be an analogy in terms of shape or function. Thus everyday objects can stand for (or connote) either the sexual organs or the sexual act itself. The transition of ubiquitous objects into sexual symbols is the product of 'censorship' and such censorship is not restricted to dreams but occurs in our cultural lives too. However, Freud reserved a special place for the interpretation of dream symbols, and indeed the importance of dreams is part of the legacy inherited by Jung and passed down to today's analysts. True, psychotherapy can also involve the interpretation of patients' dreams and the subsequent elucidation of associations, but it is psychoanalysis itself which puts the dream centre-stage in an almost reverential manner.

It is tempting at this point to apply these ideas of manifest and latent content and the ubiquity of sexual dream symbols directly to films. Perhaps the process of making a film is like the act of dream work in which disguised sexual material becomes transformed into more socially acceptable images. If so, the pleasure we get when watching a film is a type of disguised sexual pleasure in which the desire to look is a sublimation of the psyche's libidinal energy. However, a few words of caution are in order before undertaking such an enterprise. First, there is no reason to assume that dreams and films can be analysed in the same way. The interpretation of a patient's dreams is a personal psychological activity, whereas interpreting a film is a cultural undertaking that only secondarily has a psychological aspect. (This idea will be developed and somewhat contested later on in this chapter and again in the chapter on Phenomenology (Chapter 8), in particular by Hockley's idea of The Third Image.) Next, films are collective products designed for entertainment with mass appeal and their ostensible meanings are readily accessible. Dreams, on the other hand, are individual and bespoke, they do not set out to entertain and their meanings are often difficult to discern. Finally, the structure of dreams and films is different, as are their conditions of reception. Perhaps the fullest exposition of these ideas is found in the work of Christian Metz and in particular his book, *The Imaginary Signifier: Psychoanalysis and Cinema* (1982). In that work, Metz tracks the similarity between the cinematic apparatus (the physical conditions of the production of films and their exhibition) and the internal psychic apparatus that governs the Oedipal dynamic. While not claiming that films are dreams, he asserts that they are somewhat dreamlike. The act of watching a film involves the activation of internal psychological structures as, in a transgressive voyeuristic act, it becomes possible to see what is normally kept behind closed bedroom doors – the primal scene. (The primal scene is the act of the child, either real or imagined, in which parents are seen during sex.) Metz makes the interesting claim that in no small part the power of cinema comes from the way it activates such primal fantasies not while we are asleep but as part of our waking life. He argues that cinema is particularly powerful as a psychological medium because its 'delusions' occur while we are conscious.

Post-Freudians and Jacques Lacan

More than any other figure it is Jacques Lacan and his development of Freud's ideas that holds the strongest influence on contemporary psychoanalytic film theory. Indeed by the early 1980s in European universities Lacan had become synonymous with psychoanalytic theory and Freud was only studied, if he was at all, as a precursor to Lacan's ideas. Here is not the place to try and attempt to assess Lacan's work, its coherence or even the evidence that he draws on in support of his theoretical elaborations – that has been done elsewhere and in great detail (see Homer, 2004). Instead we shall focus on one of the central concepts of his theoretical approach. At the very core of Lacanian theory is the idea of the mirror stage or *stade du mirror* – sometimes also referred to as the mirror phase. It is important not only as a stage of psychological development but also because it illustrates the role that image plays in the Lacanian view of the world.

In summary, Lacan suggests that while an infant the child goes through several phases in which he or she separates from the mother and becomes aware they are a being in their own right. This is concerning for the child as what was once a unity between mother and baby is now broken. More worrying still is the new awareness of the infant's own body and that it is composed of body parts – legs, hands and so forth – 'Just how do they join up?', the child muses. According to Lacan, this is where the mirror stage has a decisive role to play. At somewhere between six and eighteen months old the child sees its own reflection in a mirror and misrecognises itself as a perfectly whole body – an ego ideal. For Lacan this opens up one of the central fissures in the human psyche, namely the desire for perfect psychic wholeness as reflected in the unity of the body, and the solidity of our ego. However, this is accompanied by the inability to achieve such rock solid cohesion because, put simply, such perfection is an illusion, a reflection if you will. It is important to note that Lacan is not suggesting that the child sees their actual reflection in a mirror (although that is not ruled out), it is more that they find their behaviour mirrored by those around them. Lacan allows for this process to also be symbolic in some way. As he notes:

> This jubilant assumption of his specular image by the child at the *infans* stage, still sunk in his motor incapacity and nursling dependence, would seem to exhibit in an exemplary situation the symbolic matrix in which the *I* is precipitated in a primordial form, before it is objectified in the dialectic of identification with the other, and before language restores to it, in the universal, its function as subject.
>
> This form would have to be called the Ideal-I. But the important point is that this form situates the agency of the ego, before its social determination, in a fictional direction, which will always remain irreducible for the individual alone, or rather, which will only rejoin the coming-into-being (*le devenir*) of the subject asymptotically, whatever the success of the dialectical syntheses by which he must resolve as *I* his discordance with his own reality.
>
> (Lacan, 1977: 2)

Film theory has seized on the ideas of reflection, misrecognition and fragmentation as a means through which to understand the function of cinema. Perhaps like the mirroring gestures of adults around children, in the cinema we find our own interiority mirrored in the apparatus of cinema. In many ways the cinema projects an image of the idealised whole and perfect body that, through the diegetic mechanism of filmmaking, viewers are encouraged to identify with. Yet at the same time these whole bodies are also fragmented through the intervention of technical and formal filmic elements including camera framing and editing. The body is in a sense dissected through these operations and then combined again by the viewer as the film is watched. Of course, this process of temporary wholeness is disrupted as soon as the next edit occurs or the shot is reframed in some way, and so the cinematic body is in a constant state of wholeness and fragmentation – a condition that mirrors our own.

There are a few problems with this approach. Perhaps the main one is that despite the intellectual appeal of the proposition that the mechanisms of cinema replicate our internal psychological mechanisms, the experience of watching a film is not one of constantly shifting between wholeness and fragmentation. One solution to this problem can be found in the suggestion that the process is in fact an unconscious one. Of course, that is hard to dispute but it does raise the question as to how it would be possible to know about it all if it, and all its effects, remained completely unconscious. Perhaps then this process is largely unconscious. This is no more help in solving the problem because again there is a disjuncture between the experience and the theory. In one sense none of this needs to be too much of a problem. Lacan himself did not offer much, if any, evidence for his theory. So too we can take the theory and apply it, noting 'it is as if'. We ask ourselves what would happen if we reframed cinema to see it through the lens of Lacanian psychology – 'it is as if' the cinema screen acts as an analogue of the early childhood mirror stage, reminding us of our fragmented condition and our desire for unity – something that is both promised and frustrated by the cinema, as it is by language itself.

Yet somehow this explanation does not feel adequate either. Is there a way to understand the psychological function of cinema that sits rather more readily with the actual experience of watching a film? For that, we turn to Jung and his theories about the psychology of the image.

Jung: sign and symbol

The symbol/sign dichotomy is one of the central points in the discussion of the relationship between Jungian theories and semiotics. It will be argued that this distinction can be used effectively to examine on-screen semiotic structures such as visual metonymies and synecdoches. In other words, that a Jungian conception of symbols does not preclude a semiotically nuanced reading or interpretation of a film. In semiotics a symbol is something that does not visually correspond to its meaning. As mentioned earlier in this sense, words are symbols as they look nothing like their linguistic meaning. However, when Jung refers to semiotics it is not this particular definition that he has in mind. Instead Jung makes a distinction between sign and symbol in psychological terms. In semiotic terms, the symbol is indexical because it points to something else – a knock on the door is indexical as it indicates that someone is outside and wants our attention. For Jung in his sign/symbol paradigm, that is a sign, as a sign stands for something concrete. By contrast, the psychological symbol goes much further. In the semiotic example the connection between the index and its meaning can be learnt and exists as a cultural code or convention. By contrast, the psychological meaning of the symbol can never be fully understood, a point that we will return to in a moment.

In the trio, sign-metaphor-symbol, a sign has the most stable meanings while the symbol is the least fixed. Metaphor has a relatively recognizable meaning yet still with a degree of interpretative indeterminacy. Further symbols can form semiotic systems when their meanings are 'pinned down', as in the Jungian reductionist approach mentioned above. Basically, we are moving along the scale of the fixedness of meaning here and its degree is always socially and culturally determined. The less fixed the meaning, the less indexical the sign/symbol is as indexicality is lost in proportion to the loss of the link between the signifier and the signified.

For Jung the symbol is a psychological image that encapsulates the current psychological situation. As such, it is at least partly comprehensible to the conscious part of the psyche. However, it also contains a strong unconscious component and it is this proximity to the unconscious that gives the symbol its affective charge and power. Put another way: the sign points to (or is indexical of) something that consciousness can readily comprehend, while the symbol provides a psychological insight that consciousness *needs* to comprehend. In this model the link between signifier and signified can be, at best, tenuous. As Jung puts it:

> The method is based, rather, on evaluating the symbol (i.e., dream-image or fantasy) not *semiotically*, as a sign for elementary instinctual processes, but symbolically in the true sense, the word 'symbol' being taken to mean the best possible expression for a complex fact not yet clearly apprehended by consciousness.
>
> (CW8: 148, emphasis as original)

Jung is careful to note that semiotic interpretations have their place. In doing so it is highly likely that he had in mind Freud's psychoanalytic interpretative conventions. Freud creates an elaborate if 'closed' semiotic system in which the chains of signification lead back to some form of sexual neurosis that has been repressed but which still manages to find expression. In *The Interpretation of Dreams* (1976), he sets up a series of interpretations in which images in dreams of objects that are long and thin in shape symbolise the penis, while enclosing shapes represent the womb, especially if they have an opening corresponding to the vagina. However, these are not really symbols (at least in a Jungian sense) but are instead better thought of as signs that point to the childhood aetiology of sexual disturbances. While the patient might not understand such causative links the idea is that the doctor is able to comprehend them and also to explain them to the patient in a clinically useful manner. Freud's paradigmatic case studies such as 'Dora', 'The Ratman', 'The Wolf Man', 'Anna O.' and 'Little Hans' all provide cogent and compelling examples of this method in action.

Freud thought that the unconscious mechanisms by which the psyche sought to protect itself could be understood and that analysis was in no small part about the conscious understanding of unconscious contents as a means by which to release affect and restore psychological harmony. While accepting the value in such an interpretation, for Jung symbols work in a quite a different manner. As he repeats time and time again, and as we noted at the start of this chapter, the unconscious can never be fully understood. It follows that a semiotic method and paradigm is always going to be of limited use. Not without utility to be sure, but certainly not comprehensive. As Jung observes:

> I am far from suggesting that the semiotic interpretation is meaningless; it is not only a possible interpretation but also a very true one. Its usefulness is undisputed in all those cases where nature is merely thwarted without any

> effective work resulting from it. But the semiotic interpretation becomes meaningless when it is applied exclusively and schematically – when, in short, it ignores the real nature of the symbol and debases it to a mere sign.
> (CW8: 88)

Philipson, in his book on Jungian aesthetics, provides a neat summation: The symbol does something while the sign is a dead end (Philipson, 1963: 15). This is why Jung describes the symbol as a *corpus et anima* – a body with spirit, and as such he regards it as alive in ways which Freudian conceptions of the symbol do not. In the Freudian model of the psyche, the meaning of symbols is always, in the last resort, personal. Further, the ubiquity of the Oedipal complex, the consistent structure and function of dream work, and the relationship between sexual content and its imagery are relatively fixed and individual – they are not cultural, at least not in the way Jung uses the term. The Freudian view of the unconscious is that it contains personal sexual material and that all symbolic expressions relate to an underlying personal neurosis. Jung came to the view that actually the unconscious is more cultural than Freud suggested. It intrigued Jung that in both the dreams of his patients and in their psychological fantasies it seemed that similar mythological imagery cropped up and that these images, themes and motifs were something about which they had no conscious knowledge. From this basis Jung interpolated the existence of a part of the psyche that was transpersonal and he referred to it variously as the 'objective psyche', the 'collective unconscious' and even the 'psychic organ'.

The existence of the objective psyche is one of the distinguishing characteristics of Jungian psychology, particularly as he suggests that this part of the psyche involves more than just having an element that is common to all of us – as is the case with the Oedipal complex. Instead, the objective psyche is something that cannot be fully contained or comprehended. It is also the repository of the shared psychological structures of humanity that Jung refers to as archetypes. In turn, these structures find a partial expression in the form of images and in particular as symbols. This is how Jung's thinking comes together: from clinical observation it appeared to him that there is collective and unconscious aspect to the psyche; this is expressed and culturally inflected in images including dreams and creative acts, fantasies and in particular symbols; these can never be fully understood as they relate to a vast and deeply buried part of ourselves. From this it follows that Jung could not agree with Freud's formulation of the psyche as predominantly individual and sexual. Nor could he agree to a semiotic and reductionist mode for interpreting symbols because the proximity of symbols to the unconscious means they cannot be fully understood. Philipson summarises this neatly:

> Thus, the principle which Jung has put into question is the Freudian assumption that *all* 'symbolic' expressions can be reduced to the structure of the personal unconscious. If the Freudian position were adequate, then it would follow that all non-literal expressions – particularly, in the light of our ultimate consideration here: all *art-works* – are reducible to the fundamental

> instinctual processes, namely, of the libido. But Jung opposes this assumption in the effort to save such content as characterises culture, most especially religion and art, from being reduced to (i.e., 'explained away' by) a casually reductive analysis in the one-sided service of 'nature'.
>
> (Philipson, 1963: 16)

This leads us to another of the distinctions between Freudian and Jungian approaches. As mentioned, Freud conceived of libidinal energy in the psyche as either displaced or sublimated sexual energy. For Jung libidinal energy is more helpfully thought of as all psychological energy that derives primarily from the unconscious, however it is expressed. In particular, libidinal energy aids in the movement of material that is unconscious into consciousness; it is that process which fuels the creation of images, and symbols. As Jung observes:

> The transformation of libido though the symbol is a process that has been going on ever since the beginnings of humanity and continues still. Symbols were never devised consciously, but were always produced out of the unconscious by way of revelation or intuition.
>
> (CW8: 92)

This is why we are able to have unconscious affective relationships with images – they mean something to us and can move us in ways that the rational and conscious part of our minds is unable to comprehend. Indeed, once we do understand the psychological meaning of an image or symbol, it ceases to 'affect' us in quite the same way. This symbolic and largely conscious dimension to images helps to understand the diversity of emotional responses that viewers have to films. Of course, in one sense we all have unique relationships with the people and things that we encounter in our daily lives. But the cinema seems particularly well set up to replicate the conditions of dreaming – not only is the environment warm, dark and comfortable, but like dreams it is also immersive as diegetically it is as though we become part of the film. We certainly respond in an emotional manner to characters in films as if they were real people, and consequently we project our unconscious selves onto them, in the way in which we do in the rest of our lives. What makes that process particularly curious is that at the same time as responding to films as though their events and characters were physical, we know that films are simply image and sound. The contradictory part is that these cinematic phantasms give us access to a level of psychological reality that is otherwise difficult to attain. These are the psychological conditions of the image, as understood by Jung – it is conscious and unconscious, bodily and outside the body, felt and partly understood, composed of me and something other than myself and as containing the psychological situation in the unconscious as it is right now. It follows that while films have relatively fixed narrative meanings, they also have shifting, changing personal meanings.

It is therefore necessary to make a distinction between narrative and textual interpretations of films, and the personal psychological meanings of films.

While these two interpretative foci are not necessarily connected, at least in a rational or obvious manner, neither are they hermetically sealed. Personal interests and concerns, along with individual psychological traits, will inflect every interpretative act as we inevitably project aspects of our unconscious selves on the world. No matter how rational or objective we think we are the world is nonetheless reshaped by the overlay of our unconscious processes. That said, to use psychological techniques to understand the motivations of characters in a film, or indeed to elucidate deep psychological structures and concerns, is to engage in an act of textual analysis, while using the same framework to understand our individual and emotional reactions to films is to engage in a personal empiricism. The debate between rationalism and empiricism is enriched by the perspective offered by Analytical Psychology that while recognising the separation between the two orientations, it also wants to see them as co-existing. For example, in therapy when a client presents a dream the therapist might well have an 'objective' interpretation of its meaning. This provides the lens through which the dream is viewed while at the same time the therapist will attempt to elucidate in working with the client the dream's personal and subjective meaning. In this way the distinction between the rational and the empirical is preserved, while at the same time it is also eroded. It follows that the psychological topography of the cinematic experience shifts depending on our focus. If our concern is the film, then we are inclined towards a more objective and detached analytical approach. On the other hand, if our interest is on the viewer and affective and emotional responses, then we will be more subjective in our concerns. In summary, we might say that this encapsulates the distinction between the sign as a semiological orientation and the symbol that exists as part of the psychological perspective, while at the same time noting that such a division cannot, and indeed ought not, be absolute.

James Hillman and the symbolic

James Hillman, the founder of the School of Archetypal Psychology, explores the hermeneutic operation of the psychological image from a usefully different perspective. While it is the case that the roots of archetypal psychology are partly found in the works of Carl Jung, the approach developed by Hillman is in a number of important ways quite different to that of Jung's Analytical Psychology. One of the key distinctions is that Jung focused on the relationship between the ego and the self, particularly as constellated within psychological maturation, the process that Jung termed individuation. By contrast, Hillman deliteralises these psychological constructs. For him there is no such thing as individuation, and the ego and the self along with other attempts to render and fix unconscious material are at best seen as metaphorical, and at worst serve to rob images of their psychological potency. It follows that while Hillman writes about classical gods and goddesses that these images should be treated in a poetic and playful manner. Hillman sees such images as rather like overtones that emanate from a deep fundamental note in the psyche. Actually it transpires that this is not so very different to the way that Jung describes the image. However, Hillman's followers and Jung's alike sometimes have a tendency to literalise what is more helpfully regarded as metaphorical.

The danger is that the mythological constructs which both Jung and Hillman use to amplify and illustrate psychological insights and psychological principles can be taken too literally, and when this happens they turn into embodied examples of psychological processes. Theoretically and clinically this is a mistake as what is psychologically beneficial for the psyche (which Hillman terms soul) is to hold the ambiguity of an image and to accept that its meanings cannot be discerned. What psychotherapy (care of the soul) needs to do is to help the client retain the affect of the image, and in so doing to let the image do its work. Of course, the temptation is to try and understand the image and to apply it in a meaningful way to the life of the client – with the best of intentions for the client, this disservice literalises what should remain symbolic and psychological. Understandable though this turn to interpretation is, it misses the point. Worse, in an act of reverse alchemy, it transmutes the affect-laden symbolic quality of the image into a leaden literal depiction.

This raises some interesting questions about how best to approach cinema. Our normal starting point is that we want to understand what the narrative of a film is about. However that is a different activity to understanding what a film means psychologically and it is also different to understanding what the psychological meaning of a film is for its viewers both collectively and individually. There is therefore a subtle interplay in our psyche in which the image on screen and our psychological and affect-laden responses exist together. In one sense the on-screen image is a narrative image, and part of the diegetic construction of the interiority of the film's structure. But the psychological affect as individually experienced requires interplay between our personal psychology and the collective image on the screen. While this might seem curious, in fact all that is happening is that the fantasy of our interior worlds is projected onto the outer world. This is a common precept in psychodynamic thinking and there is nothing particularly remarkable about this state of affairs. Indeed, we make these types of projections all the time. Interestingly, in the process of projection we come to the view that flaws in ourselves actually reside in other people and the consequence of this is that in the cinema we can have psychological responses that are quite at odds with the narrative meaning of the film. In this instance, meaning lies not in the dissolution of psychological projections but can be found in those moments where we gain psychological insight, even when forming a meaning that might be at odds with the narrative meaning of the film. As Hillman suggested, psychologically what we hear is the overtone, and not the fundamental note itself. It is in these resonances that are rich with sonorous affect and which ring out with psychological clarity that the voice of the unconscious can be heard. From the perspective of archetypal psychology, the representational meaning of an image is much less important than how it chimes with our psychology. As Hillman comments:

> The images are where the psyche is. People say, 'I don't know what the soul is,' or 'I've lost my soul', or whatever. To me the place to look when you

> feel that way is immediately to the images that show where you are with your soul in dreams . . . the place to look not only to your feelings, not to your interpretations not ask help from a third person necessarily, but ask yourself what were you in the images? Where's your imagination? That immediately *locates* you somewhere, in your own psyche.
>
> (Hillman, 1990b: 75)

This offers us two of the fundamental questions in a Jungian approach to the cinema – where is the image and where is meaning? These are significant questions as the two (image and meaning) are not necessarily connected. Ostensibly both image and meaning reside on the screen, yet the interplay of the unconscious with a film results in the creation of a new image. This new psychological image has a different relationship to the film – the psychological image created by the passage of the film's images and sounds as they awaken unconscious complexes and traumas of viewers is of a different order. The film's imagery belongs to its internal world, while the reception of the film gives the film a life off screen created by the life of the viewer. To escape the cinematic frame the film sheds its narrative mantel as it adopts a psychological attire that is fashioned by a viewer's unconscious personal and archetypal processes. To see the cinematic experience in this light is to attribute a profound meaning and purpose to the activity of watching films.

An approach derived from Hillman's ideas provides an important variation on this theme. Watching a film, as in dreaming, is without meaning, or more accurately, meaning and image are condensed in the creative act through which a new image is formed and whose purpose is not hermeneutic but psychological. The imbuing of the image with psychological qualities does little to explain the image. Indeed, according to Hillman such understanding should be avoided. Instead he suggests we should sit with images, and let them do their psychological work. As he puts it:

> To see the archetypal in an image is thus not a hermeneutic move. It is an imagistic move. We amplify an image by means of myth in order not to find its archetypal meaning but in order to feed it with further images that increase its volume and depth and release its fecundity. Hermeneutic amplifications in search of meaning take us elsewhere, across cultures, looking for resemblances which neglect the specifics of the actual image. Our move, which keeps archetypal significance limited within the actually presented images, also keeps meanings always precisely embodied. No longer would there be images without meaning and meaning without images. The neurotic condition that Jung so often referred to as 'loss of meaning' would now be understood as 'loss of image,' and the condition would be met therapeutically less by recourse to philosophy, religion, and wisdom, and more by turning directly to one's actual images in which archetypal significance resides.
>
> (Hillman, 1990a: 60)

The location of oneself in relation to the experience of cinematic affect is certainly one way of holding the image and not translating the image into a concept. Yet, it also seems problematic for as humans, we seem driven to make sense of the world, both material and psychological, in which we find ourselves. The propensity for storytelling as a hermeneutic activity is after all what underpins myths and fairy tales. Admittedly popular cinema starts from a different point and its roots are in the commercial imperative. However, as a medium its proximity to the unconscious and also to the dream-state means that its economy is as much psychological as it is financial. How then can we account for films in a psychological manner that acknowledges their existence as both materialist commodities and as modern myths through which to make sense of ourselves and how we are in the world? To use a Jungian metaphor, we might observe that watching films is an alchemical process in which the base materials of image and sound are transformed into the gold of the cinematic experience – films are both materialist commodity and psychological. Let us pose this as a question: is it possible to reconcile films as conveyors of material signifiers with their capacity to express and create psychologically potent and living symbols?

Signs and symbols in films

A partial answer to that question can be found in two articles first published in 1979 and 1980 when Don Fredericksen wrote 'Jung/Sign/Symbol/Film' Parts One and Two in the *Quarterly Review of Film Studies* (republished in a new edition, Hauke and Alister [eds], *Jung and Film*, 2001). This early piece on Jungian ideas and their relevance to understanding the meaning of films explores the intersection between semiotic and symbolic orientations towards films. Fredericksen sets out in the opening paragraph of the first article his concern with both the meaning of films themselves and, significantly, the meaning 'we behold' in films. In other words, he is declaring that he is as much concerned with the experience of films as he is with their textual meanings.

Importantly, Fredericksen reminds us that the terms 'sign' and 'symbol' do not have fixed meanings. In particular what Fredericksen emphasises is that, when viewed through a Jungian lens, those images that Freud regarded as symbols are in fact signs as these images point to something that can be known and understood. (A point already explored above.) This act of interpretation, or of understanding a symbol, in Freudian thinking becomes something of an exercise in code breaking which as that term suggests is a rather semiotic activity. By contrast Fredericksen proposes adopting a Jungian symbolic attitude towards films. As he comments:

> Within modern American and European film study there are three major semiotic approaches: film semiotics as such, Freudian and Lacanian psychoanalyses, and the various Marxist approaches. In their various guises, they have set the agenda in the field for the last thirty years. . . . If here are films partially or wholly symbolic in Jung's sense, for which a symbolic attitude

> is appropriate, if not compelling, then it follows that the notions of meaning used in semiotic approaches are too narrow and in need of augmentation.
> (Fredericksen, 2001: 21)

Fredericksen's article contains a compelling critique of the different approaches. His underlying argument is that all three modes of analysis locate both symbols and signs as part of a set of cultural and social practices. Understanding the construction of these cultural symbols and their assemblage into cultural codes is of course important. However, Fredericksen's suggestion is that in so doing such interpretative interventions fail to recognise the deeper layers of psychological signification that are contained within the symbol. Put another way, the unconscious origins of the symbol and its associated affective power are left undisturbed by conventional film semiotics.

It is Fredericksen's contention that the semiotic approaches offered by the three modes of analysis he identifies are well matched to the majority of films that for him are semiotic in character (2001: 27). What he quite reasonably proposes is to marry up the appropriate analytical mode with the film under consideration. For example, while it is perfectly possible to conduct a Lacanian analysis of, for example, *Police Academy 4* (Dir. Drake, 1984) it is unlikely to be particularly rewarding in the interpretative insights it yields. Similarly, Fredericksen asserts that the symbolic attitude should be reserved for those films that are rich in symbolic material and which speak in a personal voice. Fellini, Bergman, Herzog, Buñuel and Tarkovsky are among the directors who Fredericksen identifies as having such a voice, while a bridge between 'art' cinema and the commercial film is offered by the films of Nicolas Roeg, which in turn leads Fredericksen to directors such as Kubrick and eventually Spielberg.

For Fredericksen, what remains of the utmost importance is the expression of a personal voice in film, It follows that for him it is perfectly reasonable to shift between fiction films and documentaries. In this vein, Fredericksen goes on to offer one of the very few accounts that exist of a Jungian reading of a documentary film, namely Basil Wright's *Song of Ceylon* (1935). He does so as a means to demonstrate a symbolic and hermeneutic reading of the film. In part, this provides a demonstration of the validity and utility of his approach to 'personal voice' films, but it also illustrates a salient and often overlooked part of Jung's symbolic method – namely amplification. Amplifying an image involves finding similar occurrences of that image in different myths. The hope is that this will bypass our conscious defences. In so doing the implicit meaning of the image is rendered with greater clarity as its meaning is 'amplified'. Fredericksen provides the following quotation from the collected works (2001: 38):

> It does not . . . suffice simply to connect a dream about a snake with the mythological occurrence of snakes, for who is to guarantee that the functional meaning of the snake in the dream is the same as in the mythological setting? In order to draw a valid parallel, it is necessary to know the functional

> meaning of the individual symbol, and then to find out whether the apparently parallel mythological symbol has a similar context and therefore the same functional meaning. Establishing such facts not only requires lengthy and wearisome researches, but is also an ungrateful subject for demonstration . . . one has to launch forth into exhaustive descriptions, personal as well as symbological.
>
> (CW9, I: 103)

As Fredericksen comments, 'Wearisome as this constraint is, it is absolutely necessary if we are not to find ourselves in the situation where everything becomes everything else' (2001: 38–39). He also notes that any such amplification around the meaning of a symbol should be stopped once that symbol's meaning has been sufficiently elucidated – a necessary rejoinder if the amplification is not to continue until it embraces myth after myth after myth. Fredericksen effectively deploys these two precepts for the amplification of filmic symbolic material during his hermeneutic engagement with a short sequence from *The Song of Ceylon*. In his analysis he explores the meaning behind the 'symbolic' appearance of several in-flight birds at 'Adam's Peak' (the location at which the Buddha left the earth, leaving behind his footprints). Fredericksen's suggestion is that this sequence has more than a semiotic quality and that a representational reading of the sequence does little to explain the meaningful and significant narrative inconsistencies in it such as: How can trees suddenly be growing at the top of the mountain?; Why are all the birds flying to the left of the screen? In answering these questions Fredericksen identifies three locations that are symbolically intercut to create a new filmic and symbolic location – the mountaintop, the statue of Buddha, the sanctuary where the birds are in flight – put simply, the film has created and placed its viewers in a symbolic realm.

Fredericksen notes that at this point in the film, as indeed at many others – not least of which is the opening sequence – we have left the documentary mode behind. There's no commentary about the teaching of the Buddha, we do not know anything about the pilgrims, and there is no information about the habitat. We learn nothing about tea production or the conditions of the tea-pickers. In fact nothing that the Empire Tea Marketing Board and the Ceylon Tea Board, both of whom were sponsors of the film, might have expected. Fredericksen's amplification of the sequence is illuminating and detailed, and in it he argues the case for a symbolic reading as a means to understand just what it is that *Song of Ceylon* is actually documenting.

Extending Fredericksen's analysis it is important to note the role the remarkably experimental soundtrack has in enhancing the symbolic and affect-laden qualities of the film. The state of film production technology in the 1930s meant that location recording of sound was not easy, and that synchronised sound recording was almost impossible. Working within these technologically imposed constraints, Wright recreated the soundtrack in studio with composer Walter Leigh (and also the uncredited involvement of Alberto Cavalcanti) in which the sound for the film was electronically treated and manipulated to give it a rather artificial quality. Electronic waves were mixed with industrial sounds and the electronically hardened timbre of a gong was incorporated into the mix. The outcome was to create a dissonance between sound and image reminiscent of *musique concrète*. The result is the creation of a poetic space in which it is possible to glimpse something of an inner psychic world, where the 'primitive' and the technological wrap around the viewer in a never-ending Möbius strip. Developing this theme, Wright provides a fascinating account of the ways that sound and image work together in *Song of Ceylon*, noting:

> The [sound] track had a life of its own; and when it was allied to the picture it was clear that Leigh had achieved a new and important synthesis. The picture said one thing; the track said something else. Together, the two produced a third quality denied to either of them separately.
>
> (Wright, 1948: 17)

Seen in terms of film theory this type of montage technique is based on the ideas and practices of Soviet filmmakers and theorists of the 1930s and in particular those of Eisenstein and Kuleshov. However, those with a Jungian orientation cannot help noticing how Wright in his description of the ways in which the combination of sound and image can give rise to a new third meaning provides a description of something that is very similar indeed to the Jungian symbol. Of course, both Eisenstein and Kuleshov write about the emergence of 'thirds' too, as did their contemporaries Vertov and Dovshenko. But those filmmakers had a different conception of the third as a technique that was designed to make conscious something that was previously unconscious. For them the third meaning had an ideological and educative function while for Wright the filmic third offers something more poetic. His third does not provide an exposition of the plight of tea workers, nor does it deconstruct the colonial legacy of the British Empire, as a more ideologically motivated documentary might. Instead Wright provides viewers of *Song of Ceylon* with a portal through which to enter into a cinematic experience of the symbolic realm.

It is also worth adding the following gloss to Fredericksen's reading of the film. Basil Wright had an interest in Jungian psychology. As Wright comments in his lengthy and personal account of film history, *The Long View*:

> I wish Jung had paid more attention to cinema, especially in terms of the filmic illogicalities which are often . . . only acceptable in terms of [a] dream . . . but can, perhaps, be accepted as signals reaching us from inner rather than outer space.
>
> (Wright, 1976: 11)

This comment comes shortly after an earlier remark in which he wonders about the similarities between dreams and films. In particular, the ability of films to give voice to the collective unconscious:

> If, as he [Jung] suggests, dreams are capable of arousing in individuals 'not only the contents of personal conflicts but also manifestations of the collective unconscious', might not films, if only to a degree, have something of the same ability?
>
> (Wright, 1976: 9)

Of course, it is not entirely clear whether Wright has in mind a type of cultural unconscious or the unconscious of the filmmaker, or perhaps even some form or unconsciousness that is constellated as part of a creative outpouring during the film production process. However, what he seems to be exploring is the tension that exists between the individual and the collective, or between the personal and the social – a fault line that runs through the early British Documentary film movement positioned somewhere as it is between socialism on the one hand and the call for the individual to act in good faith on the other. While keeping this tension in mind, is there a way in which a filmic reading of the film that renders its stylistic and ideological debt to the legacy of Soviet formalism can be reconciled with a more Jungian view of *Song of Ceylon*? Unfortunately there is no neat interpretative trick that can square this particular circle. After watching *Song of Ceylon* what the viewer is left with is a 'sense impression' of the film, which certainly resonates with Grierson's attitude that documentaries need to appeal not to the reason of the public but to its animal instincts. Grierson's somewhat elitist attitude sits rather uneasily with his socialist politics, although it is perhaps less surprising when viewed in the light of his rhetorical skills that had been honed over a couple of years as a lay preacher in the Church of Scotland. As Wright remarked, 'when Grierson talks, you can't stop him, even if you want to, (he is the worst listener I have ever met)' (Wright, cited in Ellis, 2000: 14). Clearly, there are numerous contradictions and tensions in British documentary film making of the 1930s. On the one hand there is the sermonising of the documentary form that is coupled with the appeal to the heart of social conscience. It also draws on the intellectual motivation of the mind that in turn is combined with an injunction to social change – a motivation that is shared with Soviet filmmakers. However, by contrast, for Basil Wright what is of particular significance is the expression of a poetic sensibility in filmmaking. It was through that mode that he sought to communicate his own sense of what it was to be in the world and thereby change our relationship with it. To borrow a phrase from Jung, Wright sought to dream the myth onward (CW9, I: 271) and it was a myth that was both personal and transpersonal.

Conclusion

The intricacies of this discussion about sign and symbol mean that it is all too easy to forget the underlying psychology and the clinical origins on which this argument rests. While not wanting to lose sight of the value of critical theory it is important to remember that the function of therapy is, in Jungian terms, to live life in a way where we make sense of ourselves in the world. Therapists work with the individual as a microcosm of the collective as it holds the idiosyncrasies of personal psychology alongside the presence of archetypal forces. The hope is that, like Basil Wright, we find our own way to dream the myth onward, and with our clients we too gather the world to ourselves as we become more fully engaged with it, and through that activity become still more fully ourselves. Of course, there is trauma, hurt and pain in each one of us. But too often psychotherapy focuses on those distressing aspects of our lives and blots out our more celebratory moments. Working exclusively with hurt is similar to only watching films that will distress us. Of course, sometimes it is helpful to be challenged by a film and such experiences show how we can shed new light on our lives but it is not tenable or desirable to live life in constant pain. We would think it odd to meet someone who only went to films that were upsetting for them – yet in therapy it is a badge of honour to work through negative fantasies about the world and indeed the therapist his- or herself. There is something back to front here. And the pleasure of the cinema in all its cathartic release alludes to it – in this way, cinema can be of assistance to therapy. Deleuze and Guattari put it as follows:

> How odd the psychoanalytic venture is. Psychoanalysis ought to be a song of life, or else be worth nothing at all. It ought, *practically*, to teach us to sing life. And see how the most defeated, sad song of death emanates from it: *eiapopeia*. From the start, and because of his stubborn dualism of the drives, Freud never stopped trying to limit the discovery of a subjective or vital essence of desire as libido . . . the product of analysis should be a free and joyous person, a carrier of the life flows, capable of carrying them all the way into the desert and decoding them – even if this idea necessarily took on the appearance of a crazy idea, given what had become of analysis.
>
> (Deleuze and Guattari, 1984: 364)

If psychoanalysis can teach us practically to sing life and be a joyous carrier of the flows into the desert of contemporary culture, can the same be said of the cinema? There are hints of this in our everyday experiences of watching films. For example, on leaving the cinema we often feel as though the film has altered our psychological state – temporarily at least we are buoyed up or weighed down by the affect accrued during the cinematic experience. This fades quickly, like the memory of a dream on waking where, as our unconscious defences quickly seek to restrain the dream's influence on us, we return all too readily to our waking lives. So too in therapy when clients talk about films they do so in a manner that is heartfelt, and this is because some unknown complex or forgotten trauma has been reactivated. While the release of such affect is not divorced from the 'semiotic' meaning of the film it nonetheless retains a crucial difference. As Deleuze comments:

> The cinema is always narrative, and more and more narrative, but it is dysnarrative in so far as narration is affected by repetitions, permutations and transformations which are explicable in detail by the new structure. However, a

> pure semiotics is unable to follow in the tracks of this semiology, because there is no narration (nor description) which is as 'given' of images. The diversity of narrations cannot be explained by the avatars of the signifier, by the states of a linguistic structure which is assumed to underlie images in general. It relates to perceptible forms of images and to corresponding sensory signs which presuppose no narration but from which derives one narration rather than another. Perceptible types cannot be replaced by the processes of language.
>
> (Deleuze, 2005: 132–133)

Films cannot be understood in semiotic terms alone because the experience of a film cannot be separated from its meaning. Nor, as we have seen, is the definition of image which Deleuze alludes to adequate. However what is implicit in his argument, which is rather Jungian in tone, is that language is not enough. Further, the psychological image is more than the literal image, and it is our attempts at description that rob the image in all its manifestations of the very qualities that give it potency. As Hillman might put it, such a description is a failure to hold the image in mind.

The semiotic image and the psychological image are often at odds with each other and it is precisely this tension which gives rise to the formation of the psychological symbol and the activation of the transcendent function, which is Jung's term for the ability to hold opposites together, as we 'rise above' the tensions. This provides the means though which the symbol can be contained. It is the illogicality of films that is the very key to understanding their psychological significance and the variety of their meanings. If films were unproblematic (if they were denotative only) then we would have no need for them to be symbolic. However a psychological and symbolic conception of cinema is necessary as it shows how the cinematic experience contains the illogical emotional excess of finding a psychological value in what is an elaborate commercial fiction. Cinema is a medium of illusion. Its shimmering chimera, its lapses of temporality, its geospatial instability and its narrative illogicality all invite us to treat it as dream-like. We leave the material world behind and, as we look into its surface, we find ourselves partly reflected not in an act of Lacanian misrecognition, but in an act of image making in which the spectral embodies the felt reality of our current unconscious situation. This is the central paradox of cinema: that its immateriality gives rise to embodied psychological insight. In an act of *enantiodromia* (the running together of opposites) the screen reveals as much as it protects; it is both illusion and reality – material and phantasm, it takes us outside the walls of the cinema auditorium and into an imaginary world, while at the same time granting us access to the reality and depth of our own inner being.

Part II

Applications

Chapter 4

Combining different methodologies in visual narrative analysis

Helena Bassil-Morozow

Jungian Analytical Psychology has a lot to offer to film theory and film analysis, from the psychology and functioning of narrative structure to the discussion of the projective–introjective relationship between the audience and the screen. Yet, it still does not cover certain aspects of film analysis. For instance, Jungian psychology traditionally overlooks personal interaction in favour of 'the bigger picture' (individuation). In this sense, the personal is obscured by the abstract and the spiritual whereby relationships are transposed into the archetypal sphere. Yet, this does not always prove effective when discussing the interaction between characters on screen. Translating all relations into archetypal 'language' is as reductive and limiting a technique as looking for the Oedipus complex in every narrative, as theories work best in combinations and not on their own.

This chapter endeavours to define the place of Analytical Psychology amongst other methodologies used in narrative analysis as Jungian concepts can be successfully applied to visual narratives in conjunction with anthropology, sociology, psychoanalytic concepts and traditional film theory. Jungian film analysis neither replaces these methodologies nor directly competes with them, but instead can serve to fill in existing gaps and thus enrich the interpretive experience. For instance, while Jung and his disciples wrote extensively on the figure of the trickster, Victor Turner and Arnold Van Gennep's rites of passage concept takes the analysis of cinematic tricksters to an entirely new level. Both frameworks can be used in ways that can complement each other in the creation of a coherent and clear idea of the trickster figure as a psycho-anthropological driving force. Similarly, the apparatus theory, which traditionally focuses on the manipulation of the audience by the movie-making machine, can provide an interesting parallel to the Jungian analysis of mass hypnosis and the concept of the collective shadow. All these parallels, hopefully, will result in a dialogue between Analytical Psychology and existing film theory, and end the isolation of Jungian film criticism.

Jung and Freud: the mother

Certain films call for the integrative approach as if the author could not decide whether to emphasise the spiritual or the sexual, the eternal or the basic, the poetic or the everyday. Andrei Tarkovsky's films belong to this category.

The Mirror (1975) is a study of a man's relationship with the mother in its various incarnations – as a woman, a symbol, an object, a reflection in the mirror; as tempestuous force of nature, as the unconscious which gives birth to creativity and inspires men and, finally, as mother Russia – the goddess who needs protection yet also demands sacrifice. These different mothers are almost inseparable from each other as the whole film is an extended metaphor of a search for the ideal parent, for the non-existent picture of a loving and accepting woman that has been imprinted in the male hero's mind since he was a baby. In this quest, the protagonist, Aleksei, encounters all kinds of mothers as projected onto different women. Yet the perfect one, the lost one, remains missing.

The Mirror switches between three different time frames: before the Second World War (1930s), wartime (1940s) and post-war (1960s). The protagonist remains behind the scenes for most of the film and is only present in the frame as an extra-diegetic voice. The film starts with the footage of a stuttering young man being hypnotised by a female therapist and then waking up 'healed' from his speech disorder, and it ends with the protagonist on his deathbed, holding a freshly hatched chick in his hand. Throughout the film, Aleksei remembers his childhood before and during the war, his parents, their separation, his mother raising two boys on her own, the spooky country house, the military training, his wife Natalia and son Ignat, and the elderly mother (played by the director's own mother, Maria Vishnyakova).

This is a curious but organic combination of Jungian and Freudian imagery. On the one hand, the film clearly foregrounds ideas traditionally discussed using the language of Freudian and post-Freudian psychology: the mother, the mirror, the Oedipus complex, the primal scene and the absent father. The mother, Maria (Margarita Terekhova), is presented as beautiful, sexual, flirty, playful and mysterious; the images of the mother from Aleksei's childhood are almost tactile, which renders the idea of the boy's attachment to her. On the other hand, Tarkovsky's symbolism – and particularly his fascination with Russian nature and water – have an undeniable Jungian hue. The way Maria's appearance is presented – her hair, her face, her arms and hands – make her look like an icon, like someone impersonal, ephemeral, otherworldly, not least because Tarkovsky was inspired by Leonardo's 'Portrait of a Young Woman with a Juniper Twig'. This means that the mother figure in *The Mirror* is both Oedipal archetypal, physical and poetic, sexual and mysterious.

The 'Freudian mother' crops up throughout *The Mirror*, and is particularly noticeable in the pre-war scenes of Aleksei's childhood. The impression she gives is that of a mystical seductress: she is aware of her attractiveness, has large, dreamy grey eyes and often plays with stray strands of her long blond hair. She is clearly aware of her power as a woman. Aleksei (as both the child and the grown-up) is consistently used to focus the narrative, and it is through his eyes that we see the Oedipal female who will remain the uncatchable *objet petit a* of his life.

Importantly, Aleksei sees her as a strange but attractive object, and not as a person. For him, she is a fantasy, a ghost. His early memories of her are often shown in black and white, and in slow motion. One of the scenes is a variant of 'the primal scene': the little boy gets up in the middle of the night and witnesses the father (Oleg Yankovskiy) washing his wife's hair in a basin. The mother's face is hidden behind the veil of her wet hair, while the father is pouring water from a jug to wash away the soap. The son is shocked, and freezes to observe the moment of 'forbidden' intimacy between the two parents. Yet, he cannot voice his despair, and his feelings about the parents are expressed metaphorically in the 'apocalyptic' destruction of the house at the end of the scene. The ceiling begins to collapse, and water starts flooding through the roof. This is the collapse of the boy's fantasy of the maternal object belonging exclusively to him, and the beginning of the loss. Both the house and the exclusivity of the boy's position in the house are gone forever with the introduction of the father figure into the picture.

Another uncanny slow-motion sequence shows the mother in a white nightdress that reveals her legs, floating over a messy bed. A white pigeon crosses the top right-hand corner of the frame. The mother appears seductive and terrifying, dangerous yet passive, dead and alive, a vaguely remembered and misrepresented Oedipal object. There is a discernible Gothic hue in these two sequences: even though they contain nothing particularly terrifying. Their uncanniness stems from the perception of the Oedipal dynamic, and from his desire (and inability) to 'pinpoint' the maternal object. His fragmentary recollections of his mother are insufficient for an exhaustive, 'whole' picture of her. Throughout the film Aleksei is driven by loss as he is trying to remember the times when the mother was his, and no one else's.

In one of the opening scenes (shot in real time and in colour) the child is looking anxiously at a well-dressed man flirting with his mother. The man (Anatoly Solonitsyn) sees her sitting on a fence and smoking, and asks for a cigarette. He has guessed that Maria is separated, and decided to try his luck. He says he is a doctor implying that he is a good catch. Yet, the mother glances at her son sleeping in a hammock before returning any favours to the doctor. The son wakes up, and it is clear that he wishes the doctor to go away, to leave his mother alone. Now that the father is gone, the boy does not want another man to take his place, and to steal his mother's affections away from him – the child. As the rival retreats, we feel the protagonist's relief at the outcome of the encounter.

In the post-war scenes, the protagonist transfers his Oedipal tension onto his former wife, Natalia. Interestingly enough, the wife and the mother are played by the same actress, Margarita Terekhova. This enables Tarkovsky to show Aleksei's obsession with *objet a* and his inability to tell the difference between the female objects in his life. Aleksei is unable to understand them as real people, and eventually cuts both the women off. He is also a selfish father – for years he has neglected his son Ignat who is now failing school.

In one of the post-war scenes, the mother tells the son of her friend's death. The aged Maria expects comfort and empathy from the son, but gets none. The protagonist, who is too self-absorbed to deal with other people's problems, quickly brushes the subject aside. Symbolically, the conversation takes place in an empty room, where both characters are just disembodied voices and the camera is the only actor. This scene epitomises the mother–boy relationship and paradoxically shows their connection as profound and superficial, existing and non-existent. The old Maria is not the mother he wants – 'his' mother is the one who understands him telepathically, who sacrifices herself for him. She does not annoy him with her problems because only his problems matter in the world in which only two of them exist.

Similarly, Aleksei's wife Natalia accuses him of being selfish, of behaving as if he is above everyone, of being self-obsessed, of being utterly immature. Natalia naturally associates herself with the mother because the two are playing the same role in the protagonist's life, and both end up being 'not perfect enough' for him. Neither of the two women manage to become the 'good enough mirrors' reflecting his broken self.

However, not all that is happening in the film can be described in Freudian terms. Moreover, Freudian psychology's insistence on the centrality of sexuality in the human psyche is in direct conflict with Tarkovsky's vision of cinema and cinematic symbolism. In Tarkovsky's view, images have to be neither precise nor easily decipherable. Throughout his book, *Sculpting in Time*, he insists that it is not always possible to predict the unfolding of the creative process or the birth of symbols in the artist's psyche. Images remain vague and mysterious:

> It is hard to imagine that a concept like *artistic image* could ever be expressed in a precise thesis, easily formulated and understandable. It is not possible, nor would one wish it to be so. I can only say that the image stretches out into infinity, and leads to the absolute. And even what is known as the 'idea' of the image, many dimensional and with many meanings, cannot, in the very nature of things, be put into words. But it does find expression in art. . . .
>
> The artist tries to grasp [the principle that makes the image, or a life moment, unique], new each time; and each time he hopes though in vain, to achieve an exhaustive image of the Truth of human existence. The quality of beauty is in the truth of life, newly assimilated and imparted by the artist, in fidelity to his personal vision.
>
> (Tarkovsky, 2008: 104)

Here Tarkovsky's philosophy of filmmaking agrees with Jungian psychology. For Jung, the symbol is always bigger than the sum of the dreamer's (or the author's) biographical details, and significantly deeper than any literal or pre-existed meaning. In contrast to Freud and the post-Freudians, Jung's additional 'layer' of the psyche – the collective unconscious – permitted him to detach the work of art from the Oedipal, sexual or any other personal issues the artist may possess. The work of art grows out of its creator rather like a tree that draws its nourishment from the artist's psyche. It is a force 'that achieves its end either with tyrannical might or with the subtle cunning of the nature herself, quite regardless of the personal fate of the man who is its vehicle' (CW15: 114). The work of art is a 'living thing implanted in the human psyche' (CW15: 114). When he feels the need to create, the artist only answers the call of the collective unconscious. Through the artist, the unconscious speaks and the collective expresses itself.

According to Jung, the creative impulse is a living thing, an *autonomous complex*, a split-off portion of the psyche. When activated, it can be so powerful that the artist loses the ability to control it. This means that artists are often mere vehicles for the symbols of the unconscious which then attempt to escape. As he puts it, 'The divine frenzy of the artist comes perilously close to a pathological state, though the two things are not identical' (CW15: 122).

Similarly, Tarkovsky describes the creative process as something springing from the totality of the psyche, but which also involves the artist as a whole person. As he comments, when one hears its call one has no other choice but to answer it:

> The artist's inspiration comes into being somewhere in the deepest recesses of his 'I'. It cannot be dictated by external, 'business' considerations. It is bound to be related to his psyche and his conscience; it springs from the totality of the world-view. If it is anything less, then it is doomed from the outset to be artistically void and sterile. It is perfectly possible to be a professional director or a professional writer and not be an artist: merely a sort of executor of other people's ideas.
>
> (Tarkovsky, 2008: 188)

For instance, there are many mother images in *The Mirror* that are symbolic in the Jungian rather than the Freudian sense. For instance, Mother Nature is unpredictable, tempestuous, dangerous. Tarkovsky often uses long, black and white shots of Russian nature, sometimes in slow motion. They act as metaphors for Maria as a woman and a mother, as the site of the feminine enigma. Tarkovsky's depictions of nature emphasise the wind in the grass, the depth and darkness of water in a pond, the fierce movement of a bird's wings, the persistence and harmony of raindrops. This is the archetypal mother that is both cruel and kind: the mother that gives birth to the boy, and the terrible mother that overwhelms the dying protagonist; mother womb and the caring mother. The little bird, newly hatched, presents the protagonist's unbroken self; it stands for the descent into the world of the mother, and the protagonist's recreation of her in metaphors and images. He is going back 'into the womb' and being reborn simultaneously.

This is confirmed in the final sequence of the film, straight after the deathbed scene. Maria and the father (still together) are relaxing on the grass, and discussing their future baby. Maria flirts with the camera; she is aware of it. It is as if the invisible protagonist is residing in the camera, as if the unborn baby wants her undivided love, her endless attention and her perfect reflection of his self. The scene is followed by the shots of the old Maria, walking in the field with the two boys. In a way, it contains the distilled essence of the film: the mother grew old, but the boy did not grow up. He rejected the idea of maturity, and chose to remain a child forever, locked in the emotional safety of the pre-war world. The focus in this sequence, however, is not on the boys, but on the association of Maria with Mother Nature: both young and old Marias are shown against the magnificence of the windy fields, the darkened forests, against the distant, milky swirls of fog. The shots of the ageing mother are intercut with close-ups of decaying trees, an abandoned well full of rubbish, the empty house. The chick that flies off at the end of the deathbed scene is released back into the wild. It represents the protagonist's confined and suffering soul, which is now reborn, resurrected, freed from the stifling influence of urban existence, from the oppressive repetitiveness of life. His soul returns to the parental embrace of nature – the terrible, mysterious and beautiful mother.

Similarly, Tarkovsky's 'mother Russia' is a mighty goddess. This is a very traditional, archetypal vision of Russia: she is female, she is a mother and she is so strong that she does not need a man to support her. She prides herself on her strength and fearsomeness, on her lack of femininity. In the scenes portraying wartime, Aleksei and a group of other boys are shown undergoing military training with a strict drill sergeant. In freezing conditions, in the snow, the boys learn how to use firearms and to throw grenades. The sergeant is not impressed with the boy who keeps questioning his instructions. He sees that the boy is not yet a man because he is too selfish and individualistic; he does not respect his country and refuses to defend it; he does not want to sacrifice himself. In this context a Russian man, by contrast, is not an individual – he belongs to his motherland who then decides his destiny.

This view is confirmed in the newsreel footage to which the military training scene cuts. Tarkovsky watched thousands of metres of film before he found the footage he wanted: the Red Army crossing Lake Sivash in 1943. What impressed him most was the poignancy of the piece: it was 'an image of heroic sacrifice and the price of this sacrifice; the image of a historical turning point brought about at incalculable cost' (Tarkovsky, 2008: 130). The men knew that they were likely to die soon, yet they kept moving; they kept going on, defying tiredness, defying mud, defying physical pain. Common men became heroes. Tarkovsky continues:

> The film affected you with a piercing, aching poignancy, because in the shots were simply people. People dragging themselves, knee deep in wet mud, through an endless swamp that stretched out beyond the horizon, beneath a whitish, flat sky. Hardly anyone survived. The boundless perspective of these recorded moments created an effect close to catharsis. Later I learned that the army camera-man who had made the film, with such extraordinary penetration into the events taking place around him, had been killed on that same day.
> (2008: 130–131)

What Tarkovsky admires most is the man's ability to create and to make films in the harshest of conditions, when physical survival rather than creativity should be the focus of attention. When the artist keeps creating in the most difficult of circumstances, he is supported by the great mother, the mother of creativity – the unconscious.

This mother is expressed in a powerful metaphor. The film opens with the scene (a television programme watched by the protagonist) in which a psychotherapist is hypnotising a teenager suffering from a severe form of stuttering. The woman is unattractive and almost rude; her voice is firm and commanding. She is confident. Because she manipulates the young man both physically and psychologically, the scene is quite disturbing. However, this is redeemed by the result we witness at the end of the session when her patient regains his ability to speak. At first he is shocked to hear his own voice, but is not afraid of it, and he is finally able to express himself. The fearsome therapist is a version of the archetypal mother who takes the young man in and renews him – gives him his voice back.

This scene reflects Tarkovsky's perception of creativity as a force that is simultaneously benevolent, ecstatic and dangerous. James Hillman echoes Jung's ideas when he describes the creative impulse as a wild energy that poses potential psychological dangers for its vehicle. It is neither good nor bad. Its power can even make the artist suicidal, and this is almost normal when someone attempts to deal with an impulse of this scale coming from the depths of the psyche. The human frame is far too frail to contain and control something so daemonic:

> The creating Gods are the destroying Gods. As Jung said, 'Creation is as much construction as destruction' (CW3: para. 245). The ectopsychic instinctual force, because it comes from beyond the psyche, is more than human and mightier than its possessor. Its possessor is, in fact, always in danger of possession. Working as a compulsion, the force is always 'too much'. One spends one's life trying to slow it, tame it, give it enough time and space, because its haste is the destructive devil within the creative impulse itself. Suicide always remains the fundamental possibility of psychological creativity, as its reversal, since the destruction of soul is the counterpart of the creation of the soul.
>
> (Hillman, 1998: 36)

In *Sculpting in Time*, Tarkovsky echoes Hillman's view that creativity is neither good nor bad, being a neutral force, rather like Mother Nature. For Tarkovsky depression is the price to pay for the honour of being the pathway used by the unconscious to communicate its information in images, ideas and music:

> True artistic inspiration is always a torment for the artist, almost to the point of endangering his life. Its realisation is tantamount to a physical feat. That is the way it has always been, despite the popular misconception that pretty well all we do is tell stories that are as old as the world, appearing in front of the public like old grannies with scarves on our heads and our knitting in our hands to tell them all sorts of tales in order to keep them amused. The tale may be entertaining or enthralling, but will do only one thing for the audience: help them pass the time in idle chatter.
>
> (Tarkovsky, 2008: 188)

Going back to the scene with the youth regaining his voice – creativity demands sacrifice, and it is expected that the artist will suffer in some way for his talent. The creative process is a form of psychological birth, and suffering is its inseparable part. The relationship with the mother of creativity is bound to be tempestuous.

The same can be said of all mothers portrayed in *The Mirror*: the little boy, the soldier, the filmmaker, the artist, the father, the husband – he is trying to reconnect with the cunning feminine spirit which somehow always escapes him and flies away. She pretends to be owned by him, yet disappears the minute he attempts to capture her; like a bird or like the wind moving the grass and caressing the water in the pond. She is forever lost yet is eternally present in his psyche, and she gives him the strength to create and to move on even in difficult times.

Jung and Lacan: the daughter

Tarkovsky's admirer, the Danish director Lars Von Trier, is another filmmaker combining the themes of spirituality with explorations of sexuality and pre-Oedipal bonds. His notorious film *Nymphomaniac* (2013) can be analysed using a combination of approaches, including Jungian theory. In relation to this film, the concepts of the animus and individuation work particularly well when used in conjunction with Lacanian ideas (the mirror stage, *object petit a*, *jouissance*, between the two deaths, ideal ego, imaginary order, etc.). This is particularly true because Von Trier is a big fan of the works of Tarkovsky who habitually combined archetypal poeticism with what could be called 'pro-Freudian' ideas: mirroring, the Oedipus complex, narcissism and objectification. Moreover, I will conduct two analyses simultaneously rather than in parallel, for my task is to show how harmoniously Jungian ideas can be interwoven with other modes and techniques of analysing cinematic narratives.

Trier traditionally likes to toy with his audience, to shock it, to take it past the comfort zone and to thwart its expectations. Any poeticism that appears in his films (often as a homage to Tarkovsky) is usually thwarted at some point in the narrative and replaced with his trademark callousness.

Nymphomaniac's female protagonist, Joe, is a sex addict. Joe does not feel whole, and no man in the world can fill her inner emptiness. She is like one black hole herself, empty and eternally hungry, and nothing can bring her pieces together again. She is visited by as many as eight different partners per night. She has sex with random people she meets on public transport and on the street. She upsets others, destroys families and breaks hearts. She abandons her husband and son because her family cannot fill the gaping hole in her heart. She resorts to sadomasochistic practices in order to learn to feel when nothing else can make her feel anything. Nothing makes her happy, and nothing is enough. She is immature, unable to grow up and is ultimately narcissistic.

On the one hand, this is an interesting and original move on Lars Von Trier's part. The male Oedipus complex has been exhaustibly explored in literary and cinematic narratives. The boy who is attached to the mother, refuses to grow up and only gives in to the pressures and demands of social reality under the threat of castration from the father, is the kind of storyline with which we are over-familiar. Much of the visual imagery is explicitly Freudian (or what is traditionally called Freudian). For instance, after nearly two minutes of black screen, the film opens with a montage of vagina-like shapes such as holes and openings in the wall, windows, narrow corridors and doorways, and pieces of steel wire woven into round 'O' shapes. Trier often uses these internal frames as the centrepieces of the shot. The two-minute darkness and silence that open the film echo the unknown, chilly depth of the industrial hole in the wall into which the camera goes at the end of the first (street) sequence. Throughout the film, Von Trier exhausts all possible metaphors for the vagina. He even includes – rather unexpectedly – automatic double doors, which remind the protagonist of her sensitive vagina letting in and out hordes of people on a regular basis. Quite often he does not bother to use a metaphor, and shows the actual anatomy.

Yet, ever the trickster, Trier challenges the traditional Freudian-Lacanian vision of the object as being (almost exclusively) female. Joe's *objet a* – the source of her wild, maddening desire and the cause of her obsessive, painful hunt for *jouissance* – is the father. Subsequently, she turns all her sexual partners into disposable objects who fail to fit into the impossible high standards of the lost *objet a*. Some of the flashbacks in the frame narrative refer to her days as a child (played by Maja Arsovic) enjoying a perfect emotional and intellectual unity with her father (played by Christian Slater). Together they used to look at magnificent trees, collect herbarium specimens and talk about the wonders and brilliance of nature. These flashbacks are poetic if a little clumsy and out of place in the film. Trier inverts the tale of the Oedipal boy – traditional in narratives written by men – and creates the story of a girl attached to her father, and never leaving behind the initial parental ideal. The father is the one who used to satisfy her emotional needs, and she remains faithful to him. He is also the only man for whom she has real feelings instead of lies or empty words. Her (Lacanian) loss is literally shown in the prolonged hospital scene in which the father dies a slow and painful death, and the daughter agonises over her impotence and wrestles with her grief.

Meanwhile, the jealous mother's attempts to break this perfect bond fail. True to the inverted Oedipal storyline, the mother is presented as icy and unloving, despising both the father and the daughter since she cannot compete with the daughter for the father's affections. She eventually leaves him. Joe has no emotional connection with her, and thinks she is a 'cold bitch'. The Oedipal girl, Joe realises that she would never have the same closeness with a man that she used to have with her father who 'made her' in more than one sense. She is prepared to have sex with men, but she would not cheat on her father emotionally – that is, she does not want to fall in love. Whenever she falls in love, however, she loses sexual drive. For her, love cannot exist alongside sex because this would mean belonging wholly to another human being. She has only ever belonged to her father, who understands her as a woman and as a daughter.

A Jungian view can offer a more balanced outlook on the subject. What is called pre-Oedipal in Freudian psychology, in Jungian thought is referred to as the uroboric state. In part this is a state before the onset of consciousness, before gender, before civilisation – a purely unconscious, instinctive state. A serpent biting its tail is a good symbol for pure unconsciousness because it depicts complete lack of awareness of boundaries between the subject and the outside world. A baby is said to exist in the uroboric world, in which there is no boundary between itself and the mother. The two of them, Neumann points out, 'form a dual union' (Neumann, 2002: 12). In this phase, there is 'minimum discomfort and tension and maximum of well-being and security' because the oppositions and tensions of reality do not yet exist (2002: 14). Tension arrives when the child has to develop the ego – the centre of conscious personality – and learn to manage his or her relationship with the outside world. Once the uroboric paradise is gone, the newly-formed human being retains the memory of this blissful existence devoid of sorrow and doubt, and full of joy and pleasure.

Technically, Neumann's description is almost identical to Lacan's (although the two formed them completely independently from each other). Both describe the primal relationship as the one that happens between the mother and the child. The difference lies in Neumann's treatment of sexuality. In his view, the uroboric phase is pre-sexual and pre-genital. It is dominated by the alimentary drive which is a mixture of basic survival instincts: feeding, sucking and swallowing, being cared for, excretion, etc. It is also related to spirituality, as 'the symbolism of the alimentary uroboros extends linguistically to the highest levels of spiritual life'. The basic instincts experienced by the child are 'fundamental alchemical conditions of all child growth' and are metaphorically linked to 'creation and transformation' (2002: 37). Neumann also emphasises the intensity of physical sensations in this phase, and the fact that they are undistinguishable from one another.

This angle on *Nymphomaniac* takes the emphasis away from Joe's sexuality and puts in the spotlight the spiritual nature of her experiences. In Joe's case, however, this primal parent who nourishes her in the paradise of pre-conscious existence is the father rather than the mother. He then extends this bliss into her conscious development by becoming her first teacher, the giver of knowledge and the enabler of feelings. He also happens to be the only man she does not see as an object, and with whom she truly empathises. Joe, who seeks the lost uroboric unity with her father, rejects maturity and the social pressure to settle down with one partner and to have a proper family. As far as she remembers, this was a state of wonderful spiritual unity with the world, which she also experiences as sensual.

Von Trier chooses not to juxtapose but instead opts to blend the bodily and the spiritual repeatedly in the film. For instance, in several scenes there is an Orthodox-looking icon of the Virgin Mary. The icon looks like something that could have been painted by Andrey Rublev (a nod towards Tarkovsky, of course), a notoriously chaste Russian mediaeval artist who saw his creativity as something bigger than personal ambition, personal life or physical comfort. Seligman (Stellan Skarsgård) keeps the icon prominently on the wall, and when Joe notices it, she reminisces about a religious vision she once had as a child, when on a field trip she dreamt of being visited by two women, styled as saints but famous for their promiscuity: Valieria Messalina and the whore of Babylon. Joe recounts this experience as oxymoronic, as a mixture of sexual-spiritual – and at one with Mother Nature (since it happened when she fell asleep in the field).

This leads Seligman to interpret her fantasy as a blasphemous version of the Transfiguration of Jesus on the Mount, a New Testament episode in which Jesus shows his celestial nature to his companions, 'And he was transfigured before them, and his face shone like the sun, and his clothes became dazzling white' (NRSV, Matthew 17:3). Peter, James and John are suitably impressed, but what happens next really stuns them: 'While he [Jesus] was still speaking, suddenly a bright cloud overshadowed them, and from the cloud a voice said "This is my Son, the Beloved, with him I am well pleased. Listen to him!"' (NRSV, Mathew 17:5).

While Joe sees these parallels as neither blasphemous nor narcissistically inflated, Seligman is shocked because he is used to separating the spiritual (associated with abstinence) from the corporeal (associated with sex). Seligman himself is a virgin and a scholar, and he sees himself as asexual. Joe gradually realises that the world in which she is trying to keep the sacred unity with the uroboric dimension is made for normal, mature people, who have clear boundaries between the physical and the spiritual (usually delineated by morality and civilisation – by the Law, to use the Lacanian parallel). In her chase for the lost archetypal masculine, the powerful force that makes her feel attractive and sensual, she forgets that the rules of reality restrict the influence of the uroboric. What used to be the indivisible union of the sacred and the physical, in the 'civilised' world has become two separate spheres: the moral and the sexual.

Joe's inability to accept this state of things can be discussed from both Lacanian and Jungian perspectives. A Lacanian feminist view might emphasise her refusal to give in to patriarchal formulae of living, and to settle down. Marriage and motherhood make her frigid, and therefore very unhappy. Instead of peace and satisfaction with life, Joe despises her new roles and attempts to escape her prison by continuing to have sex with strangers and by visiting a professional sadist. She is trapped – not personally, but socially. Society has little variety in terms of what it can offer to women as far as female self-expression is concerned. Joe's extreme addiction can be seen as a form of rebellion against the rigidity of social norms concerning gender roles and sexual conduct.

Whereas the Lacanian analysis draws attention to social inescapability, a Jungian explanation emphasises the split in the mind of the so-called civilised Western person between the moral and the physical aspects of human existence. The protagonist refuses to put aside her uroboric fantasy because her memory of how it feels to be alive – the memory of true love and true union with 'the other' (before it had become 'the other') – contradicts the vision of love propagated by society. In her view, the sexual and the divine are the same and are inseparable. Yet, the existing norms of morality are devised to make her feel bad about her habits and to feel guilty about not preferring motherhood to sexual gratification. (At one point, in pursuit of pleasure, she leaves her son alone in the flat and the boy nearly falls off the balcony). Joe is unable to accept reality not only because it does not account for her pleasure as a woman – reality does not account for guilt-free pleasure altogether. Social reality codes human relationships in prescribed ways. It does not account for 'spiritual pleasure' – the oxymoron which is forever left in the pre-conscious world – the world of the great mother.

Combined, these two visions paint the portrait of the female individual who has her own version of reality and attempts to override the official, coded social reality out there. The official version views the human body as something that has to be managed and controlled, not allowed to celebrate its pleasure, and the freedom of instincts. Under the influence of morality, Joe sees herself as a 'bad person', and her dream of ideal unity with the object turns into a pseudo-confession. Ultimately, she has to choose between fantasy and reality, and leaves society by becoming a debt collector and joining the criminal world. Her illusory world of 'real pleasure', which she sees as the highest truth that had been revealed to her as a child because she is special, different and the chosen one, is incompatible with the normal existence expected of an ordinary citizen.

Jung and the apparatus theory

It can be argued that by writing a narrative cookbook, Christopher Vogler created a perfect way of realising the worst nightmares of apparatus theorists (Jean-Louis Baudry, Jean-Louis Comolli, Christian Metz, Peter Wollen, etc.). The principal postulate of the apparatus theory is that the film industry is a powerful and malevolent machine that is able to control unsuspecting viewers and is capable of influencing their unconscious. It follows that once the unconscious of the masses is successfully harvested, the minds of the individuals can be filled with ideological content.

In his article 'The Imaginary Signifier', Christian Metz attempts to make sense of the narcissistic processes of identification, mirroring and relating through using Lacanian theory. Film, Metz writes, is like a mirror – it facilitates identification (both primary – with the act of looking itself – and secondary identification with particular characters) in the world of difference and unfamiliarity:

> The camera is 'trained' on the object like a firearm (= projection) and the object arrives to make an imprint, a trace, on the receptive surface of the filmstrip (= introjection). The spectator himself does not escape these pincers, for he is part of the apparatus, and also because pincers, on the imaginary plane (Melanie Klein), mark our relation to the world as a whole and are rooted in the primary figures of orality. During the performance the spectator is the searchlight I have described, duplicating the projector, which itself duplicates the camera, and he is also the sensitive surface duplicating the screen, which itself duplicates the filmstrip. There are two cones in the auditorium: one ending on the screen and starting both in the projection box and in the spectator's vision insofar as it is projective, and one starting from the screen and 'deposited' in the spectator's perception insofar as it is introjective

> (on the retina, a second screen). When I say that 'I see' the film, I mean thereby a unique mixture of two contrary currents: the film is what I receive, and it is also what I release, since it does not preexist my entering the auditorium and I only need close my eyes to suppress it. Releasing it, I am the projector, receiving it, I am the screen; in both these figures together, I am the camera, which points and yet which records.
>
> (Metz, 1977: 50)

Another prominent apparatus theorist, Jean-Louis Baudry, uses Plato's famous metaphor of the cave to show the extent of media enslavement of the masses. In his essay 'Ideological Effects of the Basic Cinematographic Apparatus' (1970), Baudry is worried by the apparatus's ability to produce a mirror – a distorted, delusionary reflection of reality – which captivates the audience, enslaves their imagination and does it using tried and tested marketing methods. Cinema becomes an extension of the capitalist machine as industry executives try to work out what brings the most money, and what kind of entertainment will produce the maximum effect on the audience:

> Projection and reflection take place in a closed space and those who remain there, whether they know it or not (but they do not), find themselves chained, captured or captivated. . . . And the mirror, as a reflecting surface, is framed, limited circumscribed. *An infinite mirror would no longer be a mirror.* The paradoxical nature of the cinematic mirror-screen is without doubt that it reflects *images* not '*reality*' . . . . In any case, this 'reality' comes from behind the spectator's head and if he looked at it directly he would see nothing except the moving beams from an already veiled light source.
>
> The arrangement of the different elements – projector, darkened hall, screen – in addition from reproducing in a striking way the mise-en-scène of Plato's cave . . . reconstructs the situation necessary to the release of the 'mirror stage' discovered by Lacan.
>
> (Baudry, 1986: 286)

The most dangerous thing about this kind of substitution of off-screen reality with cinematic fantasy is that the process of identification with the moving image is intentionally seamless; we subscribe to it without thinking about the psychological consequences of such self-delusion:

> Everything happens as if, the subject himself being unable – and for a reason – to account for his own situation, it was necessary to substitute secondary organs, grafted on to replace his own defective ones, instruments or ideological formations capable of filling his function as subject. In fact, this substitution is only possible on the condition that the instruments themselves be hidden or repressed.
>
> (Baudry, 1986: 287)

Cinema is thus an apparatus 'corresponding to the model defined by dominant ideology' (Baudry, 1986: 287).

The viewer is not seen by the apparatus theory as someone making independent decisions about his or her constructions of the self, but rather as a brainwashed individual swallowing any information offered by the ideology and its extensions (including cinema). This primarily happens because the individual chases the illusion of wholeness, and is too lazy to construct his or her own identity. Instead he or she prefers to be taken back to the imaginary and plied with mirror images of the pre-Oedipal perfection which in reality had never existed. The apparatus fools the audience with false promises of bringing back the lost paradise, and delivers empty fantasies which do not last long and have to be substituted with fresh fantasies as soon as the novelty wears out. As a result, the viewer becomes addicted to the mirror, and dependent on the constant supply of narcissistic prostheses for his or her various psychological functions.

Apparatus theorists also bitterly realised that the mature, independent-thinking individual was itself an illusion as human beings are always happy to get rid of responsibility for their own identity-making decisions, and to regress to the state of 'early childhood', when things are decided for them by a parental figure – in this case an ideological apparatus. Besides, it is easier to imagine oneself to be a superhero than to accept one's own 'normality' and humanness.

Apparatus theorists have not used Jung's concept of the collective unconscious to prove their point, yet it perfectly suits their purpose. In fact, Jung even had a term for submerging into the imaginary (which could be used to describe cinema spectatorship): *abaissement du niveau mental*. It becomes felt when the intensity of conscious interests and activities gradually diminish, leading 'either to apathy – a condition very common to artists – or to a regressive development of the conscious functions, that is, they revert to an infantile and archaic level and undergo something like a degeneration' (CW15: 123). If the viewer chases the illusion of wholeness, Vogler implies in *The Writer's Journey*, by all means let's give it to him. Let's create an epic fantasy, a giant fantasy, a most impressive fantasy – and supply it to the masses.

This is when Jung's concepts of the collective unconscious and the Self come into play. Vogler bases his argument that the masses need a particular type of entertainment on the idea of the existence of a common layer of the psyche – the Jungian collective unconscious. The reason why popular films (and mass culture in general) exist and the reason why individual viewers with their unique life experiences and their different backgrounds can enjoy the same films is because they share the same psychic layer. Archetypes are universal entities residing in the collective unconscious, echoing general experiences, general life milestones through which every individual has to live. As a result, it is relatively easy to predict what kind of narrative the audience will like: something with adventures, difficulties and struggles at the end of which the hero will achieve a change of status – i.e. he will get nearer to perfection.

Vogler firmly believes that the apparatus only follows the natural proclivity of the psyche towards wholeness – towards the unachievable Self:

> The Hero's Journey is not an invention, but an observation. It is a recognition of a beautiful design, a set of principles that govern the conduct of life and the world of storytelling the way physics and chemistry govern the physical world. It's difficult to avoid the sensation that the Hero's Journey exists somewhere, somehow, as an eternal reality, a Platonic ideal form, a divine model. From this model, infinite and highly varied copies can be produced, each resonating with the essential spirit of the form.
>
> (2007: xiii)

Unlike Lacan, Jung imbued the pre-conscious universe with spiritual significance, and even singled it out into a separate archetype – the Self. The hero's journey is the journey towards the Self which is an archetype symbolising psychic wholeness. Jung writes that 'wholeness can be realised for one moment only – the moment that Faust was seeking all his life' (CW12: 321). In Vogler's hands, however, the apparatus and its perfect cookbook become an integral part of the universe's spiritual plan of giving the individual back the lost happiness.

Moreover, Vogler claims, so much more than just a writing guide, his book is a kind of spiritual guide; it is 'nothing less than a handbook for life, a complete instruction manual in the art of being human' (2007: xiii). It can also be read

> as a guide to the life lessons that have been carefully built into the stories of all times. Some people have even used it as a kind of travel guide, predicting the inevitable ups and downs of making a physical journey.
>
> (2007: xiv)

This view can be seen as an interesting take on the apparatus theory. It follows from his argument that the film industry can exploit the propensity of the human psyche to 'think' in archetypes, and to see a reflection of itself in images of wholeness – often in idealistic and non-existent images. It also exploits the impulse to individuate by showing the hero's journey on screen. In fact, such individuation by proxy can become addictive and even take away the need to individuate in real life. The perfection the audience sees in superheroes and other unrealistic characters is an illusion and, as such, is dangerous, as it aims to replace the world outside. It cancels the individual's impulse to act, to change things, to become an agent. 'The apparatus' numbs the masses' senses, and puts them to sleep by plying them with hero stories and fantasy scenarios which replace reality and, ultimately, protect the apparatus from being subverted or challenged.

Jung and anthropology: the trickster

The trickster describes the process of individual development and meaning-making in relation to socializing and civilizing structures. As a psycho-anthropological phenomenon, it is of paramount importance to the balance between the social and the personal in the individual's life. Many scholars recognise the trickster's role in identity formation as by challenging the structure, by rejecting it and by laughing at it, we find our own unique way of living and of doing things.

Jung designated the trickster as an archetype – i.e. as one of the essential elements of the individuation process. Jungian analyses of the trickster work well in combination with anthropological definitions of it. Together, they form a theory that presents the trickster as an important part of the narrative structure, as a trigger which sets the events of the story in motion and changes the established order, of which the protagonist is a part. In the course of such a narrative the protagonist goes through a complete transformation, a trial by chaos, and ends up re-establishing the order in his or her life on new terms.

Jung saw the individuation process as a sort of liveable combination of a self-narrative and a series of ritualised personal transformations. This explains his interest in anthropology, which has traditionally been interested in the link between narratives and religious rituals. Both narratives and rituals provide frameworks for spiritual and physical change in an individual's life as well as in the life of his or her society. As Nünning *et al.* argue, both these structuring devices

> create specific worlds; worlds which provide meaning as well as order. . . . Apart from the actual performance of ritual, there is an additional performative quality to both rituals and narratives, in the sense that they picture possible alternatives to the narrative's or ritual's referential context and thereby develop a transformative potential.
>
> (Nünning *et al.*, 2013: 15)

Individuation (including as a narrative) consists of a series of psychological transformations and self-illumination moments dressed up as physical adventures and encounters with mythical figures. It would be impossible without the trickster – the trigger of change and the enemy of stagnant peace. The trickster is thus a big part of any systemic and personal revival, even though, to get the best results, it is advisable to manage it lest it gets out of control and becomes pure chaos. This meaning-making framework contains and houses the trickster, and exists in a kind of unstable symbiosis with it.

The duality of the trickster's nature and his mutability are also emphasised by several cultural anthropologists among whom Paul Radin, who writes in the preface to *The Trickster: A Study in American Indian Mythology* (1956), the trickster 'knows neither good nor evil yet he is responsible for both. He possesses no values, moral or social, is at the mercy of his passions and appetites, yet through his actions all values come into being' (Radin, 1972: xxiii). He also foreshadows 'the shape of man' (1972: xxiv).

Like Radin, Karl Kerényi calls attention to that paradoxical 'creation through destruction' quality of the trickster. Mythological tricksters are silly and irresponsible; they can walk into an existing order of things and thoughtlessly ruin it – yet out of their careless actions a new life is born. As Kerényi notes in his analysis of tricksters in Greek mythology, often the folk prankster 'approximates to the figure of a beneficent creator and becomes what the ethnologists call 'a culture hero' (Kerényi, 1972: 180–181). Greek tricksters combine the sly and the stupid in themselves; in their behaviour we can discern both intention and lack of it. They symbolise the twilight of human consciousness:

> Prometheus, the benefactor of mankind, lacks self-interest and playfulness. Hermes has both, when he discovers fire and sacrifice before Prometheus did – without, however, bothering about mankind. In the playful cruelties which the little god practiced on the tortoise and the sacrificial cows at his first theft, and which conferred no benefit on mankind, . . . we see the sly face of the trickster grinning at us, whereas in the deeds of Prometheus we see the sly and the stupid at once.
>
> (Kerényi, 1972: 181)

Most trickster narratives (mythological, literary or cinematic) share a number of stock themes and motifs that serve as the backbone for the plot. Usually, a trickster narrative starts with the cunning creature being or feeling restricted (often physically), goes on to describe the trickster's escape and its adventures, and ends with the dissolution/transformation of the trickster. The most common structural elements of trickster narratives are being trapped, boundary-breaking, licentious behaviour, scatological humour, bodily transformations, the presence of animals (which I prefer to call 'the animal connection'), naming issues, loss of control over one's body and mind, and the trickster's dissolution/death/transformation at the end of the story. Not all of the elements can be present in one story, film or myth, and their place in the narrative sequence are certainly not fixed. However, the 'end result' of trickster narratives is, invariably, forced transformation of the protagonist via chance and loss of control. In other words, the protagonist achieves a new 'status' via sudden loss of shape and change.

Perhaps not surprisingly, human agency is one of the central problems of cultural anthropology. From the point of view of the British anthropologist and semiotician Gregory Bateson, the individual is permanently caught in the developmental tug of war – the process of fission and fusion (which he termed schismogenesis), the rivalry between individual initiative and cultural imperatives (Bateson, 1936: 195–196).

Another British anthropologist, Victor Turner (1920–1983), also explored the relationship between the individual and the system. He theorised that all systems were structures with an in-built internal conflict, triggered by communitas, or counter-structures. Communitas is 'over and above any formal social bonds' (Turner, 1975: 45). It can be organised and led by a group of disgruntled individuals whose vision of the system's operation and functioning differs from that upheld by those in power. The psycho-anthropological task of communitates (sic) is to counter-balance the solidifying actions of the official structure. As a result of this destabilising tension – the cultural equivalent of the trickster – the system renews itself as the fresh ideas 'feed back into the "central" economic and politico-legal domains and arenas, supplying them with goals, aspirations, incentives, structural models and raisons d'etre' (Turner, 1979: 21). Communitas is an inhabitant, and spokesperson, of liminal situations in which 'new symbols, models, paradigms, etc., arise – as the seedbeds of cultural creativity in fact' (Turner, 1979: 21).

Turner employed the term *liminal* to describe the situations in which the structure was challenged, altered or destroyed. Liminality (from Latin *limen* – threshold) was initially mentioned by the French ethnographer Arnold Van Gennep in his work, *The Rites of Passage* (1909), and later developed by Turner into a set of political and social concepts. It denotes lack of stability, temporary absence of order – a transitional, twilight state. In his analysis of liminality, Turner uses van Gennep's tripartite rite of passage: separation, transition and incorporation.

The first phase, separation, marks the end of the old state of things and the beginning of a new 'order'. The second phase is the liminal period during which 'the ritual subjects pass through . . . an area of ambiguity, a sort of social limbo which has few . . . of the attributes of either the preceding or subsequent profane social statuses of cultural states' (Turner 1979: 16). The third phase is the time of healing of the developmental rift, when 'the ritual subjects' (initiates, candidates, whole communities in social, political or economic transition) return to their new, 'relatively stable, well-defined position in the total society' (1979: 16). 'Liminality', Turner points out, refers to 'any condition outside or on the peripheries of everyday life' (Turner, 1975: 47).

In the narrative structure, the trickster represents an unpredictable element which is introduced into an existing order of things, then challenges or demolishes this order, and the new order is introduced at the end of the narrative – often after the trickster's disappearance. The trickster also changes the status of the characters in the narrative (particularly the protagonist). In this sense, the structure is reminiscent of the tripartite ritual consisting of separation, transition and incorporation. These narrative elements also hold good for the cinema where the trickster is often introduced a few minutes after the beginning of the film, after the main order is established and the principal relationships between the characters are outlined. The trickster's lessons (i.e. the lessons learned by the characters during the liminal period of the story) are chaotic but life-changing. Being a-social, anti-social and ultimately anti-structural, the trickster creates change messily and unpredictably, by introducing liminality into the existing order. It also uncovers the reverse side of normality and social reality, which consists of stagnation, predictability and lack of fresh perspective.

Paddington (Dir. Paul King, 2014), loosely based on the famous children's book series by Michael Bond, is a typical trickster narrative in that it follows a storyline in which a chaotic and unpredictable element is introduced into the seemingly stable lives of 'normal people'. A bear from 'darkest Peru' arrives in London, at Paddington Station, with a note around his neck saying 'Please look after this bear. Thank you'. He is spotted by the kindly Mrs Brown (Sally Hawkins), and invited to stay with the Brown family who soon realise that he is quite a liability. Lacking understanding of the local rules and customs, and being clumsy, Paddington keeps getting into trouble and creating mess when he cleans his ears with toothbrushes, falls off the escalator or floods the bathroom. Most of these mishaps are as endearing as they are annoying. Little does he know that he is being hunted by a vicious taxidermist, Millicent (Nicole Kidman), who believes that her father's career was ruined because of him. Her father, Montgomery Clyde, was an explorer and was expected to preserve a specimen of a bear from Peru for the Natural History Museum, but refused as he was reluctant to kill (rather human) bears. After many more adventures, and having overcome numerous dangers and difficulties, Paddington becomes an officially accepted member of the Brown family.

Paddington Bear has all the traditional attributes of the trickster. Many mythological tricksters are animals, often anthropomorphic. Animals are frequent guests in trickster myths. In fact, they symbolise the trickster's connection with the 'underworld' of instincts and animal behaviour. Many mythological and folkloric tricksters are animals, and even when they are not, some association with the animal kingdom is often present. The African trickster club boasts a spider (Kwaku Anansi), a hare and a tortoise; the Northern American group includes a raven, a coyote, a rabbit and Wakdjunkaga's numerous animal transformations. The fox is the main trickster in Russian fairy tales; Indian mythology has the monkey called Hanuman (one of the heroes of the Ramayana); the most-known Chinese trickster is also a monkey – the hero of the novel *Journey to the West* (1590); in Peruvian fairy tales the trickster's role is played by a guinea pig; Argentinean folklore has Tokwah, who is neither human nor animal; Japanese folktales mention Hare and Badger as clever shapeshifters. Their anthropomorphism also emphasises their boundary-crossing skills as well as their ability to transform into other creatures, for they don't have a permanent state, do not belong to any system and therefore lack physical, moral or social continuity.

Paddington also introduces what one character in the film terms 'a pinch of chaos' into an otherwise routine and measured family life. This fulfils the 'lack of control' condition of trickster characters. Not only can they not control their own bodies (they are also shapeshifters, remember), they cause others to lose control over theirs. Paddington brings irrational and a-systemic elements into a super-controlled environment. The Browns are a well-run family presided over by the father, who is a risk analyst by profession. Mr Brown (Hugh Bonneville) makes sure that every object in his flat is insured. He also opposes the idea of bringing home a bear – a stranger and a homeless creature. The father is the paragon of normality and order – he has to be, for he feels responsible for the safety of his family. Paddington's task (as a narrative element) is to derail the controlling order, and thus to introduce (ultimately, creative) change into the otherwise stagnating system.

The problem of control is symbiotically connected with the issue of shame. The social order uses shame to shape and control the individual. Mythological tricksters, being metaphorically pre-individual, do not claim to have mastery over their bodies or actions. When tricksters play their tricks on humans, gods and 'powerful persons', they show the power of chance and choice over rational frameworks and established orders. They also remind people that the individual is never truly perfect or complete, and that control over one's mind and body – as well as over one's surroundings – has to be constantly revised, maintained and observed.

Importantly, Paddington is an immigrant. This fulfils a whole range of trickster attributes – boundary-crossing, the problem with the name, being trapped and the fear of difference (which is essentially the fear of the loss of control over one's quiet and measured life). The immigrant bear crosses borders (he crosses several oceans), is initially nameless (the Browns call him Paddington because they find him on the platform at Paddington station) and is trapped at the beginning of the narrative (he is a stowaway who arrives in England on board a cargo ship). His behaviour is unpredictable, and he often causes chaos inadvertently. He ends up shaking up a whole range of systems, including the Browns' family habits and Mr Brown's faith in not taking risks.

Fear of chaos and losing control over one's current existence are the usual ingredients in anti-immigrant sentiments. Foreignness is one of the key themes of the film – almost its moral and social premise, in fact. Fear of all things foreign is epitomised in the character of Mr Curry (Peter Capaldi) who, despite his name, is deeply xenophobic and has nightmares about his lovely street eventually getting covered in 'their fur'. Not surprisingly, Mr Curry is also the kind of individual who rarely leaves his flat and avoids human contact. This is because, as the film's narrative goes, he had a cold and uncaring mother. His careful behaviour protects him from any risks, change or challenge. Having a stale and boring life, he nevertheless protects himself from any tricksters that could threaten it and Paddington is one such trickster. Any difference is disturbing because it breaks up the homogeneity of a particular community or the smooth working of a locally accepted order of things. Naturally, according to Mr Curry, bringers of difference should be captured and eliminated. For this purpose he teams up with Millicent Clyde, who openly empathises with his xenophobic complaints.

Paul King and his team may have toyed with the storyline, but they faithfully followed Bond's principal message. Bond admits that he got his inspiration for the character of Paddington from the images of Jewish children arriving at Reading station before the Second World War:

> I remember their labels round their necks and then I remember going to the cinema and seeing on the newsreel that Hitler had moved into some new country and seeing footage of elderly people pushing prams with all their belongings in them. Refugees are the saddest sight, I still think that.
>
> (Llewellyn Smith, *The Telegraph*, 23 November 2014)

A trickster-immigrant, Paddington shakes up the system by virtue of being different as well as being unfamiliar with the local customs. The bringer of chaos and the prince of liminality, the trickster's aim in narratives is revival of creativity and renewal of ruling structures. True to this role, Paddington takes the Browns through the liminal zone and to a more creative existence as Mr Brown re-learns to be creative (at some point he even dresses as a cleaning lady in a classic transvestite comedy twist), and family members are finally able to act together, thus rediscovering their unity.

At the end of the film they get a live-in trickster, fully integrated and managed (and thus no longer feared or seen as 'the other') into the family. Paddington the trickster guarantees them a non-stop delivery of liminal challenges and an endless stream of entertainment. Regular renewal guarantees the stability of any system while the total absence of a trickster leads to the structure's stagnation and death. 'The spirit of disorder and the enemy of boundaries' (to use Barbara Babcock-Abrahams' expression [1975: 147]), in controlled and measured quantities, ensures the longevity of the system, be it a person's mind, a family unit or a social structure.

Chapter 5

The auteur theory

A Jungian view

Luke Hockley

Introduction

The remaining chapters of this book move from the eclectic and synthesising approach of the previous chapter to explore Jungian approaches to four individual established areas of film theory. Two of these involve theories that have made the transition from the technical lexicon of the academy to become part of our everyday vocabulary, namely *auteur* theory and genre theory. While *auteur* theory is primarily concerned with the creation of films and the role of the director, genre theory examines the interrelationships between the films themselves, the studios that have produced them and how viewers 'read' such genre films. The third theory deals with questions of sexuality and representation. Finally, the book closes with a consideration of phenomenological film theory. This somewhat specialist area is included because it sets out to understand the experience of watching a film and what it is that is happening when viewers experience the unfolding flow of images and sounds in the auditorium. These are the four approaches: *auteur* theory (creation); genre theory (production and exhibition); sexuality (representation) and phenomenological theory (reception).

Providing an overview of the specific insights that a Jungian orientated approach to films can provide, each chapter examines the relationship between Analytical Psychology and the texts, structures and institutions of cinema. Each chapter has a similar structure and starts by introducing the central debates of each film theory before exploring how Analytical Psychology can inflect the ways that the *auteur* theory, genre theory, sexuality and phenomenological film theory can be understood psychologically. In so doing they will suggest the direction of travel of Jungian-orientated film theory and identify future avenues for further exploration. Informing this investigation is the following question: what is distinctive about the Jungian approach and its relationship to classical psychoanalysis, its structural variant as promoted by the journal *Screen* and subsequent Lacanian developments?

Psychoanalytic film theory has sought to find points of correspondence between the structural operation of the psyche and the machinery of cinema. In some cases such investigations were optically driven and concerned with the function of the 'scopic regime' (Metz, 1977). Put another way, psychoanalytic theory has attempted to identify just what it is that the act of looking stands for – psychologically what does it mean to look? For Freud looking was a source of pleasure and he thought of it as a sublimation of the psyche's libidinal sexual energy. Psychoanalytic film theory has wondered about the extent to which such pleasure is related to the ideological location of looking, and the objects intended to be looked at. Specifically, it has tied the scopic regime to the dominant ideology of Western culture and in so doing locates 'the look' as part of a patriarchal system of oppression in which women are objectified for the pleasure of the male spectator (Mulvey, 1975). Though rather different, arguably, there are aspects of the Lacanian position, and particularly its emphasis on the 'mirror phase', that fit into this same ocular-centric category. Others have sought to avoid such an ocular-centric approach and instead have explored how the cinematic apparatus in its projection, screen, reflection and immersive sound creates the optimal conditions for the reception of a film (Baudry, 1986). In short, such theory examines the apparatus of cinema and how it is related to our internal psychological and biological structures of perception.

By way of contrast, phenomenological theory has tended to emphasise the experience of the film as a moment where it is possible to differentiate between the narrative meaning of the film and the point of reception where other meanings come into play. The concluding chapter of this book will explore the extent to which it is legitimate, and indeed productive, to introduce the idea of the unconscious into such considerations. Historically phenomenological theory has been antagonistic to the idea of an unconscious that possesses purpose and intent, preferring instead to describe experience in terms of what is known, and what is unknown (Fuchs, 2012). While phenomenology regards the idea of the unconscious as superfluous, Analytical Psychology finds the idea of the phenomenology appealing as its focus on experience dovetails well with its interest in the relationship between deep structures and psychological imagery. Clearly, this raises the question as to the extent to which it is possible to reconcile these two rather different ways of describing the psychology of the cinematic experience.

Jungian-orientated film theory is concerned with understanding the ways in which the experience of affect has an integral part to play in the viewing experience of films and it wonders how it might influence our understanding of the films we watch. For example, how do affects relate to narrative and textual understanding of films themselves? What is the role of affect in the para-textual life of films, as they escape the confines of the cinema auditorium as movie posters, trailers, memorabilia, fan sites, DVDs and so on? Here, affect can be used to illuminate individual viewing experiences as well as means to understand films more fully. It is interesting that the concern with the structure of the psyche and the structure of film that has preoccupied much psychoanalytic film theory has meant that the crucial issue of affect has been marginalised in those discussions. Jungian-orientated film theory provides a useful corrective to that state of affairs with its emphasis on the identification of unconscious processes which are understood through the experience of affects – often unlooked for and unexpected. In turn, this provides the link to phenomenological theory as it too is intimately concerned with the experience of affect – not an intellectual appreciation of affect but its manifestation in the body as part of a hermeneutic system.

What is the auteur theory?

Outside the academy films are often identified by their directors. It is now such a normal part of our daily language that we rarely pause to think about this curious state of affairs. To routinely talk about the latest Spielberg film, or the new Fincher movie is quite normal and unproblematic to us. When the term *auteur* is used colloquially it refers to a director who has a personal style, or who seems to produce films that are in some way distinctive. For example James Cameron, George Lucas, Ridley Scott, Peter Jackson and Steven Spielberg are familiar directors who produce powerful narrative films. Arguably, Dave Fincher, Christopher Nolan, David Lynch, David Cronenberg, Woody Allen, Quentin Tarantino, Darren Aronofsky, Martin Scorsese all make more personal films.

Yet a moment's thought shows that of course it is quite possible to categorise films by producer, or writer, or any one of a number of other production personnel – yet this almost never happens. The exception to this concerns actors who have 'star' status, though even then they are often linked with the director, as in 'Scarlett Johansson in Jonathan Glazer's *Under the Skin*' (2013). The development of the director as a key taxonomic category for the classification of films emerged as the outcome of specific historical circumstances. But there are also psychological explanations that illuminate why it is that directors as powerful creative individuals have come to figure prominently in the ways we think about films – however, such psychological reasons are talked about much less frequently. This section explores the rise of the director as the author of a film, examines how Jungian-orientated film studies has utilised this development and finally looks at some of the psychological ramifications in adopting a psychological orientation to the *auteur* theory.

From early on in the history of cinema the director of a film has held a special place in the imagination of the public. Filmmaking is of course a collective enterprise as the lengthy credits at the end of any film bear testament. The complexity of commercial movie making is such that it requires vast teams of creative, technical, logistic managerial personnel. Even smaller independent productions that are not likely to be known to audiences outside of film festivals, and that might not even manage a DVD release, have significant sized production teams. For example, *The Strange Little Cat* (*Das merkwürdige Kätzchen*) (Dir. Zürcher, 2013) had a crew of over fifty people. Yet somehow the idea that the director is the equivalent of the author of a novel is a proposition of such immediate simplicity and appeal that it is hard to shake off. It is as though psychologically we need the myth of the individual creative genius. Intellectually we know that filmmaking is not a solitary activity yet somehow we hold on to the belief that in this technologically sophisticated and increasingly mediated age, the spirit of the individual survives. Perhaps this too speaks to the appeal of social media, which certainly provides the illusion that an individual and distinctive voice can be heard above the clamour of the social crowd. In the final chapter of this book we return to the role of the individual in finding and making psychological meaning in cultural products. For present purposes it is enough to register that one of the psychological functions that a 'myth' of the *auteur* performs culturally is to preserve the idea of individual identity and to foster a belief in personal creativity.

The idea that the director is the controlling and creative force behind a film was around almost from the start of the film industry. Directors such as Auguste and Louis Lumière (1862–1954 and 1864–1948) and Méliès (1861–1938) gave way to D. W. Griffiths (1875–1948), Erich Stroheim (1885–1957) and Josef von Sternberg (1894–1969). However it was really the post-Second World War period that saw the emergence of a theory of cinema that centred on the creative importance of the director. There is a historical reason for this development. During the Second World War, the Nazi occupying powers prohibited the distribution and exhibition of American fiction films. Shortly after the end of the war in 1946 America formed the Motion Picture Export Association (MPEA) (Segrave, 1997) to oversee the distribution of the American back-catalogue from the war years to thirteen different European countries. The MPEA was effective in its undertaking and subsequently Italy, France and West Germany became some the largest post-war markets for American films. For somewhat different reasons, the UK was another key market for Hollywood.

However, it was in France that the writers of the influential publication *Cahiers du Cinéma* identified an issue that they wanted to solve. The contributors to *Cahiers* who included André Bazin (its founder) and filmmakers such as Éric Rohmer, Jacques Rivette, Jean-Luc Godard, Claude Chabrol and François Truffaut came to the view that in this sea of American product, some films stood out as islands of excellence. For reasons that were not immediately apparent, some films seemed to be more compelling as works of art than the others. Formalising this observation, *Cahiers* made a distinction between the *metteur en scène* and the *auteur*. The former term relates to the *mise-en-scène* of a film. There are numerous definitions of this term but the one offered by Bordwell and Thompson (2003) identifies the following elements involved in the arrangement of the events in front of the camera as contributing to the formal properties of film: composition, props, actors, costumes and lighting (Bordwell and Thompson, 2003). Directors who mastered the formal elements of film production but who according to *Cahiers* failed to convey a personal meaning or individual vision were designated as *metteurs en scène*. On the other hand, the status of *auteur* was afforded to those directors who not only fully controlled all the elements of the film, but who also managed to explore and convey a personal set of concerns repeatedly, film after film. This distinction between *metteur en scène* and *auteur*, as promoted by *Cahiers*, had an evaluative function as for that group of critics it separated out 'good' films from those that were merely routine or everyday. The *auteurs* that the *Cahiers* critics particularly admired included: Alfred Hitchcock, Orson Welles, John Ford and Howard Hawks.

Published in 1981 John Caughie's edited collection *Theories of Authorship* provided one of the earliest assessments of the various strengths and pitfalls of the *auteur* theory and it remains a seminal account. The articles in that volume are as salient today as when they were first written, as they explore the central debates that surround questions of cinematic authorship. The book is arranged in three sections and the final section deals with 'Fiction of the author/author of the fiction' – it is the neat use of the solidus in that construction which in no small part contributes to the longevity of the formulation. Much of this book too is in different ways concerned with the creation of fictions and from a Jungian position it questions who actually is their author. Is it just the director who oversees the creation of image and sound for the screen? Perhaps we should instead focus on the institutional determinates which shape fiction films so that they are able to make a good financial return at the box office – it is all to easy to forget that the primary function of films is to make money as investors do not commit large sums on speculative ventures just to entertain themselves for a couple of hours in the cinema. Perhaps in this sense the industry itself is the author of a film – a point that is echoed in some of the writings of Andrew Sarris (1968). A third possibility is that the author of a film is actually the viewer and that the psychological meaning and its authorship rests with each individual viewer, as he or she develops a personal relationship with a film. The more likely scenario is that all three elements interact in different ways to inflect our understanding of films, their authorship and their resulting psychological meanings.

Earlier in the 1960s the American film theorist Andrew Sarris had memorably commented, 'the auteur theory is not so much a theory as an attitude, a table of values that converts film history into directorial autobiography' (Sarris, 1968: 34). And to this it is reasonable to add that in no small way, the values that convert film history into directorial autobiography belong to the viewer. In this vein, Robert Stam argues: 'Auteur studies now tend to see a director's work not as the expression of individual genius but rather as the site of encounter of a biography, an intertext, an institutional context and a historical moment (Stam, 2000: 6).

While accepting this is not Stam's intention, it remains important to note that one of the intertexts is the psychological intertext that arises in the act of watching a film. Stam has in mind institutional intertexts of the type that will be considered in the next chapter on genre. But given the psychological focus of this volume, for our purposes any theory of authorship needs to include a consideration of the extent to which the viewer's psychological authority interacts with the narrative meaning of the film to create something new, that is not inherent in the just the viewer of the film or the film itself, but which arises from the interaction of the two. Looking is not a passive activity. It is a hermeneutic activity in which the subject exists in a reflexive relationship with the object. Subject and object are not separate categories as the one needs the other. As we look at film, so too it looks back at us and in so doing the co-constellation of the gaze sets up an iterative dynamic in which ever-changing meanings circulate from screen, to viewer and back to screen and this generation of meanings is the site of the psychological vortex of the viewer–viewing relationship.

Jungian approaches to film directors

Jungian-orientated film scholars have been drawn to the idea that Jungian insights can offer fresh perspectives on the work of well-known directors. To date there have been book-length studies on Howard Hawks, Nicolas Roeg and Tim Burton. Additionally, there have been scholarly articles and chapters that have explored, amongst others, the work of Baz Luhrmann, Federico Fellini, Derek Jarman and Ingmar Bergman. The next part of this chapter considers if this interest in directors might find its origins in something other than the prevalence of the *auteur* theory – perhaps there are psychological reasons too for wanting to focus on the creative work of (male) individuals.

One of the first books to attempt such an *auteur*-based Jungian analysis of the films of a single director was Clark Branson's *Howard Hawks: A Jungian Study* (1987). It consists of a series of short analyses of each of Hawks' films. It makes for an interesting read as Hawks' work is famously diverse with very little apparently linking films as disparate as *Only Angels Have Wings* (1939), *His Girl Friday* (1940), *The Big Sleep* (1946) and *Gentlemen Prefer Blondes* (1953). The eclecticism of Hawks' work was one of the areas that the *auteur* theorists struggled with, as it is difficult to spot the thematic consistency and personal themes that they were seeking to identify. Often when looking at the work of an '*auteur*' it is possible to detect motifs that run across the films and it is not unusual for similar characters and narrative concerns to reoccur – the films of Alfred Hitchcock are a good example of just that. In a way, Branson's Jungian readings attempt to reveal psychological threads that are woven into the body of his films and in so doing answer a question that the French theorists of the 1950s were unable to.

Branson sets out in the early chapters of the book the classical Jungian approach that he is about to adopt. However, he does not really pull the directorial and psychological strands together for the reader, who is left with the gauzy impression that there is something important here but that it lies behind a veil. Some of the analyses are rather short (sometimes just a paragraph) while others go into more detail. What gradually becomes clear in Branson's analysis is how Hawk's films repeatedly deal with the emergence of a male peer group with all the opportunities for heroism and comedy that this suggests. What is unclear is why a Jungian method is needed as this insight could have emerged from any number of close textual readings. Somehow the reader is left with the impression that in this seemingly diverse body of films there is something further that needs to be excavated. Branson notes (1987: 274) that even though Jungian psychology can use grandiose terms, it is nonetheless concerned with intimate relations. That observation does actually provide a way into Hawks' films, each of which seeks to reconcile big themes such as love, war and identity with more intimate and personal relationships and experiences – the idea that what we find in the personal is an expression of the collective is a very Jungian idea indeed.

The film theorist Don Fredericksen offers a rather different take in his approach to studying *auteurs* and it is one that is redolent with psychological reflections. He is particularly interested in personal voice filmmaking which, of necessity, means that the psychological life of the director is bound into the films themselves. He has conducted a book-length study of Ingmar Bergman's film *Persona* (1966), and at the time of his death was working on another book about *Illumination* (1973) by the Polish director Krzysztof Zanussi. This would have complemented his existing work on Fellini and in particular *8½* (1963), and an early piece that while not *auteurist* in its orientation analyses the poetic documentary film *Song of Ceylon* (1934), directed by Basil Wright (see Chapter 3), one of the key members of the British Documentary Film Movement (BDFM).

For Fredericksen, all these films fall into a special category that he refers to as 'liminal cinema'. It is his contention that such films exhibit a particular proximity to the unconscious mind. The etymology of the word 'liminal' is found in the Latin word '*limen*', meaning threshold. Thus it refers to the start of something, to a crossing over into a new project or phase of life. In that sense it is rather like a doorway into a home, where we cross from the outside world into the domestic interior. However these threshold spaces are not always as fixed as a doorway – for example, the boundary between the sea and seashore changes depending on the tides. Fredericksen uses the term in both senses, as something starting and also in a more permeable manner, to explore how some films seem to exist in a space somewhere between the conscious world and the unconscious.

His revealing analysis of *8½* locates it as a work of midlife in which the director is crossing from one part of life towards another. Fredericksen undertakes what he refers to as 'a functional analysis'. He elects not to explore any of the dream sequences in the films, nor does he produce a detailed textual reading. Consequently he eschews any reflection on the tempting and famous Asa Nisi Masa motif which is a thinly disguised rendering of the Jungian term 'anima' (AsaNIsMAsa). Instead he choses to interweave into his analysis of the film speculations about Fellini's childhood that are based on comments made by the director himself, and in particular the lack of parental mirroring that Fredericksen infers took place in Fellini's early life.

In his analysis of *Persona*, Fredericksen undertakes a similar process of moving between the life of the director and the film itself, though this time the focus is very much more on the text, and he produces an insightful account of the film in which its Jungian themes are revealed. In particular he uses the idea of liminality to very good effect to reveal how doors, windows, mirrors, etc. support the idea of transition as one moves from each psychological state to the next. There is a thin line to walk here between using biographical information to inform textual interpretations and the much more problematic use of films to make psychological claims about a director's psychological life. In his analysis of *Persona* Frederick stays on the interpretative side, whereas with *8½* he arguably adopts a more interpretative and 'liminal' approach.

In her monograph *Tim Burton: The Monster and the Crowd* (2010), Helena Bassil-Morozow is in similar territory, though here the lines are more clearly drawn.

Bassil-Morozow clearly sets out to locate films not as just the creation of an *auteur*, but as social and psychological sites of meaning that exist in relationship with one another. In fact she states that her study is not attempting to find a correlation between the personal psychology of a director and the films, but rather that it is establishing a more intertextual approach that, as it unfolds, uncovers something meaningful about the psychological condition of post-modernity. For her, films have as much to say about our cultural condition as they do about the psychological state of their directors. As Bassil-Morozow comments:

> I deliberately eschewed extensive use of the psychobiographical approach because, in a way, Tim Burton's art and his vision are bigger than any number of childhood complexes that he may harbour. *Edward Scissorhands*, *Batman* and *Sweeny Todd*, far from reflecting a narrowly personal set of problems, map out the psychological face of the contemporary world.
>
> (Bassil-Morozow, 2010: 178)

The particular significance of her work is encapsulated in the final sentence, in which Bassil-Morozow makes it clear that the function of her *auteur* analysis is only in part to understand the films. More significantly what she is actually attempting is to see what the films reveal about the psychological and ideological state of society, as mediated through the figure of the director, in this case Tim Burton. What is it, then, that Bassil-Morozow uncovers? What her perceptive analysis of Tim Burton's films reveals is an enduring preoccupation in the films with the threat to individuality in which the agency of the individual is something fragile and frail, and in which the unthinking, unaware social collective threatens to drown out individual voices – something that is enacted by many of Burton's characters.

Tellingly, in the preface to her book, Bassil-Morozow comments on how growing up in the Soviet Union there was a collective mentality in which the life of the individual is actually not personal but belongs to the community. This gives her analysis of the characters in Burton's films a particular personal relevance. It also gives a different take on why Burton as a 'maverick' creative director, who produces films that are different to the mainstream product that comes out of the American film industry, is a figure of such importance for her. The director, and the psychology of his films, is ideologically inflected. In this world, it becomes increasingly important for strong individuals to stand out against the collective, even if those characters are fundamentally flawed. Arguably, it is precisely those flaws, or, to use a more psychological language, complexes, which are what give Burton's central characters both agency and affect. As Bassil-Morozow reminds us, they are embodiments of the trickster and child archetypes – the future hero whose life from his or her early days is full of all kinds of dangers and adventures. Moreover, it is in this imperfect childhood, with imperfect, often wounding parents, that the unstoppable drive to survive and to create, characteristic of true heroes, is born. Being flawed also means being able to recreate one's life – and the life of others – despite all the pain, loss and unfairness. Ultimately, it is the effort and the ability to get up and move on that helps one win.

John Izod sets up a similar, yet significantly different, set of parameters in his analysis of the films of Nicolas Roeg. In the introduction to his unjustly little known 1992 study, Izod first elucidates the Jungian dichotomy between the inner world of the unconscious psyche and that of our more conscious daily life:

> [the] juxtaposition of the universe with the microcosm of the individual psyche typifies a structure which embodies major themes [in Roeg's films]. Since the films employ myth to relate the outer and inner worlds, they are peculiarly well suited to an analysis that uses Jungian methods.
>
> (Izod, 1992: xiv)

It is worth pausing here to note that for Izod, at least at this point in his writing, the inner and outer (conscious and unconscious) are indeed separate worlds. As we will see in a moment, while he posits such a differentiation he was already beginning to question if the distinction is quite so clear-cut as it might appear. Izod is also setting up a typically Jungian view of the psyche in which each individual carries with him or her something of our contemporary collective experience and also a collective history as represented in the world of myth. The idea might seem a curious one, yet we know that ideologically we are impregnated with cultural attitudes and that these cultural values and beliefs are the result of an historical accretion that is formed as the sediment of social experience and its contingent values are gradually laid down to form the bedrock of our being.

In an intriguing and insightful moment Izod wonders what would happen if we struck a fissure through this stratum and the accumulated cultural meanings of films were cracked open? Put another way, just what is it that occurs when we read against the grain? Izod attempts just that as in a bold move he sets out to interpret Roeg's films in the light of Jungian sensitivities. This is curious because on the face of it these films appear to be rather Freudian in much of their imagery and in their thematic concerns. The oedipal dynamics of *Don't Look Now* (1973) the sexual perversions of *Bad Timing* (1980), the unrelenting images of trains going into tunnels (!) in *Track 29* (1988) all suggest that a Jungian reading of these films is not likely to be a promising undertaking. Again, Izod's intention is to use the Jungian perspective to reveal something that other ways of looking at these films have missed. The intention is not to remedy the deficiencies of the *auteur* theory itself, but rather to offer a set of different perspectives on these films to the ones that are afforded by more Freudian psychoanalytic interpretations.

Yet, informative though Izod's interpretations of each film are, what shines through is the prescient strength of the analytical position that he adopts. Izod is keen to differentiate between 'Roeg' the director as a mediated presence and Roeg the man who exists outside the immediacy of the mediated frame. This is a crucial distinction as in Jungian terms it distinguishes between persona and self. The director's mask, his persona, is the archetype of social adaptability that is needed to transform the film from script to finished product. Just as the persona that each and every one of us has is a part of who we are, it is also just the surface, the patina of the psyche.

If it were to transpire that Roeg turned out to be no more than the sum of his films, then he would be stuck in a form of persona identification. Thus, semiotically the distinction is made between 'Roeg' as director (persona) and Roeg as an ego identity that exists in relation to, but different from, his films.

However, as viewers we are inquisitive and keen to get behind the surface of the films, to tear off the director's mask and to find out more about the film and the man himself. Izod suggests that the lifting of the authorial mask comes with the interpretative impulse and that it complements the drive to understand a film in all its theoretical, aesthetic and psychological complexity. Along with this viewers project their own needs and desires into the film. Izod notes:

> we ourselves actively construct the idea of an author. Such a figure ('Roeg' rather than Roeg, to pick up [Peter] Wollen's distinction) is a compound firstly of elements encoded into the film texts together with, secondly, our own inscription of the psychological and moral characteristics that seem to us to explain those traces and, thirdly, our projection of our own needs and emotion into the text. To these diverse forms of knowledge we add whatever we can glean from sources outside the cinema such as interviews and reviews.
> (Izod, 1992: 249–250)

Izod's is a neatly multi-layered analysis. It reveals how the meanings that accrue in films are the result of three elements: the structure of the films themselves; knowledge of the films from sources other than the films (intertexts) and finally the individual psychology of viewers. (This approach to the psychology of cinema will be given further consideration in the chapter on phenomenology – Chapter 8.)

Auteur as father

What then is it that underlies the psychological appeal of the *auteur* theory to the Jungian-inclined film theorist? Of all the areas of film studies the *auteur* theory has attracted the attention of Jungian film scholars like no other. Curiously, some aspects of film theory have gone untroubled by Jungian concerns. There is almost no writing on film stars, just a little on genre and almost nothing on the institutional aspects of film production. To help in exploring the significance of the *auteur* here we will co-opt the Lacanian concept of the *nom du père* (the name of the father). It is used to indicate the role of the father in the symbolic realm. (The symbolic realm is one of the three Lacanian orders of being – the other two are the 'imaginary' and the 'real'. These technical terms are highly specified in Lacanian thinking and have meanings that are rather different to the ways in which they are used colloquially, and the Lacanian symbolic should not be confused with either the Freudian understanding of symbols or indeed the Jungian.) For Lacan the symbolic order is the determining order of being. It is roughly equivalent to an order of 'culture'. In turn, this cultural order is expressed through language. As Lacan notes in *Écrits*: 'It is in the name of the Father that we must recognize the support of the symbolic function which, from the dawn of history, has identified his person with the figure of the law' (1977: 67).

Here Lacan is implicitly acknowledging the father's role in the oedipal dynamic that, as he puts it, has existed 'from the dawn of history'. In so doing he plays with the term's phonological similarity to *le non du père* (the 'no' of the father) and as a result he emphasises the legislative and prohibitive functions of the father and also the need to extricate oneself from the prescribed vision that is enacted when the world is seen solely through the father's paternal eyes. Of course such a shift is not simple for, as Lacan implies, we cannot make such a clean-cut escape as we remain perpetually both inside and outside the *nom du père*. To use a more Jungian language, as Anthony Stevens reminds us, the work of the father is centrifugal in that it moves the child from home out into society while at the same time the child remains within the matrices of familial relations.

Psychologically speaking, as well as conceptually, Freud, Lacan and Jung are the founding fathers of our discipline. It is therefore understandable that in an oedipal manner it would be necessary to 'murder' or dispose of their intellectual inheritance. Yet, as Stevens pointed out, it is impossible to escape our familial relations. And so Jungian-orientated film studies become a site of contestation with more established approaches, with more mature approaches or as we might put it, more 'adult' views of the world. As the relative newcomer, the angry child needs to both kill the father and retain the positive aspects of family lore. The field of Jungian film theory is then both the *non* and *nom du père*.

In place of our psychological fathers we have reinstated our cinematic fathers – the directors who, like us, have undergone a crisis of identity. It is surely no accident that Tim Burton, Federico Fellini and Ingmar Bergman are all intimately concerned with questions of being and of identity. In their films they each explore issues of personal transformation, of what it means to be in a state of tension with society, and what it means to find one's own path through the world. In short, they are all concerned with individuation and arguably all use films as part of their own individuation process too. This, then, is how Jungian-informed film studies has co-opted *auteurs* to aid the individuation of the subject itself.

However, this psychological take on the *auteur* also provides a rather different perspective on the personal vision of the *auteur*. Alongside an *auteur*'s ability to exercise control over the medium (the *metteur en scène*) and the use of the medium to give personal voice to individual creative concerns (*auteur*) we need to add the psychological significance of the films themselves. Here, it is important to distinguish between the psychological potency of the films and the psychology of the director. Of course the personal life of the director is intertwined with the films. Naturally it is significant that Fellini was in Jungian analysis while he was making *8½* and it would be a mistake to ignore such biographical information, especially when Fellini left a dream journal (2007). However, it would be no lesser mistake to make the error of trying to psychoanalyse a director through his or her films. First, as we have seen, unlike dreams, which are bespoke and individual, films are collaborative and cultural. Second, there is very little opportunity to open up a dialogue with a film's director – either they are no longer alive or they are for other reasons inaccessible to us. Thirdly, there is little reason to assume that the personal psychological traces left in films are a reliable indication of the director's psychological state.

Yet it remains significant that a Jungian approach to films has been particularly interested in the creative work and personal vision of film directors. Central to a Jungian conception of the world and the psychological development of individuals is the idea of individuation. This is the psychological task, often associated with mid-life, of being more fully ourselves. It is the point in life when typically careers and families are established and so perversely it is also the time when it is necessary to escape from such societal norms and to forge a personal way of being in the world. Of course, this is a somewhat romantic notion and Paul Bishop (2009) has explored how intertwined Jung's psychological ideas are with those of nineteenth-century German romantic aesthetics and philosophy. Nonetheless, and laden as it is with this cultural history, individuation remains a central and distinguishing quality of classical Jungian psychology.

One of the contributions of Jungian-orientated film studies (romantic though it is) is a reminder of just how important personal creativity is and of the ways that it is central to our individual understanding of both who we are and how we are, in the world. Yet, significantly, Jung also stressed the limitations of such an approach:

> The essence of a work of art is not to be found in the personal idiosyncrasies that creep into it – indeed, the more there are of them, the less it is a work of art – but in its rising above the personal and speaking from the mind and heart of the artist to the mind and heart of mankind. The personal aspect of art is a limitation and even vice.
>
> (CW15: 156)

Here, then, is a good example of one way in which Jungian psychology can be helpfully contradictory. On the one hand it identifies the importance of individual psychology in both the creation and interpretation of films, while on the other it stresses the importance of the collective appeal of film as a medium that transcends the personal. The tensions between individual and collective qualities that run throughout Jungian psychology accurately reflect the way that watching a film is both a personal and collective activity. There is an *enantiodromia* (a running together of opposites) that is central to how films are understood psychologically. In terms of production, while the *auteur* might well direct films with a personal voice, his needs must sit alongside the collective appeal of films and also accommodate the individual psychological meanings they evoke. Thus the psychological meanings of films are not fixed but instead are liable to change as our personal and cultural perspectives alter – an observation that we will explore more fully in the next chapter.

Chapter 6

Film genres and archetypes

Luke Hockley

Introduction

This chapter is concerned with the idea of film genres. It will explore the extent to which the emphasis on the creative role of the individual as exemplified by the *auteur* theory is actually a reactionary view that fails to account for the complexities that are intrinsic in the production of films. To adopt the *auteur* theory is to adopt a polemical position and arguably the same holds good for many of the major film theories. However the *auteur* theory is distinctive in the way that it seeks to privilege the creative contribution of one person in the production process, namely the director. By doing so it evokes the somewhat romantic notion of the individual creative 'genius' who while railing against the commercial constraints of the film industry itself nonetheless manages to bring something that is both personal, creative and of artistic value to the cinema screen. As we have seen, this is to caricature the argument and actually when seen from a more psychological perspective the question of 'authorship' becomes more supple and sophisticated. As mediated through the lens of Jungian psychology, authorship is not just about production, it is also concerned with reception as shown through the psychological relationships viewers have with films in which they are re-authored repeatedly, as each viewer constructs afresh the notion of authorship on each viewing of a film.

From this vantage point it becomes clear that every film has numerous authors, only one of whom is the director of the film. This is somewhat different to the point made by structuralist theory (Barthes, 1977) as the emphasis here is not so much on the hermeneutic activity of reading but instead on the emotional responses viewers have with films and the psychological ramifications of such experiences. Barthes proclaimed the 'death of the author' but this does not necessitate the death of the director. Instead what the current argument emphasises is the importance of the complexities of the individual and cultural psychological relationships that we have with films – in other words we position films as part of a matrix of personal and collective meanings that might very well all be in tension with each other. The containment of such irreconcilable tensions, pulls and even opposites is one of the key psychological tasks of life and Jungian theory terms this role 'the transcendent function'.

As a result the question becomes the extent to which it is desirable to foreground the director and to privilege his or her contribution over and above the other participants in the production process, including those involved in its financing, its distribution and, crucially, in its reception. Further, the longevity of films outside the immediate contexts of their production and their subsequent translation into other media requires something more than a theory of authorship if such shifts and changes are to be adequately accounted for. The proposition is that while not without its strengths, the *auteur* theory fails to account fully for the new ways we have of interacting with films and other media, be these questions of distribution (DVD, on-demand services, Web-based distribution etc.), or the relationship of the original film to related ancillary artefacts such as computer games, fan media, websites and so forth. Finally, while the *auteur* theory is productive in the ways it establishes connections within a director's body of work, it is less successful in establishing links with other related films from other directors. The danger is that the intricacies of the ways in which meanings are circulated in culture along with the complexities of media consumption are marginalised by a view of films that is predominantly concerned with the question of authorship.

An alternative way of thinking about how meanings are created by films is offered by genre theory. The idea of film genres provides a means to see how an apparently common-sense idea is actually more complicated than it first appears – after all, we all know when we are watching a Western, or a war movie, or a comedy, don't we? Following the introductory section, Jung's definition of the image is added to the established debates about film genres. This provides a more psychological account of how meaning is constituted with genre systems and in so doing it offers a particularly Jungian understanding of the role of 'image' in the creation of meaning. With that psychological foundation established the idea of intertextuality emphasises the ways that films can usefully be seen as constituting a relationship both with other films and also with other media artefacts. Providing another explicitly Jungian take on genre and intertextuality, the idea of 'amplification' is used to see how these 'intertexts' shed psychological light on the original source text, and also on each other. As will become clear, the Jungian concept of amplification offers an intuitive and playful way to bypass our conscious defences and to tease out deep psychological meanings. Finally, the role of the audience in the creation of meaning is once again woven into the fabric of our discussion.

What is a film genre?

If the *auteur* theory sought to evaluate and analyse films according to their directors, then the genre theory attempts to classify films by their themes. It seems quite an obvious way to think about films. We have all seen detective movies, horror films, musicals and so forth, and can identify them. For example, we know what to expect in a Western film, in terms of characters, the look and feel of the location and to some extent the plots too. The landscape is familiar to us, the clothing, the weaponry and we know the stock characters even before we meet them in the film, and these narrative tropes and visual motifs reoccur as a theme and variation across numerous films. In other words, what we understand by the genre 'Western', relies on our previous experiences of watching similar films (Grant, 1986). It follows that it is impossible to have a genre that is composed of a single film. This is a great help to producers in the marketing of films, who can promote them by invoking their genre. When the marketing of *Alien* (Dir. Scott, 1979) stated 'In space no one can hear you scream' the audience knew without doubt what type of film it was. Therefore there is a match that marketers have fostered between the genre of a film and the expectations of film viewers. After all, clearly it helps to sell a product when the customer knows what the product is – it is an unusual customer who hands over money without having a pretty good sense of what it is that they are purchasing. The trick, however is to meet some of those expectations, while subverting others, thereby balancing predictability with an element of surprise and innovation (Buscombe, 1977).

Thus, the marketing of a film by genre describes to potential viewers the type of film they are going to see. However, film theorists use the term 'genre' for a different purpose, namely as an aid to the analysis and interpretation of a film. Pat Berry neatly summarises the difference, noting:

> Current debates on the status of film genres arise, in part, because of the different reasons for invoking them: film scholars tend to define genres for purposes of interpretation and critical analysis, while producers, publicists, and audiences may use them as descriptive tools.
>
> (Berry, 1999: 26)

Film theory notes how genres are built up from an assemblage of character, iconography and narrative theme. So in *film noir* audiences know to expect a detective who is a loner, normally investigating a murder in a city. The lighting will be low key and high contrast, with the darkness of the shadows reflecting both the grim nature of the crime and the off-kilter state of the detective himself. A romantic comedy, by contrast, will be naturalistically lit, have bright and breezy characters, and witty dialogue. Curiously, what genre theory reveals about both Westerns and romantic comedies is that the social order needs to be restored by the end of the film. In Westerns the figure of the outsider who arrives unbidden has to restore order to a community by the end of the film, only to leave that community or marry into it. In some ways his special ability to overcome danger needs to be relinquished. In a similar manner, the female lead in a romantic comedy needs to have her sexuality constrained and normalised by getting married (Brook, 2015). In both cases the genre serves to contain something that threatens to upturn social norms. Genre theory allows the identification of deep structural patterns that might otherwise have gone unnoticed. The reader familiar with Jungian theory might already be alert to the similarity here to Jung's archetype theory – in both genre theory and archetype theory, imagery clothes deeply concealed formal patterns and structures, of which more later.

It follows that there is a connection between social values and attitudes and genres. In the ways that film genres give expression to social beliefs, or we might say embody ideology, they have an affinity with myths. Genre theory has not ignored these similarities and as Berry puts it: 'Early genre theorists often argued that, like myths, genres have an organic relation to social consciousness – an assumption arises from traditional literary studies as well as art history' (Berry, 1999: 29–30).

Alongside the textual elements of film genres, and the ways in which they provide cues for viewers before and while watching a film, genre theory is also concerned with the cultural circulation of meanings and the manner in which genres accumulate and change meanings as a result. As we have been exploring, one way to understand this interaction is in terms of text and how viewers read and respond to genre cues – in other words, how viewers respond to the codes and conventions of a given genre.

In film studies genre theory makes a useful distinction between the semantic and the syntactic aspects of a genre (Altman, 1984). The semantic elements can be conceptualised as the building blocks of genre – very roughly they approximate to the words in a sentence that will subsequently be combined according to syntactical rules and linguistic conventions. Typically in a film the semantic elements include: character roles, settings or locations, imagery (often symbolic in quality), plot and story, and themes and values.

For example, in the Western genre characters include: the Outsider, who will save the day; the Sheriff, old fashioned and out of his depth; the Old Timer, comic relief with flashes of wisdom; the Barmaid with a heart of gold and so forth. The setting is typically a frontier town or the plains of Monument Valley on the Colorado plateau with its now iconic wind-shaped rocky outcrops; the imagery includes: stagecoaches, six-guns, the landscape itself. The plot and story of this genre asks: What are the problems? – Being attacked by 'Indians'. Who solves the problem? – The 'Outsider'. By what means? – Violence. To what end? – It doesn't pay to attack a frontier town. Themes and values: What is the problem? – White man's civilisation is under threat. Who solves the problem? – The Heroic Outsider with the co-operation of the townsfolk. By what means? – Galvanising the innate heroic qualities of the town. To what end? – To show that white man's civilisation will always triumph.

No small part of the appeal of genre films rests in the ways in which these semantic elements are combined syntactically, either to meet the genre-informed expectations of viewers or to subvert such expectations. This suggests that genre films presuppose an ideal viewer who will be sufficiently familiar with the genre to gain pleasure from watching the genre system in operation. More technically, as Steve Neale (1990) points out, genres are not systems *per se* but are more usefully thought of as processes of systemisation. It follows that they exist in a state in which they are always coming into being. Perhaps some of the points of contact with Jung's theory of archetypes are already clear. Archetypes, like film genres, are structures that change and evolve over time. These patterns take on visual images that are culturally and ideologically inscribed. In some ways, individual archetypes (trickster, hero, shadow) represent a sort of psychological genre – the more familiar we are with each archetype the more it is possible to see the subtlety of each instance of its appearance. Put succinctly, archetypes are like genres in so much as they are dynamic patterns of meaning that are never fully realised and which are embedded in a mythological context.

To these semi-linguistic and formal concerns it is necessary to add the institutional dimension of film production. Here, then, are the three interlocked components of traditional genre theory: audience, institution and text, and the locus of concern in genre theory is around how these different aspects of a genre interact to create genre systems, which in turn circulate in culture as ever changing forms. By far the least understood and analysed of these areas concerns the institutional aspect. This is because such information is difficult to come by. The ways that film production companies finance films, shape them during production and market them on release, before ushering them into the post-cinema release arena is shrouded by a cloak of commercial secrecy. Less conspiratorially the decisions that are made surrounding the production of films are often simply not recorded. That said, the extras that accompany many DVD releases can include behind-the-scenes footage, and also scene-by-scene audio commentaries from the creative team. However, the extent to which such commentaries can be taken at face value varies enormously from film to film, with some serving mainly to reinforce the mythology of the director as *auteur*.

However, where films have been in circulation for some time it is interesting to see how they take on an intertextual life that would not have been predicted during the production of the original film. If we encounter 'Rick's Bar', or hear 'You must remember this . . .', the image of Humphrey Bogart and Ingrid Bergman in *Casablanca* (1942) come instantly to mind. Interestingly, not many will think of the original stage play on which the film was based *Everybody Comes to Rick's* – partly because Warner Bros. implemented a tough contract in which the authors of the play, Murray Burnett and Joan Allison, were prohibited from staging their work – it would be understandable if the refrain, 'you must remember this' struck a sour note with them for some time. Here, then, we do have an instance of how institutional determinates come to shape a media product directly. Some films, such as Woody Allen's *Play It Again Sam* (1972), require familiarity with the original film – not that the phrase 'play it again Sam' actually appears in *Casablanca*, which provides an example of how genres can be self-perpetuating and how they contribute to their own mythology. The intertextuality of *Casablanca* is so widespread that it is almost impossible to know where a reference to the film will crop up next: there is a perfume, comic books (*The Bogie Man*), Diane Shah's novel *As Crime Goes By*, a biography of Ingrid Bergman more predictably titled by Laurence Lerner *As Time Goes By*, a board-game and so it goes on and on. What is significant here is the way in which our knowledge of the original film serves to cue, frame and in part shape our understanding of both the original and its many intersections, as meanings circulate and accrue though culture and over time. There is a difference between *Casablanca* the film and '*Casablanca*' the generic intertext.

Genre: foreknowledge, expectation and dreams

Steve Neale provides a helpful summation of the way in which film genres and their viewers are tied together in a complicated system of hermeneutic mutual reliance. He notes how genres need viewers, and how viewers need to be knowledgeable about genres if the viewing experience is to be meaningful:

> genres are not simply bodies of work or groups of films, however classified, labelled, and defined. Genres do not consist only of films: they consist also, and equally, of specific systems of expectation and hypothesis that spectators bring with them to the cinema and that interact with films themselves during the course of the viewing process. These systems provide spectators with a means of recognition and understanding. They help render films, and the elements within them, intelligible and therefore explicable.
>
> (Neale, 1990: 46)

It is important to note how Neale stresses the ways in which meaning is tied to expectation. To provide an example, in the horror genre when the camera frames a character's head to one side of the screen, leaving a large space on the other side viewers are cued via that generic convention to expect that something unpleasant might well fill the empty part of the frame. The same framing in a romantic comedy does not elicit the same genre-specific response. There is something important in the idea that the meaning of a film comes out of the relationship that viewers have with films, and that viewers are in no small part cued to understand highly specific generic conventions in particular ways. In other words, viewer and film collude to establish meaning. The insight that meaning arises within a culturally inflected relationship is something that Jungian theory has not emphasised. Instead it tends to suggest that meaning is created psychologically in a realm that exists outside of culture and ideology. The idea that Analytical Psychology itself is a type of ideology and that it too has its own cultural expectations is not often discussed. However, it is only necessary to open *The Book of Symbols* (Ronnberg and Martin, 2010) published by the Archive for Research in Archetypal Symbolism (ARAS) to see how a Jungian world view with its own codes and conventions shares and promulgates very particular interpretations of images.

Indeed, the idea that psychoanalytic interpretations are free of cultural conventions and expectations is in many senses a problematic one. Yet that statement seems a world apart from the daily work, say, of dream interpretation in the consulting room where hours can be spent discerning how the bespoke meaning of a dream is fitted to the life of a particular client. Despite the desire to provide highly individualised interpretations of dreams, in many ways the interpretations that are made are influenced by 'generic' expectations. This is not a definitive taxonomy but here are some of the expectations which underpin the process of Jungian dream interpretation: the assumption that dreams are of relevance to the life of the person whose dreams they are; that the meanings of dreams are primarily psychological;

that elements in dreams can be thought of as parts of either the life of the dreamer or as representing something from the unconscious. There is nothing wrong with these interpretative conventions, provided that we know that is what they are and that client and therapist are together entering into a relationship with the dream image and setting out to interpret it, according to prior knowledge, experience and assumptions. Just as a genre film exists in a system of expectation with its viewers, so too the analytical work of interpreting dreams involves the adoption of codes and conventions.

Interestingly, genre films like dream imagery evolve in sequences over time. Each new film needs to be sufficiently like its predecessors to cue the correct generic expectations, yet it also has to be sufficiently different to ensure novelty. Therefore there is a relationship between each film in a genre. In some ways this is not unlike the ways in which motifs and themes span a series of dreams, sometimes over years and even decades. In such sequences the understanding of a particular dream can influence how the others are understood. Additionally a dream that occurred early on in therapy that had one meaning at that time can come to mean something else when viewed with hindsight.

The suggestion is that far from being strange or unique in the way they communicate (a claim that is sometimes made in psychodynamic theory) dreams actually perform in a fashion that is somewhat similar to the ways in which film genres operate. In both cases, images give expression to deep structures the understanding of which is governed by systems of expectation that are in turn highly culturally codified. Genres exist in series and so too dreams exist one with another. Of course there are differences too, not least that genre films are collective cultural products that exist to make money, while dreams are individual and bespoke, and are not financially motivated. However, both exist as part of an unfolding series, the understanding of which arises from the interplay of experience, interpretative conventions and cultural location.

Image: a Jungian reformulation

Genre theory can usefully give pause to consider some of the limitations of the ways in which dreams are understood clinically. But Analytical Psychology offers up a useful addition to film theory in the way it understands that most basic of terms, namely 'image'. In Jungian theory the image exists somewhere in the space between the unconscious and consciousness, and in many ways it can be thought of as existing in a liminal territory between unconscious contents and outer reality. Jung puts it as follows:

> When I speak of 'image' in this book, I do not mean the psychic reflection of an external object, but a concept derived from poetic usage, namely, a figure of fancy of *fantasy-image*, which is related only indirectly to the perception of an external object. This image depends much more on unconscious fantasy activity, and as the product of such activity it appears more or less abruptly

> in consciousness, somewhat in the manner of a vision or hallucination, but without possessing the morbid traits that are found in a clinical picture. The image has the psychological character of a fantasy idea and never the quasi-real character of an hallucination, i.e., it never takes the place of reality, and can always be distinguished from sensuous reality by the fact that it is an 'inner' image.
>
> (CW6: 743)

It follows that such images need not be pictorial; rather, they are metaphorical, like the image 'heard' in a piece of music, a point developed by Nagari in his formulation of the music-image (2016). In other words the image exists not just on the screen but also somewhere in the space between the viewer and the screen. This is consistent with the view that meaning in genre films comes not just from the text, but also from what the reader brings to the text – a process which, while largely codified in genre films, is indicative of the more general process that takes place while watching a film.

Jung maintained that images are central to the construction of the psyche. Put another way, the psyche is image:

> the psyche consists essentially of images. It is a series of images in the truest sense, not an accidental juxtaposition or sequence, but a structure that is throughout full of meaning and purpose; it is a 'picturing' of vital activities. And just as the material of the body that is ready for life has need of the psyche in order to be capable of life, so the psyche presupposes the living body in order that its images may live.
>
> (CW8: 618)

The structure to which Jung alludes in the preceding quotation is the structural makeup of the archetypes within the unconscious. He is at pains to note that these structures have meaning and purpose. He claims that they put us in touch with the unconscious and that they act as guides to our inner life, and that they do so as we come to realise how aspects of our unconscious selves can affect our everyday relationships and our engagement with the world, including the films that we watch. As such the image captures the psychological reality of a given situation as it encapsulates the complex dynamics that arise from the interplay of archetypal forces and their relationship with consciousness, as the psyche attempts to come to an informed understanding of what is at hand.

> The inner image is a complex structure made up of the most varied material from the most varied sources. It is no conglomerate, however, but a homogenous product with a meaning of its own. The image is a *condensed expression of the psychic situation as a whole*, and not merely, nor even predominately, of unconscious contents pure and simple . . . . Accordingly the image is an expression of the unconscious as well as the conscious situation

> of the moment. The interpretation of its meaning, therefore, can start neither from the conscious alone nor from the unconscious alone, but only from their reciprocal relationship.
>
> (CW6: 745, emphasis as original)

This is, as Jung puts it, a 'vital activity' as the drive within each one of us towards individuation requires us to understand the complexities of the contradictions that are housed within us. In his book *Re-Visioning Psychology* James Hillman develops this theme:

> Since we can know only fantasy-images directly and immediately, and from these images create our worlds and call them realities, we live in a world that is neither 'inner' nor 'outer'. Rather the psychic world is an imaginal world, just as image is psyche. Paradoxically, at the same time these images are in us and we live in the midst of them. The psychic world is experienced empirically as inside us and yet it encompasses us with images.
>
> (Hillman, 1992: 23)

The important points to focus on are firstly that the psyche is imagistic, and secondly that such images are both inner and outer, *at the same time*. At first this may sound a little confusing. To shed some light on the situation we need to understand what Jung means by the term 'projection'. For Jung, the projection of unconscious material happens partly as a defence mechanism and is something over which we have very little control. It is the psyche's way of taking a complex (an unresolved psychological problem) and bringing it to the attention of consciousness, often through an experience of intense affect. In the cinema too it is quite possible to have an unlooked-for outpouring of affect. This happens partly as a response to the film itself, but it is also the result of a personal psychological response to the film. In other words, meaning is co-created between a film and its viewers. These co-created meanings are partly a response to the way the film is made, its codes and conventions, but they also arise from the interplay of personal unconscious concerns with the cinematic construction of the film itself.

Institutional amplification

One of the distinguishing features of Analytical Psychology is its use of an interpretative technique termed 'amplification'. Admittedly this is not an area that Jungian-orientated film scholars have been particularly concerned with, though Hockley's (2001b) analysis of *Blade Runner* (Dir. Scott, 1982), in which he traces the individuation of the film's central character, the detective Deckard (Harrison Ford), is a notable exception. (The same book also contains a lengthy amplification of the zombie 'B' Movie, *Trancers* aka *Future Cop* [Dir. Band, 1984].) The purpose of amplification is to bypass our conscious and unconscious defences as a means to explore the possible psychological meaning of images. These images might be dream images, found images, or images created by the client. However, there is no reason why the technique can not be used to explore the psychological meaning of feature films. The process of amplification is reasonably straightforward though it does require a good working knowledge of mythological themes and motifs. In essence, a selected image is compared to its appearance in other mythological material. As the images build up it is sometimes possible to see the emergence of psychological themes. For example, the *mise-en-scène* of *Blade Runner* is that of neo-noir, and it is a dark city setting. It also rains almost all the time. In amplifying the image of 'rain' it would be necessary to look at rain in mythology, and perhaps water symbolism more generally. Coming straight to mind is the story of Noah in which rain symbolises both death and renewal. Might it be that the psychological theme of death and renewal has a greater relevance in understanding *Blade Runner* than might be immediately obvious?

The problem with this type of analysis is that it can lead in rather unpredictable directions, and great care has to be taken to ensure that the amplification does indeed shed some light on the film, and that mythological parallels are not forced onto the text in an attempt to make it fit a preconceived psychological idea (see Fredericksen, 2001). In other words, great sensitivity to the fidelity of the text is needed and any possible interpretations should be seen in the light of the actual contents of the film. Here it is important to note that in this context amplification is being used to understand the text of a film while in a clinical setting it is used to understand the psychology of the client. This is a significant distinction and it is why any interpretative claim that arises from amplification must be tested against the film itself. Just because there is iconic similarity between several images it does not necessarily follow that such a resemblance will be a guarantee of interpretative insight and relevance. A further potential issue is that as an intuitive method, any analysis of a film might actually become more about the psychology of the interpreter than the psychology of the film itself. Of course, this is entirely appropriate in a clinical setting and many clients find it helpful to talk about their personal understanding of films, and their emotional responses to them. Whether this is quite so helpful in promoting a scholarly understanding of a film is more debatable.

On a related note it is interesting to wonder if the intertextual life of films can be understood as a type of unwitting amplification. Perhaps the imagery and the themes of a film are as 'amplified' in marketing material, movie posters, interviews and websites. To regard such paratexts as part of a system of institutional amplification would position them as products in their own right and also explore their relationship to the original material, thereby revealing something that was not immediately obvious. For example, 'slash fiction' focuses on the sexual attraction of fictional same-sex characters, who are not engaged in sexual relationships in their fictional worlds. The question arises whether such fantasies help to illuminate the original texts – does such fiction, perhaps about Kirk and Spock in the *Star Trek* world, reveal anything that is relevant to the films, or does it remain a quite separate fantasy? To provide a somewhat different example, do the various ways in which we identified paratexts of the film *Casablanca* shed any light on the original film? It is certainly the case that such paratexts do influence how we understand *Casablanca*. The prevalence of imagery and music derived from the film has come to influence how we see the original – to the extent of inventing dialogue. In a way, they all become part of the 'myth' of *Casablanca*, a myth that is of course no more or less real than its purely celluloid incarnation.

To ignore such paratexts is akin to a therapeutic process that ignores dreams, or the client's creativity. When the movie poster of *Edward Scissorhands* (Dir. Burton, 1990) proclaimed 'His story will touch you, even though he can't', it was partly setting out to tell potential viewers what to expect but in another way the paratext also functions as part of a psychological system that influences how the film is understood. Similarly, the marketing of *Inception* (Dir. Nolan, 2010) stated, 'Your mind is the scene of the crime' and in so doing it blurred the distinction between the viewer and the characters in the film in a way that, while suggested by the film, is not explicit in its narrative. The film is concerned with the mind of its characters, and not its viewers – at least ostensibly. The tagline removed the ambiguity and in so doing it inflected the psychological relationship of the viewer, and the result is that those viewers who know the tagline of the film approach it differently to those who do not.

Regarding paratexts as part of the system of amplification that sheds light on both the paratext and the original film itself is an area that requires further development. In many ways the existing work on intertextuality, as originated by Genette (1982) established the importance of understanding how texts work together to create complicated matrices of cultural meanings. However, Genette did not include a psychological dimension to his analysis and so the idea that amplification might do so has been mentioned here as part of a sign-posting exercise for the field. While it has not been developed, this is an aspect of 'therapy thinking' that offers a fresh way to understand how contemporary mythologies are made, and through which to comprehend their shifting psychological significance.

A particular type of paratext that is closely related to the genres is composed of what can be thought of as 'movie star' genres and such films open up the possibility of a different type of amplification. Here it is important to remember that C. G. Jung regarded the persona as one of the most accessible and readily identifiable archetypal patterns of the psyche. The function of the archetype is literally to put a mask over the individual's psyche as a means to fit into a social situation. Each one of us has many masks: parent, employee, friend and so forth. The danger is that it is possible to become overly identified with a particular role and take it home with us, so to speak. That would be a case of the policeman who enforces the law at work and at home. In such an instance the persona ceases to be helpful and our sense of self has to separate from what should be a temporary role

For example the persona of John Wayne is clearly identified with the Western genre. Over forty years or so from about 1930 to the late 1960s viewers came to identify Wayne with roles in films such as *The Searchers* (Dir. Ford, 1956), *Rio Bravo* (Dir. Hawks, 1959), *The Man Who Shot Liberty Valance*

(Dir. Ford, 1962) and *The Alamo* (Dir. Wayne, 1960). When he appeared in war movies like *Sands of Imo Jima* (1949), *Operation Pacific* (1951), *The Wings of Eagles* (1957) the inter-fictional carryover was clear. The mythologem (underlying central myth themes) of the Western were transported into a different genre. Psychologically we might say that while the mythology (genre) had changed, the underlying ideological values as encapsulated in the mythologems remained the same. The persona of Wayne and the ideological values for which it came to stand played an important role facilitating the shift of values from one genre to another. Of course, other factors are important too, not least of which are the plot and story elements in the films themselves. However, the role of the persona as the archetype of social adaptation confers on each of these genres an ideological perspective which at first sight seems natural – the persona of the film star fits between culture and ideology in such a manner that what in other circumstances would appear troubling is now socially acceptable and normative.

Two brief case studies: *film noir* and the Western

The idea that film genres operate in ways that are partly unconscious or psychological has not escaped the attention of film theorists. However, the application of that insight has resulted in an approach that tended to be somewhat structural. The reason for this is that structuralist approaches were seen as ways of interrogating the transmission and development of cultural codes and values. Put another way, to approach culture structurally, semiotically and using postmodern insights is to deconstruct how media artefacts contribute to ideology. Of course it is the case that the narrative of genre films that textually might appear regressive, actually turn out to be more ideologically subversive and expressive than they might on first sight appear to be. Berry provides a neat summation, noting:

> The notion that genres can manifest 'unconscious dynamics' which contradict the ideological values implied by their narratives suggest that they are both symptomatic and ideologically structured. Such an account rests on Althusser's notion of overdetermination, whereby texts are seen as sites of unconsciously conflicting structural forces.
>
> (Berry, 1999: 37)

However, an alternative perspective on this issue of conflicting structural forces in genres is offered by a more straightforwardly psychological explanation. Of course any genre will be full of ideological inconsistencies. The reason for such inconsistences is that genres are partly unconscious forms and do not conform to the rational logic of the thinking mind. There is an interesting and complicated relationship that exists between implicit acquired knowledge about film genres and the explicit rendering of such knowledge in a film. From a depth psychological perspective, it is inevitable that every creative product will be tinged with unconscious elements. Genres represent deep structures that underpin and give meaning to the narrative of films. As we have seen, this act of interpretation is itself a creative process and it is one that is also inflected by psychological concerns. In part these arise from the narrative of the film, but they also stem from our personal psychology and also our collective cultural complexes.

Before moving on to two examples of film genres, the Western and *film noir*, it is worth pointing out the relative instability of generic categories. On the one hand it is tempting to cookie-cutter film genres – a war movie is a war movie, clear and simple. However, actually genre boundaries are more plastic and elastic (Neale, 1990 and Altman, 1999) than this suggests. This echoes the point made by the Russian theorist Boris Tomashevsky (1925) that it is not possible to make clear, firm and fixed logical classifications of genres. While he was writing about literature, and also from the explicit position of Russian Formalism, this insight can nonetheless be usefully extended to film genres. For example, a film such as *Apocalypse Now* (Dir. Coppola, 1979) is in part a war movie but it is also about a quest, and an inner journey as much as it is concerned with outer and more explicitly ideological engagements. *Good Morning Vietnam* (Dir. Levinson, 1987) is a comedy, a war film and a film about personal psychology. Films such as *Inglourious Basterds* (Dir. Tarantino, 2009), in an act of cultural cross-fertilisation, deliberately seek to combine generic conventions, in this case between the Western and the war genres. Berry notes:

> The instability of generic labels thus arises not only from the Bakhtinian 'heteroglossia' of generic allusion that limits any attempt at film classification, but from the fact that genres function as tools for predicting and regulating the reception of texts.
>
> (Berry, 1999: 40)

However, it might also be that because genre structures function rather like archetypal structures that something more psychological is occurring. If the premise that genres are inherently psychological is accepted then it is not unreasonable to expect genres to behave in a manner that is psychological: they will be non-rational, polysemic, polyvalent and consequently resistant to definitive and reductionist interpretations. A single archetypal pattern finds expression in a variety of images, each of which is influenced by its cultural location. There is therefore a relationship between the deep unconscious structure and its expression in consciousness. So too, the pattern of a film genre finds numerous ways of expressing an underlying concern. Of course, this does not exclude a more structural and ideological understanding of genres. Rather, it sees the ideological and the psychological as enmeshed in the fabric of the cinema – it is not a question of either or, but of both.

Film noir

In the article *Film Noir: Stereotype or Archetype?* Hockley (2001a) begins to outline some of his thinking in relation to the Hollywood detective films of the

1940s and early 1950s. In it he identifies how many of the formal elements of the genre have their origins in the stylistic practices of 1920s and 1930s German Expressionistic filmmaking. In particular Hockley notes how canted camera angles and lighting that is low key and high contrast (which ensures dark shadows and piercing white highlights) combine to provide a set of genre conventions that are well suited to exploring psychological themes. It might at first sight seem odd that Hollywood should adopt German film production techniques while it was at war with that same country. In fact the adoption of these elements of film production is explained when it is realised that it was done by German Jewish émigrés who came to work in Hollywood in the 1930s. In so doing they unsurprisingly brought with them their professional knowledge and skills as film directors, cameramen, composers and suchlike.

The fortuitous part, some might suggest synchronistic aspect, was that those professional skills in film production would chime so well with the narrative content of the hard-boiled detective story. Popularised by the authors Raymond Chandler and Dashiell Hammett, the figure of the tough, but psychologically isolated detective had a cultural resonance for a country that found itself for the second time in just a few decades embroiled in a European war that was outside of its own making. The persona of the detective became a familiar figure in the filmic night-time, rain drenched city streets. So too his wise-cracking patter with the insightful and often cutting put-down became as much a part of the clothing of the private eye as his iconic trench coat. Always flawed in some way, through an over reliance on alcohol or some other drug, the psychology of the tough detective was emblematic of the broken state of a culture that had become over reliant on its materialistic achievements.

In part, the potency of the private eye came from his independence. He is not a policeman and more often than not he is in a state of considerable tension with the official structures of law and order who regard him as quite a challenge to their own investigations – which of course, he is. The private detective won't be found in a police station (unless he has been arrested) and instead operates at the margins of Western culture and is as likely to be found in Chinatown as he is actively tracking down the murderer. Those foreign cities within a city symbolise the need for something of the 'other' as means by which to comprehend the cultural conditions of the present moment. There is something of the unconscious, or at least a fantasy of the unconscious, in Chinatown. Seen sociologically, the depictions of Chinatown in classic *film noir* verge on the racist and orientalist. However, taken psychologically, Chinatown symbolises how in the very midst of that great materialist achievement of the twentieth century, the city with its skyscrapers and thriving downtown area, something else has been kept alive – something altogether more ancient and less rational.

What that image of Chinatown, as a city within a city, expresses is the Jungian insight that we are composed not of just one character but of numerous subpersonalities. Often these aspects of ourselves remain unconscious. However, that does not mean they do not have an effect on our conscious lives as these unconscious components are projected onto people and places. From this perspective, Chinatown is a sub-personality of the psyche of the city. It represents both its shadow side and its intuitive qualities. If downtown represents thinking materialist achievement, then Chinatown embodies the reflective and intuitive aspects of the city's inner life. While not wanting to ignore the ideological issues surrounding the representation of Chinatown, such imagery also speaks to the Jungian process of looking in the forgotten, rejected and seemingly 'unimportant' parts of our lives for the psychological gold of insight and transformation. In this regard, Chinatown challenges the presumption that the materialist and capitalist culture has the answers to life's problems.

While the process of detection, of solving the crime, appears to be a rational one, in fact the systematic following of clues is the stuff of police work. The 'shamus' (a term that might have its origins in the Yiddish *shammes*, which also lexically possesses a certain similarity to shaman) has an altogether more intuitive approach and it is one where each clue appears to lead to the next. In fact the detective relies on his intuitive 'hunches' to do what an overly rational society cannot – but of course it comes at some personal cost. The detective embodies the psychological 'truth' that the process of ratiocination is insufficient and that the intellect alone will always prove inadequate when it comes to psychological understanding. The forensic work of thinking is best left to the police, even if they are one of the institutional structures that contributed to the problem in the first place.

Ostensibly, the work of the private detective is to solve murders and normally those are committed in the city. But actually this masks his true purpose, that is to try and make sense of a world that actually makes no sense; his search is for truth and it is as much existential and psychological as it is criminological. As such, the figure of the hard-boiled detective is emblematic of a mood in which it seemed that there was no escape from war and destruction. With that in mind, from the Jungian perspective it is unsurprising that the figure of the *femme fatale* should play such a prominent role in the *film noir* genre and in the life of the detective. Psychologically she is the figure the detective needs, as she connects him to the intuitive part of himself that he is going to be important if he is to get the job done and to get the crime solved. Yet he is also deeply resistant to her, recognising that there is danger in this split-off form of his own being. The *femme fatale* is as likely to destroy the detective as she is to be of assistance to him. As an agent of social change, it is this type of duality that the detective needs to hold onto as it points to the unknowing opposition of the contemporary dominant values that drive society.

What *film noir* offers as genre, and, as others have argued, as a style of filmmaking more generally (see Silver and Ursini, 1999), is an example of how cultural and ideological values become intertwined in fiction films. Some of the explanation for this lies in the transmigration of filmmaking techniques and practices. But there is a more unconscious aspect too in which a complicated system of interactions is set up between the Hollywood studio system, the influx of new creative talent and the political conditions of the time. *Film noir* did not set out to suggest the need for a more female approach to the issues of the day, yet the figure of the *femme fatale*, at once glamorous and also deadly in her seduction of the detective, presented part of the remedy for the psycho-social upheaval that was central to the 1940s.

The Western

Film noir is, of course, not the only genre to intertwine psychological and ideological concerns. In his book of 2006, *Screen, Culture, Psyche: A Post-Jungian Approach to Working with the Audience*, John Izod devotes a chapter to the Western in which he undertakes just such an integrated analysis by exploring the contemporary rendering of the Western genre. In many ways the chapter is an audacious piece of writing as it seeks to find connections in the Western genre by going backwards into its literary origins, and in turn, back still further into the religious underpinnings of the genre. At the same time, Izod locates the genre in a more contemporary political landscape and in so doing he explores how it weaves in and out of psychological concerns that while deeply historical find a particular relevance in the twentieth and early twenty-first centuries.

It is Izod's contention that the Western as a genre contains one of the central psychological myths of contemporary times. This is not in and of itself a particularly striking claim as film studies has long held that the Western is an important site of cultural myth making (Carter, 2014; Cawelti, 1999; Kitses, 2007; Kitses and Gregg, 1998; Wright, 1977). However what remains distinctive about Izod's claim is the psychological emphasis he places on the genre and its ability to express not just ideological and political concerns but also deeply unconscious qualities. As he puts it:

> If Western movies do indeed constitute a primary locus in which the struggle for the collective soul of the USA has been fought out and that struggle implicates its characters, how does it involve the deep psychology of the audience? Does the Western of the early twenty-first century differ from its predecessors in ways which reflect changes in the audience's circumstances and reveal psychological shifts associated with those societal changes?
>
> (Izod, 2006: 181)

For Izod the roots of the Western can partly be found in the literature of James Fennimore Cooper's 1823 novel *The Pioneers*. That much is not particularly surprising. But more significant for him is the way they reworked older English pastoral concerns and specifically the English literature of the seventeenth and eighteenth centuries. Such writing was concerned with an exploration of the idea of the rural idyll, and the ownership of land. Importantly, the main readership for this literature was not the relatively few landowners, but those who worked on the land that they could never hope to possess. The writing embodies a myth of paradise that Izod identifies as a re-imagining of the Edenic myth.

Izod goes on to tease out the interplay between shadow and anima in the Western, giving the land a certain *topos* that has the capacity, albeit unfulfilled, to unite thinking and feeling, *logos* and *eros*. His analysis is careful and convincing in the way it moves between the imagery of the Western, its themes and variations across a range of films and in the emergence of a critical perspective that is revealing about both the psychological and political aspects of the genre. As the piece concludes, Izod brings the Western into alignment with the imagery that conjuncturally and synchronically surrounded the representation of Osama Bin Laden in North American-mediated political discourse. In so doing the landscape of the Western becomes the landscape of political and ideological power. He positions the Western as a new type of revisionist genre. The Western has a long tradition of revisionism, notably the way in which in the 1970s the Western inverted many of its traditional tropes. A marked example of this is the film *Soldier Blue* (Dir. Nelson, 1970) in which rape and murder are committed by the cavalry. The saviours of the traditional Western have become the villains. The violence of white people, once shown pursuing the advancement of civilisation, is now shown as repugnant and racist.

To return to Izod's point, he conjectures that a less mythic and demonising discourse around Bin Laden would have had benign effects – his claim is a bold one: that media imagery can have a positive effect on the popular conception of world political events, and that it can psychologically contain difference and ambiguity, good and evil. He argues that genre films are particularly well placed to act as such a container, noting:

> A more ambivalent picture emerges in the case of genre films. Such films, because of their ritual quality, are more likely than any others to engage energies active not too far beneath consciousness in the cultural unconscious. Where the cultural unconscious is stirred, a film may arouse strong emotions in large numbers of the audience or touch on a collective repression. The force of emotional arousal or repression may then be such that it does not wholly lie within the power of the filmmakers to control or even direct it . . . . Some spectators will take the force of archetypal and symbolic representations more or less as the filmmakers intended; others will appropriate a film to their own world view.
>
> (Izod, 2006: 218)

Film genres are socially and psychologically organised through the structuring agencies of audience, institution and text. As such they allow a psychological relationship to come into being between the viewer and the film. The personal history of the viewer is significant here in coming to an understanding of how the textual cues of films are read through familiarity with genre-specific conventions. Film genres are organised both semantically and syntactically, which results in a type of genre grammar with which viewers are familiar. Indeed, the knowledge of the codes and conventions of individual genres is indispensable if the viewer is to engage fully with a genre film.

Conclusion

Archetypes function rather like genres – as expressed in an image, they circulate meanings between the text itself, the institutional conventions of Analytical Psychology and the viewer of the image. It is therefore quite legitimate to think of the archetype of the shadow, for example, as a type of psychological genre – its meanings are institutionally framed, we rely on previous similar experiences to understand the shadow and yet we have a unique and personal relationship with it. Just as archetypes cannot be fully understood, so too genres cannot be fully defined as both are quasi-organic psycho-social structures. It is in the interaction of these psychological structures with the filmic that the richness of the generic experience rests.

We should not underestimate the complexities of this process. It is important to be clear that the suggestion is not that processes through which genre systems come into being and change are identical to archetypal processes. Rather, it is more that it is productive to explore the interaction between the psychology of the archetype's image and the psychology of genre images. In so doing genre and archetype are eased into a relationship in which similarities and differences can be productive for both parties.

In the above statement Izod points to the ways in which the narrative of films, and in particular genre films, interacts with other narratives, both personal and cultural. Jungian-orientated film theory frequently finds itself engaging in psychological archaeology. Sometimes this involves the excavation of the recent past, though just as often this only serves to unearth the complexities of historical archetypal images whose origins are often deeply buried. The work of this type of psychological and cultural criticism is to bring to life what other forms of film theory leave untouched. The difficulty is that it is all too easy to get drawn into the mythological past. The Jungian antennae are well tuned for such an undertaking and can quickly detect the ancient archetypal signals in contemporary media texts even though they are less well suited to holding such historical resonances with the lived reality of contemporary social and cultural events.

Chapter 7

Jungians vs. Freudians

Gender, identity and sexuality on screen

Helena Bassil-Morozow

This chapter compares the Freudian and Jungian ways of looking on women as actors, agents, spectators and individuating agents. Particularly in the past twenty years or so moving image narratives have been confused as to the nature and structure of female individuation. Traditional cinematic narratives present women as mesmerising things, as passive objects of desire, as fragile yet dangerous creatures; they are shown by men who make films to men who watch films, whereas women, both as actresses and as spectators, are largely excluded from the creative and decision-making processes as well as disregarded as spectators. Up until relatively recently, female passivity in cinematic narratives has only been questioned and challenged theoretically rather than practically. These outdated practices are now contrasted with the new breed of female protagonists who are happy to wield a sword, master the art of archery, fight a bloody battle or approach a man sexually.

As Freudians were analysing films and explaining the political importance of the moving image well before Jungians discovered the field, Freudian theories are outlined in this chapter first. Then the applicability of Jungian theory to feminist film criticism is discussed. Finally, this chapter gives an overview of 'woman as a man on screen' – a phenomenon which emerged in cinema and television fairly recently, and which is likely to become mainstream sooner or later.

The question of female individuation

Judging by myths and fairy tales in which the protagonist is a woman, female individuation is structurally different from the traditional hero myth. Most traditional fairy tales present the woman either as a mysterious part of the male individuation process, or as a helpless creature in need of support, guidance and protection (all of which, predictably, are provided by men). Cinematic narratives grapple with the same issues regarding the feminine as the other art forms: activity and passivity, objectification and identification. If the woman is passive, does she mirror male activity and become an object to be consumed and admired? If she is active, is she not a threat to the man who would feel inadequate next to her? If the man's position as a result of the hero activities changes from dependent (uninitiated) to independent (initiated), could the same be true for a woman? Or does she just 'change hands': her parents pass her on to her husband?

A traditional female individuation narrative, as exemplified by *Little Red Riding Hood*, *Bluebeard*, *Beauty and the Beast*, *Sleeping Beauty* or the Russian fairy tale *Morozko*, shows a young woman at the mercy of a tyrant (male or female) who tries to destroy her, and being rescued by a kind man (a stranger, a brother or a prince) at the end. The young woman is often sent on a dangerous journey that is beyond her physical or moral strength, and cannot endure it due to her fragility and lack of experience. Her inability to make decisions and to be independent is emphasised. For instance, Little Red Riding Hood is far too small for a journey through the forest, the Beauty's dangerous task is to tame wild masculinity, and Nastenka from *Morozko*, who is thrown outside by her cruel stepmother one freezing winter night, mentally prepares to die because she can no longer fight both the severity of the Russian winter and the cruelty of human nature. Both in the Eastern and the Western European traditions the young woman is often bullied by some kind of evil mother figure (rarely by a father figure), and is pushed to go on a journey that she has not chosen. This implies a certain passivity, which stands in contrast with the activity of the masculine hero in traditional narratives.

In one of her famous reworkings of traditional fairy tales with female protagonists, *The Bloody Chamber*, Angela Carter gives a voice to the otherwise silent 'new wife' of the rich old man who is going to murder her like he murdered all his previous wives. The heroine of the tale notes that her journey from the moment when she leaves the parental home will be lonely and heavy. Contrasted with the typical male journey, which entails seeking freedom (including the freedom of self-expression) by going away and trying to become psychologically and physically independent, the aim of the woman's journey entails finding a suitable man, establishing a new family and finding a sense of belonging and community. In other words, the transition is from one family to another; from the old to the new.

The meaning of the female journey is 'relating' (as opposed to 'discovering', which is the focus of the male journey). When a female attempts to copy the masculine journey model (such as, for instance, *Little Red Riding Hood*), she is immediately warned of the dangers of seeking independence (and particularly of seeking a personality that is not dependent on a community), and sent back home accompanied by a 'male guardian'. Shortly before she marries the old Marquis, Carter's heroine laments her single life, and is mentally preparing for eternal loneliness and 'exile' (Carter, 1995: 7).

Carter mocks the classic female individuation pattern: changing hands, signing a contract to be someone else's property, getting yourself into a trap, losing (or even never tasting) independence, being passive and expecting to be saved by a man. Surprisingly, in her feminist version of the tale, Carter changes the finale, and instead of being rescued by her brothers, the heroine is saved by her mother who breaks into the castle and shoots the Marquis who is about to cut his unruly wife into shreds. In this and other tales in *The Bloody Chamber and Other Stories*,

Carter attempts to find a new path for the individuating female, a path that would not involve victimisation, objectification, silence or stereotypes.

The female characters in the other stories are allowed to be aggressive or sexual. They can even be evil, for instance, Little Red Riding Hood from 'The Werewolf' who kills her grandmother; or Vampirella from 'The Lady of the House of Love' who preys on young men. Carter is showing that a woman does not have to be a victim; and she does not always have to 'belong' in a community or family. Her individuation goal is not 'getting into a relationship' in which she would have a passive role. She can be a loner who cannot and will not learn 'social graces' for the sake of losing her animal nature. In fact, Carter implies that women do have animal nature, only centuries of training in relational skills had blunted and repressed it, turned it into a seat of shame and fear.

Can there be a balance between the 'passive' and the 'active' positions? In other words, can a woman represented on screen 'be herself' and 'individuate' without simply becoming a man and adopting male strategies for dealing with the world such as proactive behaviour, aggression and attack? This is what we will try to find out in this chapter by comparing the Freudian and Jungian ways of dealing with this issue.

The female journey on screen: psychoanalysis

Freudian and post-Freudian feminist film criticism focuses on the fact that women (both on and off screen) are silent and silenced, their roles and behaviour dictated by directors, managers and other 'owners'. From its early days, Hollywood has been a male-dominated industry, and to expect gender equality from it would be too hopeful. Women on screen, the Freudian film circle maintains, have always been regarded as mere objects, as having no reference point of their own, lost and waiting to be directed, as having no gaze – or even no right to have a 'gaze'. They are 'things' whose role is to be consumed. They have to present themselves, physically and behaviourally, in such a way as to maximise the enjoyment of the males looking at them. Preferably, they should only move when told to, and say the things included in the script. They should be dolls with a limited number of choices and options, pre-destined to perform prescribed roles and to follow certain patterns.

Many theorists of feminist cinema (perhaps unsurprisingly) have approached the difficult subjects of women on screen and women as spectators from psychoanalytic points of view, using the concepts of the gaze, voyeurism, fetishism, the mirror, scopophilia, objectification, phallus, etc. Theorists such as Laura Mulvey, Mary Ann Doane, Jacqueline Rose and Kaja Silverman have written extensively on the issue of the silent, passive female both as an object and as a spectator. In their texts they have particularly focused on the subject of looking, and being looked at – on the concept of the gaze and obsessions associated with it. Moreover, they argue that the industry is simply not interested in the female spectator as it assumes that she wants the same as the male spectator, and does not have psychological needs of her own.

Traditionally, male philosophers of culture using Freudian and post-Freudian theories have presented a limited at best, and sexist at worst, view of women, their sexuality, self-expression and place in society. In this sense, Freudian-Lacanian feminists have always been torn between the usability and applicability of Lacan's theories and his marked refusal (or inability) to see woman as equal to man, or to abstract himself from the importance of the phallus in all its incarnations in culture. Despite the claims that Lacan de-biologised Freud, his stereotyping of women is quite visible in his philosophy. For instance, Lacan writes in *On Jouissance* that the woman's 'sexual organ is of no interest' and she is defined as 'not whole' in respect to *jouissance*. Regarding her sexual characteristics, 'it is those of the mother that take precedence in her' (Lacan, 1998: 7). His famous controversial proposition, repeated in many of his essays, that 'the woman does not exist' (1998: 57) can be interpreted in a number of contradictory ways, including the refusal to objectify the feminine, and the insistence that women are of no importance because of their 'castrated' sexual organs. In any case, in this phrase Lacan emphasises the 'absence', the 'lack', the incompleteness inherent in female nature and determined by her body.

The woman is excluded from the nature of things for being not-whole, and even her *jouissance* has a 'supplementary function' (Lacan, 1998: 72–73). Yet, despite this lack of phallus and 'proper' *jouissance*, the woman is the one who controls the man with her sexuality:

> contrary to what people say, it is nevertheless they who possess men. . . . He is the one who obeys orders, not her. Since Rabelais, we have known that phallus, her man, as she says, is not indifferent to her. But, and this is the whole point, she has different ways of approaching that phallus and keeping it for herself.
>
> (1998: 73–74)

His ideas about what constitutes women's manipulative ways of 'keeping the phallus for themselves' are echoed and elaborated by Jean Baudrillard in the 1984 interview with Salavatore Mele and Mark Titmarsh. Baudrillard notes:

> In itself, the masculine doesn't seem to be seductive. Perhaps it is powerful, strong. Perhaps it holds in some way the controls – those distinctive oppositions in the order of the world. For the feminine it is the matter of dissolving this order, of bringing everything down to zero. In the end it ensures that everything is played ironically, seductively, and so on. For the masculine, nothing plays, things must function; it is different.
>
> (Gane, 1993: 86)

In another interview, he extends his views on seduction and the power, and benefits that come with it:

> I am not in agreement with hardline feminist ideology which says that woman as seducer is a degrading role. In my view the strategy of seduction is a happy,

> liberating power for women. It feeds into the simulation. Unfortunately, in feminism everything that happens to be female is defended . . . . It seems to me that the feminine strategy of seduction is not an alienation of woman, as the feminists believe. One must rise above the battle of the sexes and get away from sexist alienation. Men and women should not oppose each other. I believe one can regain feminine seductiveness as a positive virtue and that this is one way to rise above it.
>
> (Gane, 1993: 154)

Although Baudrillard keeps adding disclaimers such as 'the "feminine" is not strongly connected with "woman"' and 'I risk being misunderstood', his statements exemplify a typical male view of imaginary female seductiveness – as a product that is comfortably consumed, and therefore should be kept unchallenged and unchanged (1993: 86–154). Seen in this light, the woman is an object of desire, a seductress who sells her body in exchange for power. As such, she is not expected or even allowed to be the generator of power, or the builder of an order.

Baudrillard sees seductiveness as a form of activity, albeit a rather passive one. In his view, it leads to subverting the existing order created by men. Ultimately, he asserts, seductiveness leads to reducing the male power to zero. Applied to women on screen, this argument simply does not hold. A woman on screen is almost always beautiful, and in traditional Hollywood narratives – also passive. Is she capable of bringing down the social order with the very fact of being seen, of being looked at, of being admired, of having the power of sexuality? It can be argued that Marilyn Monroe had more social and political power, and was more influential, than the men with whom she slept, the men who made films with her, or the men who enjoyed watching her ethereal, childlike beauty on screen. The epitome of the traditional Hollywood actress, she was a successful object, a professional object, in fact, whose real voice was not welcome, on or off screen. Her seductiveness was not just in her looks, but also in her roles, which included a wide range of sensuous and provocative females, and some beautiful mothers and wives.

Seduction is closely related to the dichotomy of activity and passivity, the silence and the gaze, when the object is being watched and expected to absorb projections in order to be accepted into the social order. The logic of Baudrillard's argument would lead us to think that seductiveness is powerful precisely because it is all about sex, and that sex, being the most basic of all instincts, is capable of bringing down the social order, the civilised froth on the top of our unconscious lives. Both Lacan and Baudrillard imply that the force of sexuality is so strong that men could become obsessed with the object, and give up parts of their power in order to keep it and to enjoy it. In other words, one should pay for a good object in order to claim ownership of it. Likewise, a good object should feel 'not-whole' and seek a phallus-saviour for completeness and protection. It should be suitably passive and have space for male projections of power and control.

Freudian film feminists primarily discuss female behaviour on screen in terms of passivity. They see women as disenfranchised, stereotyped, objectified, branded as castrated (and therefore defective and incomplete) and enslaved within the linguistic framework of the patriarchal order. In other words, women are seen as victims whose rights to be individuals and to make their own life choices are limited and controlled. This line of criticism stems from Lacan's analysis of *objet petit a* – the object of desire – as an imaginary thing, as 'no being', as 'the void presupposed by a demand' (1998: 126). This means that the desire is based 'on no being', and that in every demand 'there is but the request for *objet petit a*, for the object that could satisfy jouissance' (1998: 126). Worse even, the object's role in the relationship boils down to basic pre-Oedipal functions:

> the partner of this 'I' that is the subject, the subject of any sentence that constitutes a demand, is not the Other, but that which is substituted for it in the form of the cause of desire – that I have diversified into four causes, insofar as the cause is constituted diversely, according to the Freudian discovery, on the basis of the object of sucking, the object of excretion, the gaze, and the voice. It is as substitutes for the Other that these objects are laid claim to and made into the cause of desire.
>
> (1998: 126)

The object's power, however, is rather dubious. As it is not a real person, it could be replaced by another object at any moment if that new object better reflects the owner's inner core, or better absorbs his projections (including sexual fantasies). Moreover, the object is replaced the very moment it dares to show its real personality, its real wishes and desires, which are always a challenge to the owner's claim of control. The object has no individuation of her own – her individuation is in belonging, either to a person or a community. Luis Buñuel's 1977 film, *That Obscure Object of Desire*, brilliantly outlines the unstable relationship between the owner and the object in Lacanian terms: a wealthy middle-aged man Mathieu (played by the Spanish actor Fernando Rey) attempts to purchase an eighteen-year-old woman from her Catholic mother. The girl, Conchita, is played by two actresses, Carole Bouquet and Angela Molina. They are used interchangeably in different scenes. Yet, the protagonist is so inflamed with the idea of possessing Conchita sexually that he does not even notice her radically changing appearance. In Buñuel's language this means that women exist for Mathieu only as things, and the pretty ones could be bought and discarded depending on the circumstances. Although Conchita's constant rejection of Mathieu makes him madly obsessed with her, and does give her a certain power, the real power – money, social status, decision-making – still remains with the man. In fact, Mathieu even buys her a house in an attempt to melt her heart and finally enjoy her body. Conchita accepts the house but does not let him in, and even has sex with a young man while Mathieu is watching, horrified.

The tale is a reworking of the *Bluebeard* tale, only in Buñuel's version the woman, in the absence of all other sources of power, uses seduction as a way both to gain status and to bring down the man who attempts to use her. Her seduction turns into poison, and is eventually replaced by open insults such as having sex with a young man in plain sight of the older suitor who bought the property. She is not a victim, but an active and decisive female, a fatal hunter as predatory and dangerous as her suitor. Although at some point Mathieu beats her up, leaving her bruised, she soon retaliates by pouring a bucket of water over him. Her seduction is a torturous mimicry of Mathieu's desires. Instead of the perfect mirror and the perfect object, the protagonist got a very imperfect, distorted mirror ridiculing and insulting him. This kind of mirror is not silent but brave in its insolence. Its aim is to show the extent of the male obsession with the controllable object and the extent of masculinity's obsession with itself.

Mulvey's analysis of the traditional Hollywood approach to depicting females on screen, although out of date, is still influential in feminist film criticism. Writing about the classical Hollywood cinema of the 1940–1950s in her article 'Visual Pleasure and Narrative Cinema', she famously outlines the ways in which the silent female is manipulated and commodified by the industry. In her view, cinema is only a reflection of the general social attitude towards women as the bearers of meaning, not the makers of meaning, condemned to be silent, both on and off screen:

> the function of woman in forming the patriarchal unconscious is two-fold, she first symbolises the castration threat by her real absence of a penis and second thereby raises her child into the symbolic. Once this has been achieved, her meaning in the process is at an end, it does not last into the world of law and language except as a memory which oscillates between memory of maternal plenitude and memory of lack. Both are posited on nature (or on anatomy in Freud's famous phrase). Woman's desire is subjected to her image as bearer of the bleeding wound, she can exist only in relation to castration and cannot transcend it. She turns her child into the signifier of her own desire to possess a penis (the condition, she imagines, of entry into the symbolic).
>
> (Mulvey, 1975: 6)

Mulvey sums it up by describing cinema as generating an illusion of reality created by the symbolic order for the purpose of enjoyment of objects without responsibility or obligation – rather like a strip-club. Women are mere props for male fetishism, unwilling participants in male scopophilia:

> During its history, the cinema seems to have evolved a particular illusion of reality in which this contradiction between libido and ego has found a beautifully complementary phantasy world. In *reality* the phantasy world of the screen is subject to the law which produces it. Sexual instincts and identification processes have a meaning within the symbolic order which articulates desire. Desire, born with language, allows the possibility of transcending the instinctual and the imaginary, but its point of reference continually returns to the traumatic moment of its birth: the castration complex. Hence the look,

> pleasurable in form, can be threatening in content, and it is woman as representation/image that crystallises this paradox.
>
> (Mulvey, 1975: 10)

Feminist film criticism focused on the issue of proximity and availability of the object via the concepts of the gaze ('looking'), the voice ('speaking') and curiosity ('looking', 'investigating'). All these are linked to the woman's Oedipal position in society. If she speaks or looks, she will cease to be a mirror, she will be misrecognised, will become 'the other' – a potentially traumatic experience for the man.

Kaja Silverman writes that, as a castrated object, women are not allowed to speak because they represent 'an alien and unwanted quality' (Silverman, 1988: 17). They are desired, but from a distance, in a fetishist way so as to prevent the fearful male subject from getting affected by 'castration'. A castrated object who speaks is a male nightmare personified. It is important that women remain silent, which proves to be difficult in real life. The screen therefore provides an ideal safe distance for such consumption of the silent object, for it is a fantasy life in which the male can look but not be looked at; in which he can consume females without having to deal with the actual woman and in which the woman is guaranteed to be silenced without any chance of her being out of control. The woman is absent from the process of signification as she represents lack. Lack, loss and castration, film feminists have argued, are at the base of both the production and consumption processes of the film industry.

Silverman notes in *The Acoustic Mirror* (1988) how the female voice is manipulated by the industry to match the fetishised screen image, while the authentic woman is never heard. Silverman evokes the silent cinema star Lina Lamont (Jean Hagen) in *Singin' in the Rain* (1952), who is not allowed to give interviews by the studio for which she works, Monumental Pictures, because she has a shrilly annoying voice. Lamont was perfect for the silent cinema, but in the wake of the sound era she suddenly became a liability, and the discrepancy between her silly voice and polished appearance needed to be concealed (Silverman, 1988: 45). Voice, Silverman notes, significantly changes the meaning of the image as it makes it all too real, it destroys the beautiful illusion (and the illusion of control over the object): 'When the voice is identified . . . with presence, it is given the imaginary power to place not only sounds but meaning in the here and now' (Silverman, 1988: 43).

The silent woman is not just the woman who does not speak – she also does not look. In other words, she does not act. Throughout her texts, Mulvey keeps exploring the link between proactive behaviour (traditionally criticised in females) and the act of looking, which reflects the desire to penetrate, to investigate, to set something free, to uncover the hidden. One investigates first, and then voices one's opinion – and women are not expected to do any of these. An active female is the woman who directs her look at the objects; she is a detective, acting out of stubborn curiosity. By so doing, she defies male orders and wards off male attempts to direct the gaze *at her*. She does not accept the fact that she is 'castrated' – that (as the patriarchal order would have it) she has nothing to penetrate the mystery with.

Mulvey explains this exclusion of the female from the cinematic space using the allegory of Pandora's box. In the myth, Pandora, out of curiosity, opens the box containing all the evils of the world. Her drive to discover and to investigate 'is directed at a culture in which woman has not, traditionally, been the possessor of knowledge and which has, traditionally, tended to consider femininity as an enigma' (Mulvey, 1995: 4). Pandora's compulsive desire to look and to explore instead of passively mirroring the male gaze is a serious threat to male dominance, and thus is presented as 'the end of the world'. This mythological character, Mulvey argues, represents feminist defiance of objectified passivity expected of women in male-dominated cultures:

> While curiosity is a compulsive desire to see and to know, to investigate which is secret and to reveal the contents of a concealed space, fetishism is born out of a refusal to see, a refusal to know, and a refusal to accept the difference that the female body symbolises. Out of this series of turnings away, of covering over, not the eyes but understanding, of looking fixedly at any object that holds the gaze, female sexuality is bound to remain a mystery, condemned to return as a symbol of anxiety while overvalued and idealised in imaginary. Hollywood cinema has built its appeal and promoted its fascination by emphasising the erotic nature of the female star concentrated in a highly stylised and artificial presentation of femininity. . . . The myth of Pandora and the box are similarly imbricated with the structure of fetishism. But Pandora opens the box containing everything that fetishism disavows. The box is, in this sense, a fetish that fails.
>
> (Mulvey, 1995: 18)

Curiosity, Mulvey notes, sets up a 'configuration of space through its association with investigation' (1995: 9). The box lures Pandora, and prompts her to act and to discover, thus breaking down the 'regime of fetishism' (1995: 18). Transgressing the rules of the regime, exposing it to unsafe objects, forcing it to look at the horror of castration without the distance, is seen by the patriarchy not just as a mere act of defiance as it creates an association between the feminine and fear of evil (1995: 18).

Like Pandora, other women in traditional narratives are either politely asked to comply with the rules of the male world or, failing that, threatened into submission. Such narratives are full of warnings about the dangers of curiosity expressed by women:

> Although Eve's story highlights the knowledge theme, the epistomophelia, as it were, inherent in the drive of curiosity, the myth associates female curiosity with forbidden fruit rather than with forbidden space. The motif of space and

> curiosity can be found again symptomatically in the fairy story *Bluebeard*. The story is about his last wife, a young girl who is given the free run of his vast palace with the exception of one room which her husband forbids her to enter. Its little key begins to excite her curiosity until she ignores the luxury all around her and thinks of nothing else. Then, one day, when she thinks her husband is away, she opens the door and finds the bodies of all his former wives still bleeding magically from terrible wounds and tortures.
>
> (Mulvey, 1995: 9)

In her essay 'Woman's Stake: Filming the Female Body', Mary Ann Doane writes that 'to those who still ask, "What do women want?" (a paraphrase of Freud's famous line), the cinema seems to provide no answer' (Doane, 1988: 216). She also equates 'the simple gesture of directing a camera toward a woman' with 'a terrorist act' because 'cinematic images of woman have been . . . consistently oppressive and repressive' (1988: 216). This state of affairs, which is:

> the result of a history which inscribes woman as subordinate – is not simply to be overturned by a contemporary practice that is more aware, more self-conscious. The impasse confronting feminist filmmakers today is linked to the force of a certain theoretical discourse which denies the neutrality of the cinematic apparatus itself. A machine for the production of images and sounds, the cinema generates and guarantees pleasure by a corroboration of the spectator's identity. Because that identity is bound up with that of the voyeur and the fetishist, because it requires for its support the attributes of the 'noncastrated', the potential for illusory mastery of the signifier, it is not accessible for the female spectator, who, in buying her ticket, must deny her sex. There are no images either *for* her or *of* her.
>
> (Doane, 1988: 216)

Similarly, Joan Copjec notes that women are

> the external, who are repeatedly excluded by the homeostatic system – the constant reproduction of the male by the patriarchal mechanisms of film, language. . . . the point of view and the structures of voyeurism, exhibition, identification which follow from it are always, repeatedly, male. Women, therefore, cannot look, cannot be represented – as women.
>
> (1988: 233)

Freudian and Lacanian film feminists emphasise that women are banned from participating in male activities – i.e. activities that involve investigating and discovering, speaking one's mind, killing and conquering, and pursuing the grail awaiting at the end of the journey. Their discussion of women's position both on screen and in society is also deeply politicised, and their psychological analysis of the situation is linked to social and political issues.

Female individuation on screen: the Jungian approach

Jungian discussion of women as actresses and spectators differs significantly from the one employed by the Freudian and post-Freudian theorists. Firstly, Jungian feminist analysis is not as politicised as its Freudian counterpart. Andrew Samuels rightly notes that Jungian discourse on the feminine is 'directed away from political and social action' (Samuels, 2015: 102). This is also generally true of Jung's writings, for he was more interested in the spiritual than in the socio-political applications of psychological phenomena – though, as noted in the Introduction to this book, he was also concerned with the relationship of the individual to society at large. As with all Jung-influenced analyses, a Jungian feminist approach to women on screen is bound to be mildly spiritualised and discussed in terms of the woman's transcendental journey instead of being a closely focused examination of the social and political conditions that oppress her.

This, however, does not mean that Jungian concepts are completely apolitical or could not be used to discuss social issues such as the position of women in society or gender fluidity. Jung's concepts of the anima, the animus and the mother are certainly useful in the discussion of the cinematic representation of women as well as female spectatorship. Moreover, with Jung's emphasis on the feminine, his psychology may even be more relevant for the study of women on screen. Unlike Freud's psychology, which is explicitly patriarchal and father-centred, Samuels argues, Jung provided 'a mother-based psychology in which influence is often traced back much earlier, even to pre-natal events' (2015: 213).

Moreover, Jungian thought has never stressed gender differences the way its Freudian counterpart did. Rather than emphasising the 'lack', sexed or sexless, Jung writes about both the genders lacking something on their own, without each other. Hence his extensive use of the gnostic idea of syzygy – the divine unity, the double-gendered nature of God. Psychological wholeness is a matter of equality and enlightenment, not a retrospective exercise in eliminating difference or an immature search for similarity and perfect mirroring.

For Jung, gender differences were more symbolic than social, or of actual importance. Susan Rowland writes:

> where a Freudian interpretation reduces visual pleasure to a sexuality organised around the phallus as the significant organ of pleasure and meaning, Jung regarded psychic energy as essentially neutral and *hence not privileging one gender*. Where Freud (and Lacan after him) considers the Oedipus myth to possess an originating role in the structuring of the psyche, Jung makes room for many potential myths of being. Some of them can even emphasise the feminine!
>
> (Rowland, 2011: 148–149)

Secondly, Jungian discourse on the feminine tends to be structuralist – it is concerned with the peripeties of female individuation and how they compare to the stages of the traditional hero myth. This approach inevitably involves the discussion of archetypes and their role in the woman's journey of self-discovery. The anima, the animus and the great mother are particularly pertinent to this approach. The issues of the female voice and her right 'to look' are also included in this discussion.

In an attempt to ward off accusations in sexism, one of the key figures in 'individuation screenwriting', Christopher Vogler, explains that his version of the individuation process, *The Writer's Journey*, has unjustly been viewed as a masculine theory, 'cooked up by men to enforce dominance, with little relevance to the unique and quite different journey of motherhood' (Vogler, 2007: xxi). He emphasises the universality of the process rather than any differences the hero's gender may bring to the journey:

> There may be some masculine bias built into the description of the hero cycle since many of its theoreticians have been male, and I freely admit it: I'm a man and can't help seeing the world through the filter of my gender. Yet I have tried to acknowledge and explore the ways in which the woman's journey is different from the man's.
>
> (Vogler, 2007: xxi)

Vogler insists that, since the call for better self-understanding is universal, gender differences are not as important as the essence of the journey, which is learning about yourself in the world: 'I believe that much of the journey is the same for all humans, since we share many realities of birth, growth, and decay, but clearly being a woman imposes distinct cycles, rhythms, pressures, and needs' (2007: xxi).

In fact, what Vogler is trying to do here is circumvent the issue which has never been properly resolved in any approach to gendered narratives: a formalist narrative analysis of female self-discovery. What is it that constitutes a 'female' narrative? What are the specifics of 'female individuation'? Moreover, are the schemes offered by Jung, Campbell and Vogler applicable to women? Or if they are not, since at the centre of the hero myth lie what traditional societies regard as 'male qualities' – activity (often accompanied by aggression), decisiveness, independence, assertiveness, power (achieved by any means), endurance, ability to overcome obstacles – how can this original scheme be changed to incorporate the 'female qualities'?

First, what are these mysterious female qualities? The hero myth, for instance, is packed with action which forms the base of all the 'spiritual' elements of the male journey: self-reflection, self-knowledge, individuation, maturation all happen via being proactive and spreading your influence. By contrast, a typical female individuation narrative emphasises 'modest' character traits: patience, passivity, dependence on some kind of 'master' or 'parental figure', helplessness, fear of sexuality, fear of male aggression, dependence on male benevolence, fantasy of being rescued (usually by a prince), etc. Vogler proposes, in a rather muddled way, that women's journeys are not as linear and clear as a typical male hero myth:

> men's journeys may be in some sense more linear, proceeding from one outward goal to the next, while women's journeys may spin or spiral inward and outward. The spiral may be a more accurate analogue for a woman's journey than a straight line or a simple circle. Another possible model may be a series of concentric rings, with the woman making a journey inward towards the center and then expanding it again. The masculine need to go out and overcome obstacles, to achieve, conquer, and possess, may be replaced in the woman's journey by the drives to preserve the family and the species, make a home, grapple with emotions, come to accord, or cultivate beauty.
>
> (2007: xxi–xxii)

A male hero, as described in Campbell's and Vogler's narrative schemes, is summoned on a journey either by an inner voice or some kind of external mentor figure – usually an old wise man (such as Obi Wan in George Lucas's *Star Wars*). He may initially refuse the call (step two in Campbell's seventeen-stage journey), but he nevertheless overcomes his fear, and eventually sets out on a journey for enlightenment and individuation.

In *The Heroine's Journey: Woman's Quest for Wholeness* (1990), Maureen Murdock notes that preoccupation with the masculine narrative structures in the West is caused by the fact that society is still not interested in a woman who can see, speak and act:

> We live in an androcentric society, which continues to view the world from a masculine perspective. Despite women's advances in academia, business and the professions, stereotypes persist that impede women's economic, political and professional progress into top leadership roles. Research from psychologists about stereotypes informs us that there is still a double standard when it comes to human behaviour. Behaviours such as being active, independent, objective and logical are still equated with males, while more dependent, subjective, emotional and illogical behaviours characterise females.
>
> (Murdock, 2013: 1)

Murdock notes, in an understandably annoyed tone, that Campbell himself had little interest in the nuances of female individuation,

> My desire to understand how the woman's journey relates to the journey of the hero first led me to talk with Joseph Campbell in 1981. I knew that the stages of the heroine's journey incorporated aspects of the journey of the hero, but I felt that the focus of the female spiritual development was to heal the internal split between woman and her feminine nature. I wanted to hear Campbell's views. I was surprised when he responded that women don't need to make the journey. 'In the whole mythological tradition the woman is *there*. All she has to do is to realise that she's the place that people are trying to get

> to. When a woman realises what her wonderful character is, she's not going to get messed up with the notion of being pseudo-male.'
>
> (Murdock, 2013: 7)

True, in traditional female quest narratives, the individuating woman does not choose to go on a journey; she is pushed out of the house. Her initiation and maturation are associated with remaining weak, fragile and dependent on other, stronger people. The task of her individuation, it seems, is to find nice people on whom to depend (a prince, a brother, a kind stranger) instead of nasty ones (nasty elder sisters or a cruel stepmother). An attempt at independence results in yet another affirmation of physical or emotional fragility in the face of the cruel world in the form of big animals (a wolf, a monster), extreme weather conditions, envious older women (stepmother, half-sisters) or a horrible new husband (a maniac or a murderer).

The other option for the individuating female is to copy the male maturation scheme, i.e. to become a 'hero' and to follow the path of adventures, monster extermination and treasure hunting. This would mean abandoning the 'fragile' feminine nature, as well as dependency on others and relational (as opposed to forceful) ways of dealing with conflicts. Yet, as Murdock notes, her years of experience as a therapist show that direct transposition of the male version of the hero myth onto a woman's life would not necessarily make her happy. She witnessed all kinds of emotional consequences of this kind of transposition, which has become normal in contemporary Western societies: 'a sense of sterility, emptiness and dismemberment, even a sense of betrayal' caused by the fact that the original male goal is to 'attain a success in the marketplace' (Murdock, 2013: 10). The boon, at which women who adopt the male model aim, is associated with exhaustion, overscheduling and suffering from stress-related ailments. They end up asking themselves 'What is all of this for?' (2013: 10). This model, just like its passive counterpart, denies 'who [the women] are' (2013: 10). In other words, Murdock advocates combining the relational with the heroic in the feminine journey towards self-discovery.

In a way, Campbell's and Vogler's views on what constitutes female individuation are quite similar. The woman does not have to 'go somewhere' in order to achieve some kind of self-fulfilment or to gain a change of status, for this would mean an initial sense of self-dissatisfaction, a sense of non-belonging, an ambition, a desire to influence the environment. Meanwhile, as Vogler puts it, the true vocation of the woman is to 'preserve the family and the species', 'to grapple with emotions' and 'to cultivate beauty' (Vogler, 2007: xxii). In this sense, their views are in line with psychoanalytic thought in general, which tends to regard female narratives as coming from the passive position, lacking an aggressive impulse, and achieving a change of status – essentially a liminal change – with the help of a man (or men).

Vogler attempts to preserve some semblance of equality in his book by using examples of female protagonists in cinematic narratives alongside examples of male protagonists. Predictably, he uses Dorothy from *The Wizard of Oz* (1939; directed by Peter Fleming). Yet, Dorothy's individuation, either in L. Frank Baum's novel or in MGM's famous adaptation, still has recognisable 'female' attributes: motherly behaviour towards others, community-making, kindness and endearing naivety.

In other words, the girl from Kansas's 'hero myth' is more relational than heroic *per se*; or maybe it is a kind of combination of the two, the very 'third way' which Murdock advocates. Murdock also proposes her own version of female individuation, which entails the integration of masculine qualities with feminine values. This version begins with the stage called 'separation from the feminine', and ends with the integration of masculine and feminine qualities (Murdock, 2013: 12). The realisation of the importance of feminine qualities, according to Murdock, happens somewhere in the middle of the journey, and in this the heroine makes a decision to unite the two parts of her psyche through heroic effort. This happens, Murdock insists, because the heroine, having started her journey as a male hero and met the unavoidable dragons and ogres, decides that being a man is neither satisfying nor brings her closer to her personal goals – which are self-realisation, spiritual growth and wholeness.

On the one hand, novels such as Lewis Carroll's *Alice in Wonderland* (1865) and Baum's *The Wonderful Wizard of Oz* (1900) symbolised a turning point in female individuation narrative: the woman is finally allowed to 'travel' in pursuit of self-actualisation, albeit presented as a dream in a frame narrative. On the other hand, these narratives, influenced by modernity as they were, were still focusing on the relational attributes of the female quest. The heroine is still not the one who fights but the one who creates links with others; she achieves her goal of self-discovery by being kind and patient. In this sense, her self-actualisation proceeds by winning people over with her 'mother hen' qualities. It mostly happens via others, via connecting, relating, helping and being sympathetic. By listening to others and by taking their problems seriously, she becomes 'herself'.

Dorothy, Vogler writes, meets her miserable companions during the hero myth stage which he calls 'Tests, Allies and Enemies', when the protagonist figures out who can be relied upon and who cannot be trusted:

> Dorothy encounters her Tests, Allies, and Enemies on the Yellow Brick Road. Like Psyche or the heroes of many fairy tales she is wise enough to know that requests for aid should be honoured with an open heart. She earns the loyalty of the Scarecrow by getting him unhooked from his post and by helping him learn to walk. . . .
>
> Dorothy wins the affection of another Ally, the Tin Woodsman, by oiling his joints and listening sympathetically to his sad story of having no heart. . . .
>
> She protects her dog Toto, Dorothy stands up to the blustering of the Cowardly Lion, a potential Enemy or Threshold Guardian, and ends up making him an Ally.
>
> (Vogler, 2007: 137–141)

The main problem of this analysis is that Dorothy's 'quest for wholeness' is based on her qualities as a motherly female: she looks after all the broken men she finds on her way. Even better – she mends them with her kindness, optimism and purity of heart. No male approach would have cured the Scarecrow (Ray Bolger), the Tin Woodman (Jack Haley) and Cowardly Lion (Bert Zahr) from their respective complexes. As such, Dorothy is a 'good mother' in the making.

Another problem is that Vogler compares Dorothy to Psyche rather than to a male mythological or folk hero. Far from being an individuating fighter, Psyche, from Apuleius's *Metamorphoses*, is a martyr condemned to suffer for love and to pursue a man while also being punished for her beauty by the jealous and envious Venus. This is certainly not a favourable comparison. It is also incorrect, for Dorothy is not looking for her lost love, but her lost home.

Looking for a home, or going through a liminal, transitional state between losing the 'old' home' and acquiring a 'new' one, is a typical component of the traditional female individuation myth. It is presumed that homemaking is a large part of the woman's life in which family is her main aim, and therefore her maturation process consists of moving away from her parents and establishing a family of her own. True to this scheme, Dorothy's trials mostly teach her to solve problems by love and empathy instead of tackling them head-on. Her change of status (both in the book and in the film) is achieved via suffering and motherly behaviour.

The good news, however, is that at least she is allowed to travel the road by herself and to act decisively and independently. This is a far cry from the traditional female individuation narratives in which girls venturing outside the house get into trouble, and are eventually saved by men. At least Dorothy, who calls herself 'small and meek', is the one who *saves men*, while the main man, the god figure, the carrier of the world wisdom, the Wizard of Oz, happens to be a fake and a 'a good man but a bad wizard'. He is exposed and deposed in his narcissistic, overinflated guise while Dorothy triumphs as the leader of her tribe. Her tactics of overcoming obstacles, however, are communal rather than individualistic – she summons the strengths of everyone in her circle to solve problems instead of relying on herself. Her quest is a sort of triumph of the 'feminine' way of doing things, the victorious female quest for wholeness in which the said wholeness is achieved by gathering everyone around you instead of relying solely on yourself, and by befriending the monsters instead of fighting them.

The silenced woman and her hidden voice: the Jungian perspective

The issues of the voice and the gaze have also been tackled by Jungian and post-Jungian authors. Although their theoretical framework is different from that employed by their Freudian colleagues, they touch upon similar themes such as the female voice in a society that does not encourage women to have opinions, or to be proactive. Jungian psychology does not operate with traditional psychoanalytic terms such as castration, fetishism or the gaze to express the male fear of the woman as an agent. Instead, it uses archetypes called the animus and the anima, which represent 'the image of the other sex that we carry with us as individuals and also as members of the species' (Jacobi, 1973: 114).

Jungian psychology has traditionally been biased in its representations of these 'soul images': the anima has been depicted either as a dangerous seductress (Circe, a siren, a water nymph) or as a beautiful and passive angel waiting to be saved (Cinderella, the Sleeping Beauty or the Frog Princess). Both the 'angel' and the 'whore' versions of the anima are part of the male individuation: one is to be subdued and conquered, the other protected (and often represents the 'boon' at the end of the journey).

The good thing about Jungian psychology, however, is that it accounts for the active, aggressive and masculinised forms of female behaviour when it discusses the 'whore' aspect of the anima. Although it still objectifies the feminine and brands it 'mysterious' or 'dangerous', it nevertheless does not try to diminish its importance or restructure it to suit the patriarchal order. Jung's approach to the feminine, although largely tainted by the general patriarchal attitude to women prevalent at the time, nevertheless accounted for its power – not passive power, but the active and unpredictable type of power. This is largely due to Jungian psychology's emphasis on the spiritual and its relative neglect of the physical, the bodily, the difference between the sexes on which Freudian psychology is practically built. As Susan Rowland argues,

> where the Oedipus complex is the Freudian first principle, the idea that is *productive* of the whole psychology, Jung's originating principle is that the unconscious is independently creative of the ego and in part unknowable. Such a belief means that the human body cannot fix meaning. Gender becomes a dialogical process between the creative unconscious . . . and the cultural meanings bestowed upon the sexed body.
>
> (Rowland, 2011: 149)

At the same time, it is undeniable that Jung, both as a man and as a psychologist, was burdened with prejudices of his time. For instance, his views of the anima are quite romantic:

> If the encounter with the shadow is the 'apprentice piece' in the individual's development, then the encounter with the anima is the individual's development, then with the anima is the 'master-piece'. The relation with the anima is again a test of courage, an ordeal by fire for the spiritual and moral forces of man. We should never forget that in dealing with the anima we are dealing with psychic facts which have never been in man's possession before, since they were always found 'outside' his psychic territory, so to speak, in the form of projections. For the son, the anima is hidden in the dominating power of the mother, and sometimes she leaves him with a sentimental attachment that lasts throughout his life and seriously impairs the fate of the adult. On the other hand, she may spur him on to the highest flights. To the men of antiquity the

> anima appeared as a goddess or a witch, while for medieval man the goddess was replaced by the Queen of Heaven and Mother Church.
>
> (CW9, I: 61)

Jung's writings, particularly about the contrasexual 'soul image', imply that male narcissism is rarely individuated to the point when the mystical aura of the anima dissolves and real women take her place:

> She [the anima] is not a shallow creation, for the breath of eternity lies over everything that is really alive. The anima lies beyond all categories, and can therefore dispense with blame as well as with praise. Since the beginning of time man, with his wholesome animal instinct, has been engaged in combat with his soul and its daemonism.
>
> (CW9, I: 60)

Even worse than the seductive anima is the little demonic, opinionated man who lives inside the female psyche and occasionally escapes to nag everyone in the vicinity. This man is called 'the animus'. Marie-Louise von Franz writes that the animus is 'the male personification of the unconscious in woman' which 'exhibits both good and bad aspects, as does the anima in man' (Jung and von Franz, 1964: 198). It is akin to a loud, stubborn voice in a woman's head and it needs to be restrained:

> the animus does not so often appear in the form of an erotic fantasy or mood; it is more apt to take the form of a hidden 'sacred' conviction. When such a conviction is preached with a loud, insistent masculine voice or imposed on others by means of brutal emotional scenes, the underlying masculinity in a woman is easily recognized. However, even in a woman who is outwardly very feminine the animus can be an equally hard, inexorable power. One may suddenly find oneself up against something in a woman that is obstinate, cold, and completely inaccessible.
>
> (Jung and von Franz, 1964: 198)

Moreover, it is not a single figure, but a whole chorus of men ready to argue and to fight at any moment. These men, Jolande Jacobi argues, are full of

> uncritically accepted opinions, prejudices, principles, which make women argue and bicker. . . . They seem to make up a fairly high percentage of their sex, though there may have been some change since the turn of the century, perhaps as a result of the emancipation of woman.
>
> (Jacobi, 1973: 121)

It is interesting that Jacobi links the rise in the power of the animus to female emancipation. Both Jacobi and von Franz imply in their respective analyses of the animus that women should always be 'supervised' by a man who would be able to control, manage and direct their 'inner voice' should they start expressing any 'uncritical opinions'. Meanwhile, both of them worked under Jung's supervision, were part of his school of thought and expanded his ideas. In a way, Jung played the role of their animus whose 'stubborn voice' sounded in their heads.

Their teacher's opinion of the animus was no more favourable than their own. For Jung, the animus expresses itself in 'opinionated views, interpretations, insinuations and misconstructions, which all have the purpose (sometimes attained) of severing the relationship between two human beings' (CW9, II: 32). Shockingly, in extreme cases Jung even advocates applying physical force to the woman whose animus 'just would not shut up':

> No matter how friendly and obliging a woman's Eros may be, no logic on earth can shake her if she is ridden by the animus. Often the man has the feeling – and he is not altogether wrong – that only seduction or a beating or rape would have the necessary power of persuasion. He is unaware that this highly dramatic situation would instantly come to a banal and unexciting end if he were to quit the field and let a second woman carry on the battle (his wife, for instance, if she herself is not the fiery war horse). This sound idea seldom or never occurs to him, because no man can converse with an animus for five minutes without becoming the victim of his own anima.
>
> (CW9, II: 29)

Yet, the animus also plays a positive role in a woman's life. For instance, it is in charge of creativity, being 'a psychopomp, a mediator between the conscious and the unconscious, and a personification of the latter' (CW9, II: 33). It also 'gives to a woman's consciousness the capacity for reflection, deliberation, and self-knowledge' (CW9, II: 33). It follows from this analysis that female creativity is something that has to be controlled and managed by a male guide.

The woman is thus both the anima and the container of the animus. Either way, she is the victim: patriarchal culture sees her animus as 'the loud evil thing', and, as the anima she is not even a real woman – she is a cluster of someone else's fantasies. The animus needs to be restrained lest its uncritical opinions destroy the aura of mystery surrounding the feminine; and the anima needs to be maintained in order to keep the woman a suitable vessel for projections.

Amongst male directors, Hitchcock is particularly adept at showing the 'female enigma' which is usually stalked, investigated, deciphered or violated in some other way, physically or psychologically. Traditionally analysed from a Freudian perspective with the use of such terms as voyeurism, scopophilia, objectification, phantasy and narcissism, Hitchcock's films have been regarded by feminist criticism as perverse, extreme examples of Hollywood's treatment of women as well as faithful reflections of society's moral brutality towards the feminine. Yet, his films equally lend themselves to Jungian analysis which, although not as blunt or straightforward, still clearly shows the patriarchal biases.

Hitchcock's heroines, who have since become archetypal, are inexplicable enigmas that male protagonists attempt to solve. Thus, the role of the aggressive and penetrating one – the role of the investigator – is exclusively played by a man. As a rule, Hitchcock's protagonists have 'penetrating' professions, hobbies or criminal proclivities: detective, photographer, policeman or even maniac. For instance, the protagonist of *Vertigo* (1958), Scottie (James Stewart), is a retired detective. He is asked by an old friend to spy on his wife, Madeleine (Kim Novak), who has recently been behaving in a strange way: leaving home and going to various places all by herself. The friend (Tom Helmore) claims that she is possessed, and that she needs help. Scottie starts following Madeleine, who indeed appears to be possessed by a ghost of Carlota Valdes, a woman who happens to be her great-grandmother and who had committed suicide. Throughout the film, Kim Novak's character says very little, thus solidifying her status as a fantasy figure. Scottie becomes obsessed with the silent object on the brink of hysteria and in need of male intervention. Only a man, a rational creature, the one who takes charge and makes decisions, can save her from madness.

Madeleine's silence both positions her as Scottie's seductive anima and emphasises her silenced yet stubborn 'animus'. Her very desire 'to see' is suicidal, as the film's narrative would have it. By contrast, as Mulvey puts it, Hitchcock's male protagonist 'does see precisely what the audience sees' as well as 'takes fascination with an image through scopophilic eroticism as the subject of the film' (Mulvey, 2013: 65). A woman who wanders inexplicably in the streets, and visits hotels and cemeteries when she is supposed to be at home waiting for her businessman husband (even though his wealth was her dowry), evokes certain cultural connotations. The investigating spirit working within her must be following a shadow, an illusion. Her desire to investigate, to penetrate, to go on a journey must be misguided, for a woman's journey is different; it is supposed to be about passive waiting and victimhood. Being active, going outside the confines of her home, are the elements absent from the 'traditional' structure of the 'female' journey. If a woman sets out on such a journey, she is likely to run into difficulties or face danger (fairy tales such as *Bluebeard* present us with good examples of this), and that's when she needs to be rescued by a man. In fact, it is even better if a male guardian follows her everywhere in case something bad happens (and it will, because of the narrative necessity: the woman has to be returned 'home' and handed back to her 'owner').

Male aggression towards 'the anima', as well as male attempts to silence the rival voice 'the animus', are consistently shown in Hitchcock's films. In *Rear Window* (1954) the protagonist, a journalist played by James Stewart, is stuck in his flat with a broken leg. This temporary disability is usually interpreted in Freudian terms – as a metaphor of castration. In fact, this is exactly how he feels. An adventurer and investigator, he is used to being proactive and to taking risks, but is now immobile and looked after by two women. Ever the hunter, he channels his adventure spirit into spying on his neighbours from his windows. He sees his beautiful girlfriend Lisa (Grace Kelly) as a nuisance who is trying to tie him down until he will 'never be able to go anywhere'. In fact, he finds more fun in watching other people's lives:

'Miss Torso', a sexy showgirl entertaining hoards of men in her flat; a lonely lady who dreams of having a lover, and sometimes enacts scenes of affection with an imaginary male guest; a middle-aged sculptor; a married couple who like to sleep on the balcony; two female friends who take off their pyjamas and sunbathe, etc. This kind of fantasy life fuels Jeff's imagination, and fills his hero journey.

Jungian theory deals with the question of reality versus narcissism by contrasting projections with real people. Often archetypes, and particularly the anima and the animus, become the false standards, the formulas, the ideals by which we measure others. Being mature, and growing up, means learning to separate one's own projections from real people out there. Jeff's life is one long hero myth, full of adventures, danger and escape from reality. By contrast, Lisa exists in reality and makes demands on him. Worse, she is a successful woman in her own right, a writer and a socialite whereas Jeff wants someone ordinary who would accept his lifestyle as her own and would follow him anywhere. Lisa is many a man's fantasy anima, but not his. She eventually earns a ticket into his life by helping him investigate the murder of a woman by her husband. She risks her life by doing this, but it brings her closer to Jeff.

Hitchcock's most famous work, *Psycho* (1960), invites Oedipal interpretations, but can equally be approached from a Jungian point of view; for instance, by referring to the archetype of the mother. The mother archetype, even more so than the anima, symbolises the power of the feminine. Unlike in Freudian psychology, Jung did not see the mother as something silent, innocuous or dominated by the masculine. In Jungian psychology this archetype is regarded as a real force, as a metaphor for power. Moreover, Jung is not prescriptive in his assessment of the mother, either real or metaphorical. She is not only the one who cares but also the one who destroys. Although the terminology he uses is still rather sexist, Jung does not downplay the influence of the feminine. He writes in 'Psychological Aspects of the Mother Archetype':

> The qualities associated with [the mother archetype] are maternal solicitude and sympathy; the magic authority of the female; the wisdom and spiritual exaltation that transcend reason; any helpful instinct or impulse; all that is benign, all that cherishes and sustains, even fosters growth and fertility. The place of magic transformation and rebirth, together with the underworld and its inhabitants, are presided over by the mother. On the negative side the mother archetype may connote anything secret, hidden, dark, the abyss, the world of the dead, anything that devours, seduces, and poisons, that is terrifying and inescapable like fate.
>
> (CW9, I: 158)

Thus, the mother is both 'loving' and 'terrible', and the two aspects of this archetype are often inseparable. The mother is 'unsafe', and it's fine for her to be unsafe. Like the unconscious, the feminine is something that should be reckoned with, something untameable and potent.

Possession by an archetypal figure is one of the key motifs of Hitchcock's films; and possession by a mother is a particularly prominent moment. The protagonist of *Psycho*, Norman Bates (Anthony Perkins), thinks that he must kill people on behalf of his mother. He also dresses like his mother when he murders his victims. Some time ago Norman murdered her and her lover out of jealousy. Then he assumed her guise in order to be as close to her as possible. Like a spider, he waits at his hotel hoping for a suitable victim to appear. One such victim is Marion Crane (Janet Leigh) who is on the run from her employer after embezzling 40,000 dollars from him. She takes the wrong turn, and the road takes her to Bates's motel. She does not suspect that the shy and youthful proprietor is a maniac who sees her every move through a hole in the wall. In the famous 'shower scene', Bates, dressed as his mother and brandishing a giant knife, murders Marion in the bathroom. In the last scene but one, Bates is sitting at the police station, wrapped in a large shawl and 'thinking' in his mother's voice who is telling the audience that she is not even capable of harming a fly. The final shot is a double exposure showing Norman's face merging with the face of his dead mother.

From a Freudian perspective, this looks like a typical Oedipal dynamic. Bates murders his mother and her boyfriend because he is jealous and cannot stand the thought of the mother 'replacing' him with another man. He also tells Marion that 'a boy's best friend is his mother' and admits that he cannot leave his mother even though he sometimes wants to curse her. Meanwhile, Marion is fooled into thinking that the mother is still alive and that she is a disturbed tyrant mistreating her nice son. In reality, Norman is so attached to his parent that he behaves like a shy, compliant boy (and calls himself a 'boy' with no outside friends). He cannot overcome the trauma of separation from the mother or accept the pressures of reality which demand that he becomes an independent man. In order to preserve the pre-Oedipal unity with the parent, he chooses to murder her. He also murders other women because they remind him of the treacherousness and volatility of the feminine which cannot be trusted, and which needs to be kept under lock and key. The woman should be controlled; she should not have a will of her own. Bates finds that the best way of ensuring a woman's constancy is by murdering her and keeping her corpse, seated on a rocking chair, in the house, in a room of her own.

Yet, a Jungian perspective reveals something entirely different about the movie. Whereas the Freudian perspective paints women as helpless victims of male objectification, a Jungian analysis shows the dark power and the anger of the repressed feminine. Far from being helpless, women in the film are capable of being proactive, of retaliating, of being aggressive, sexual and disloyal.

True, the film depicts a patriarchal society in which women are mothers, secretaries and subordinates whereas men are in charge: the masculine, in the form of the boss, the policeman or a resident maniac controls the woman and administers punishment if she oversteps the boundaries of expected behaviour. The boss, the policeman and the car salesman all follow or chase Marion, and Bates murders her. Yet, it is the feminine that has the real influence in the film. Through the layers of patriarchal oppression, the great terrible mother rises and shows her power.

On the one hand, Marion and Mrs Bates are victims of male control. On the other, both the characters display a degree of defiance to the patriarchal system, and in both this defiance comes out via emotional excess and illegal behaviour because 'legality' in the social system is defined and guarded by men.

First of all, Marion has a lover, Sam (John Gavin). 'A lover' here is opposed to 'a husband' who, supposedly, would be able to support her financially. Sam has debts, that's why the two cannot get married. Marion's stealing and lying make her a criminal and yet they also represent the ability to take charge of the situation. Moreover, after breaking the law, she sets out on a dangerous quest of her own, trying to break free from dependence on the society. Marion has sex with a man of her choice and enjoys it, steals, lies and goes on a road trip on her own. No wonder she triggers the suspicion of the policeman (who starts behaving like a stalker): a lonely woman on the road is an unusual sight, unlike a lonely man. When Marion is speaking with Norman, she comes across as mature and confident, in contrast to Bates who is boyish, bashful and immature.

Through Marion's victim shroud, her true nature is visible – that of the woman who wants to make her own decisions. As Fred Botting writes in his book *Gothic* (1995), Hitchcock's reworking of Bloch's novel

> draws a linear narrative of transgression and punishment of a sexually attractive and independent single woman drawn into the gloom of a decaying family house and isolated motel . . . the maternal figure is felt to be oppressively alive . . . the killer is also a victim.
>
> (Botting, 2013: 176)

Similarly to Marion, Norman's mother 'refuses' to be branded a victim. Prior to her death at the hands of her own son, she also used to be an independent, sexually active female. In terms of symbolism, she is also depicted with a large knife in her hands – a phallic symbol as well as a symbol of aggression. Symbolically, she is associated with the great mother hermaphrodite described by Erich Neumann in his essays on the feminine as well as in his book *The Origins and History of Consciousness* (Neumann, 1989: 46). Neumann writes:

> the uroboric character of the great mother is apparent wherever she is worshipped in androgynous form, for instance, as the bearded goddess in Cyprus and Carthage. The woman with a beard, or with the phallus, betrays her uroboric character in the nondifferentiation between male and female. Only later will this hybrid be replaced by sexually unequivocal figures, for its mixed and ambivalent character represents the earliest stage from which the opposites will subsequently be differentiated.
>
> (1989: 46)

Neumann also evokes the Swiss nineteenth-century anthropologist Johann Jacob Bachofen whose chief research interest was prehistoric matriarchy. In his analysis of the feminine, Bachofen emphasises the power of the feminine as a giver of life and asserts that the masculine principle is subordinate to its feminine counterpart:

> The first earthly manifestation of masculine power takes the form of the son. From the son, we infer the father; the existence and nature of masculine power are evidenced only by the son. On this rests the subordination of the masculine principle to that of the mother. The man appears as creature, not as creator; as effect, not cause. The reverse is true of the mother. She comes before the creature, appearing as cause, the prime giver of life, and not as effect. She is not to be inferred from the creature, but is known in her own right.
>
> (Bachofen, cited in Neumann, 1989: 48)

Similarly, in *Psycho*, although there are attempts to quell the power of the mother, ultimately her influence is unquestionable. Bates assumes his mother's guise; he also fails to grow out of the immature, uroboric state of unity with her. Women in *Psycho* are sexually active, decisive and confident. On the surface, they are punished (murdered) by men for being all these, but deep down, the power of the great mother – the female power – endures. Mrs Bates has the last word when she appears as a voice-over in the last scene but one. Ultimately, it is the terrible great mother who is in charge while the man himself is silent and compliant. The son is 'subordinated' to the mother while her numinous power is seeping through the surface of the patriarchal society.

Woman as a man on screen

In the last twenty or so years there has been a proliferation of 'women as men' both in films and in television. In these narratives, the proactive female protagonist is neither a fragile maiden waiting for a prince to save her nor a mother hen tending to men's weaknesses and being patient with everyone. In other words, she is neither the anima nor the great mother. She is a man. She does everything traditional mythological female protagonists are not supposed to do: goes on quests, actively uses her sword or gun, drives cars and lorries, trains for difficult times ahead, has physical strength and endurance, often gets in trouble, gets hurt and recovers, and is relentless towards her enemies. Often her curiosity leads her to dark and dangerous places, and she is not afraid to enter them. This new heroine fights, murders, investigates and penetrates. Nothing can stop her if she gets curious. Her instincts are to chase, to seek, to find, and not to look for a new home and a partner, or to be maternal towards 'broken things'. As early Jungians would have put it, she is possessed by her animus.

Charismatic, powerful and mysterious, heroines of this kind quickly enter the cultural imagination: Lara Croft, famously portrayed by Angelina Jolie (*Lara Croft: Tomb Raider*, 2001; developed from the video game series *Tomb Raider* [Eidos Interactive/Square Enix]); Beatrix Kiddo (Uma Thurman) from Quentin Tarantino's *Kill Bill* (2003–2004), Trinity (Carrie-Anne Moss) from The Wachowskis' *The Matrix Series* (1999–2003), Lisbeth Salander (Noomi Rapace), the protagonist of the trio of films based on Stieg Larsson's *Millennium* series, Imperator Furiosa (Charlize Theron) in *Mad Max: Fury Road* (2015), Rey (Daisy Ridley) in *Star Wars: The Force Awakens* (2015) and many others. Even Tim Burton made a film with a defiant female protagonist going on a quest of self-discovery (*Alice in Wonderland*, 2010). Many of these action heroines came to screen from video games, comic books and novels. They also come from a variety of genres, from high fantasy to martial arts and procedural.

Of course, the contemporary action heroine has older role models such as Ridley Scott's Ripley (*Alien*, 1979) and Jordan O'Neill (*G.I. Jane*, 1997). Another early prototype is Jodie Foster's character in *The Silence of the Lambs* (1991, directed by Jonathan Demme). Clarice Starling is a detective who is entrusted with the task of dealing with two serial killers: Jame Gumb/'Buffalo Bill' (Ted Levine) and Dr Hannibal Lector (Anthony Hopkins), a former psychiatrist turned cannibal. Clarice regularly has to interview Lector in prison in the hope of finding out more about Buffalo Bill. In exchange for bits of information about the maniac, Lector demands that she tells him more about herself, and often torments her with his insight and shrewd offensiveness. Even though Clarice manages to shoot Gumb, throughout the narrative she is not entirely in control of the situation. She is nervous in Lector's presence, and is more or less like Little Red Riding Hood dealing with, despite his incarceration, a still dangerous and manipulative Wolf. Lector remains in control through to the end of the film when he calls Clarice to 'reassure' her that she is safe, and asks for a similar guarantee concerning himself. Moreover, rather than being independent, the young detective keeps relying on the dangerous man's insight and experience, which implies that she would not have caught Buffalo Bill without Lector's help.

Television, which in this instance is more progressive than Hollywood, abounds in examples of 'women as men' in individuation quests: *Xena: Warrior Princess* (1995–2000), *Buffy the Vampire Slayer* (1997–2003), *La Femme Nikita* (1997) and *Nikita* (2010–2013), Nordic Noir series *Forbrydelsen* (*The Killing*, 2007–2012) and *The Bridge* (2011–), the international 'high fantasy' blockbuster *Game of Thrones* (2011–), *Orange Is the New Black* (2013–) and *Jessica Jones* (2015). Again, the genres are varied and include both fantastic and realistic narratives. Yet, they are united by the theme of independent women on a quest for self-realisation. Their female protagonists are confident and prefer adventures to family life. Lone fighters rather than community-makers, they often pursue their quest regardless of what others might say, and the 'grail' they hunt is placed higher than their personal life, their own wellbeing, or even the safety of their family. Focused and sharp, when the time comes, they see nothing but the goal ahead. Netflix seems to be particularly keen on creating narratives that have strong females in the lead (*Jessica Jones*) or explore taboo social issues that do not correspond to gender stereotypes, such as female crime and aggression (*Orange Is the New Black*).

A good example of the almost total loss of feminine qualities in a heroine is Tarantino's *Kill Bill*. Tarantino himself struggled to define the film's genre, calling it a mixture of *giallo* (a sort of Italian noir) and a Japanese Yakuza film

(Latham, *BBC Website*, 6 October 2003). Its protagonist is Beatrix Kiddo, devoid of any empathy for or patience with others. Her behaviour is the opposite of what is traditionally expected of women: she is ruthless, focused on her goal and is a martial arts genius wielding her knife and sword better than any man would.

Beatrix is on a mission to kill Bill (David Carradine), the former leader of an assassination group to which she used to belong. In the past, Bill murdered Beatrix's unborn child (who, Beatrix insisted, was his), and also tried to kill her. When Beatrix wakes up after four years in a coma, she finds her former squad members and kills them one by one. The last one to kill is the notorious Bill, who is a tough nut, but she accomplishes her mission successfully.

Beatrix is an interesting character in terms of gendered behaviour. It could be argued that she is traumatised into becoming a man, and that she goes on her brutal quest – the killing spree, during which she leaves behind blood-splattered walls and rooms full of body parts and dead enemies – because she had lost her potential family, and because her lover had betrayed her. Since the woman in her feels offended and betrayed, she has no choice but to adopt male behaviour. Her injured femininity pushes her to the limits of endurance and violence. Beatrix's looks still betray her former femininity – she is lithe, pretty and has long blond hair. In a way, she does not choose her quest – she is pushed into it by a man whom she – symbolically – murders in the end. Since she cannot be a woman, she will be a man.

By contrast, Tim Burton's colourful and radical version of *Alice in Wonderland* (2010) has as its protagonist a woman who chooses a male quest not because she failed on a female one, but because she wants to be like her father – an explorer and adventurer who died when she was a child. For this purpose, Burton and the writer Linda Woolverton completely reworked Carroll's linguistically puzzling original. A rebellious nineteen-year-old who feels stifled by Victorian high society and its conventions replaces the hyper-imaginative girl. A frame narrative is wound around the core storyline telling us why exactly Alice (Mia Wasikowska) fell through the rabbit hole: it was her surprise engagement party; she did not like her ridiculous fiancé Hamish (Leo Bill), even though he was a lord; and suddenly, in the midst of the engagement ceremony, when she was expected to say 'yes' in front of the crowd of overdressed Victorians, her mind went into a kind of overdrive. She was struggling to find the answer within herself, and, speaking metaphorically, fell into her unconscious. The unconscious did not give her the answer straight away. It took the girl and umpteen bodily transformations, monster battles, nonsensical conversations and aristocratic encounters, to regain her 'muchness', and to answer the question she inherited from the original Alice – 'Who am I?' This question suits Burton's experimental protagonist very well because it is not just Alice who is going through a crisis – the Burtonian hero is looking for a new definition and a new direction.

In his search for a new direction, Burton attempts to transform Carroll's lost little girl into a Victorian feminist. 'Defamiliarisation' ('the world upside down') is both Carroll's and Burton's narrative device of choice to show the artificiality of social norms. Woolverton's frame narrative idea – marriage and sexual initiation – might have come from *Beauty and the Beast* (1991), on which she had previously worked for Disney, but Carroll's original text is also abound in references to female identity – and its crisis. Being too small or too big for your surroundings, not being able to fit in, being a pawn in someone else's game, being forced to accept the rules without questioning them – this is what Burton responded to, and made the film about. Johnny Depp's Mad Hatter and Helena Bonham-Carter's Red Queen are transformed into two warring figures on the female quester's path. The outcome of their conflict determines Alice's future in the real world. Alice's 'empowerment story' is lovingly embellished with Burton's favourite visual symbols that he traditionally uses to illustrate male quests: an assortment of cutting and piercing objects, a narrow staircase, gloomy castles and weird topiaries. The dragon Jabberwocky is promoted to the rank of the arch-villain, with whom our heroine, dressed in shiny armour and equipped with a magical sword, has an archetypal climatic hero-fight. Burton's masculinised Alice, with the phallic sword in her hands, metaphorically severs herself from her Victorian contemporaries, with their prim eccentricity and thinly-veiled social games. She then emerges from the hole of her unconscious, ready to announce her decision to the distraught relatives.

Even Disney/Pixar followed suit, albeit reluctantly and somewhat accidentally. *Brave* (2012), directed by Brenda Chapman and Mark Andrews, is a tale of Merida, a rebellious Scottish princess, who refuses to follow in her mother's footsteps (i.e. get married and become a queen). The flame-haired Merida is her father's daughter, a real tomboy who despises all things 'feminine' and 'decent', and loves riding, running in the woods, climbing trees and rocks, and shooting arrows at difficult targets. When expected to choose a husband from an array of silly-looking suitors, Merida outshoots them in an archery competition, and runs into the woods. There she encounters a witch (who does not like being a witch because 'there are too many dissatisfied customers'), and asks her for a spell which would make her mother change her mind. The witch gives her an enchanted cake which turns her mother into a she-bear. Merida's task now is to find a way to remove the spell and to help her mother regain her human form.

Chapman admits that sneaking such an innovative narrative into the Disney-owned company was challenging. Even worse, the computer animation industry, due to its 'techy' reputation, traditionally has very few women. She was distressed when the story was taken away from her and given to Mark Andrews; particularly because the story is inspired by the relationship with her daughter (Chapman, *The New York Times*, 14 August 2012). In the end, however, her vision came through in the film:

> So I kept my head held high, stayed committed to my principles, and was supported by some strong women (and men!). In the end, it worked out, and I'm very proud of the movie, and that I ultimately stood up for myself, just like Merida, the protagonist in *Brave*'
>
> (Chapman, *The New York Times*, 14 August 2012)

Brave is revolutionary in many ways. It is the first Pixar film directed by a woman. It is also a masculinised female individuation narrative. This is very unusual for the children's animation genre, which tends to be heavily gender-coded. Merida is no typical Disney Princess with pretty hair and wearing dangling earrings, a shiny necklace and a pink ball gown. Neither is she a victim, oppressed or controlled by some evil witch like Ariel (*The Little Mermaid*, 1989), Rapunzel (*Tangled*, 2010), Snow White (*Snow White and the Seven Dwarves*, 1937), Cinderella (appearing in a range of Disney films from 1950 to 2015) and Aurora (*Sleeping Beauty*, 1959). Merida is self-reliant, and is not expecting to be saved by a prince. Throughout the film, she gets into difficult situations – but she also successfully solves them. Merida is capable of expressing anger, aggression and frustration. She does not like the idea of being weak, nice or polite. Importantly, even though the narrative starts with the traditional female individuation element (the oppressive mother figure stifling the younger female's self-expression), Merida takes on the mother and attempts to destroy her before coming to her senses and seeking reconciliation. She deals with her beasts, witches and monsters herself. Killing (meaning integrating) the evil great mother and the beastly animus is the task of every hero-woman on the quest for self-actualisation.

Recently, the latest instalment in the *Mad Max* franchise, *Mad Max: Fury Road* (2015, directed by George Miller) made waves in the cinema world, and became an unusual platform for many a debate regarding the role of women in society. Charlize Theron's character, Imperator Furiosa, is a fearsome rebel warrior, undaunted and unstoppable despite missing one hand. She enrages the cult leader Immortan Joe (Hugh Keays-Byrne) by stealing his five beautiful wives (used for 'breeding'), and taking them away in a war rig in the hope of settling in a place where women are respected more. Joe sends his army of brainwashed 'war boys' to kill Furiosa and to reclaim the wives, one of whom is pregnant with his child. The film's title character, Mad Max (Tom Hardy), is almost side-lined by Furiosa who is as aggressive, angry and as capable as the embittered man accustomed to survival in the post-apocalyptic world. Her disability (which can be seen as a metaphor for her belonging to 'the weaker sex') does not make her a lesser soldier. Moreover, her disability, along with her shaved head, war paint and dusty face, visually challenges the traditional perception of the female character (and a Hollywood actress!) as someone ethereal in its feminine 'completeness'. Furiosa eventually blows off Immortan Joe's face and frees the cult members from oppression and humiliation.

This is certainly an unusual angle on the feminine, and a far cry from the traditional objectification of women in commercial cinema. In an interview with *Vanity Fair* Miller explains his choices by the gradual changes in the attitudes towards gender in Western societies: 'We've gone from being very male dominant to being surrounded by magnificent women. I can't help but be a feminist' (Rich, *Vanity Fair*, 14 May 2015). Theron herself salutes such a radical destruction of the double 'mother-whore' stereotype of women prevalent in screen media: 'You're either a really good mother or you're a really good hooker. The problem with how movies represent women goes right back to the Madonna/whore complex. You can't be a really good hooker-mother. It's impossible' (Shoard, *The Guardian*, 14 May 2015).

Several recent television projects present a similarly radical reversal of gender roles and reworking of the female quest. Two Nordic Noir series, *Forbrydelsen* (created by Søren Sveistrup) and *The Bridge* (created by Hans Rosenfeldt) are police procedurals in which the detective is a woman who tackles the most difficult and dangerous cases. Although female detectives have existed in narratives since 1926, when Agatha Christie's Miss Marple appeared in a short story for the first time, the Nordic Noir version of the investigating woman challenges the traditional notions of gender: the female protagonist *looks and behaves like a man*. Instead of using her 'female' qualities (patience, carefulness, intuition, wisdom) to solve problems, she tackles them head-on, often putting herself and others around her in danger. She thrives in adrenaline-infused atmosphere, and shoves any feelings or doubts into the furthest corner of her mind.

Throughout its three seasons, *Forbrydelsen*'s detective Sarah Lund (brilliantly played by Sofie Gråbøl) is so focused on catching the criminals that she neglects her teenage son (Eske Forsting Hansen) who, by season three (2012), tired of being rejected and ignored, cuts off all communication with her. In season one (2007) she drives away her boyfriend Bengt (Johan Gry) and regularly upsets her mother by being cold towards her. Sarah is a loner who cannot cultivate relationships with others because it is both time consuming and requires being able to process and release one's emotions. Relationships are risky, emotionally taxing and involve effort. Sarah does not know how to handle them. Besides, when an idea or a goal appears in her life, she becomes so obsessed with it that she cannot think about anything else. Her solution is cutting her family off, and concentrating on her work since pursuing both seems like an impossible task. She defies gender stereotypes and stays on her quest regardless of whether she is needed by her community. Moreover, the idea is that her goal, the treasure that one gets rewarded with at the end of the quest – catching the murderer – is higher and more valuable for the community than the treasures a 'typical' woman would be happy to get at the end of her quest: the love of others earned by patience, kindness and care.

Yet, being a detective – the penetrating one, the focused one – is not compatible with 'the vocation of the woman'. Sofie Gråbøl herself admits that playing a character who behaves like a man was both a difficult and a rewarding task. She says in an interview with BBC's *Newsnight* that immersing in the role has changed her own perceptions of masculinity and femininity:

> We all felt that the story of a woman in a dilemma between work and the family, work and love – there's a whole battle which, of course, as a woman, I totally know how it is – we all thought that it's not relevant, that it has been told so many times.
>
> (Gråbøl, interview by Kirsty Wark, *BBC Newsnight*, 1 November 2011)

Forbrydelsen's competition, the Danish/Swedish series *The Bridge*, has a similarly obsessive woman detective who lacks pretty much any feminine qualities despite looking like a blond bombshell. Saga Norén (Sofia Helin) is incapable of analysing her feelings, prefers casual sex to relationships (which surprises and shocks men who sleep with her), is not planning to settle down or to have children, takes her work home with her and stares at disturbing pictures from crime scenes until late in the night. As a questor, she is very male and very focused on catching the killer. Everything else falls out of the picture.

High fantasy is another rich ground for challenging gender stereotypes. The creators of *Game of Thrones* invert the traditional genre expectations which delineate the man as the hero on a quest and the woman as the princess to be saved, the monster to be killed, the passive wife waiting at home or the treasure to be found. Based on George R. R. Martin's fantasy series *A Song of Ice and Fire* and created by the screenwriters and producers David Benioff and D. B. Weiss, the show boasts an array of powerful and aggressive female characters, including Cersei Lannister (Lena Headey), the murderous, ambitious and beautiful Queen of the Seven Kingdoms; the naïve but charismatic Daenerys Targaryen (Emilia Clarke); the powerful and treacherous priestess Melisandre (Carice Van Houten); the deadly Sand Snakes; the shrewd and manipulative Margaery Tyrell (Natalie Dormer) and her grandmother, the clever, wise and political Olenna Tyrell (Diana Rigg). Women in *Game of Thrones* have real influence and power despite the fact that men still rule the world.

Notably, and very unusually for a medieval epic of this scale, several feminine characters are completely masculinised and only ever follow the male quest: Arya Stark (Maisie Williams), a rebellious, angry and adventurous teenager who chooses her sword nicknamed 'Needle' and a vagabond life over any settled lifestyle; the redhead Ygritte (Rose Leslie), a 'wildling' and a fearless warrior; Yara Greyjoy (Gemma Whelan), whose father entrusts her with leading a bunch of brutal men of the Iron Islands into battle; and the knight Brienne of Tarth (Gwendoline Christie), a tall and muscular master swordsman who is fond of challenging men to fight with her, and almost always wins.

Such a concentration of female fighters is impressive, particularly coming from a male writer and two male producers. George R. R. Martin explains to *The Telegraph*'s Jessica Salter that, although deep down he considers himself to be a feminist, he cannot call himself one because of the restrictions contemporary feminists place on who can wear the badge:

> There was a period in my life when I would have called myself a feminist, back in the seventies, when the feminist movement was really getting going . . . I thought if the current crop of feminists believes that no man can be a feminist, then I guess I'm not one.
>
> (Salter, *The Telegraph*, 1 April 2013)

Martin also says, in another interview:

> It's one of the things that please me most. I'm lucky that I've got such a big project; it means I can have lots of different types of female characters and so avoid stereotypes, which is what fantasy writers can end up doing.
>
> (Salter, *The Telegraph*, 25 March 2013)

Most of Martin's female warriors are 'father's daughters' who want to be like their fathers; that's why they learn sword fighting, archery and military leadership. Yet, amazingly, in Martin's fantasy world, this is a normal and an almost accepted path for a woman. Ned Stark (Sean Bean) has nothing against his daughter having sword lessons, Balon Greyjoy (Patrick Malahide) raises his daughter as a man and a legitimate heir to the throne (having lost his son to captivity), and Brienne of Tarth is the only surviving child of her father. During her wanderings, Arya keeps befriending scary-looking grown men who she views as both role models and brothers in arms: her fencing teacher Syrio Forel (Miltos Yerolemou), the 'faceless man' Jaqen H'ghar (Tom Wlaschiha) and the disenchanted knight Sandor 'the Hound' Clegane (Rory McCann). Not only does she think that having formidable men for friends is normal – she trusts them and wants to be one of them.

Far from being viewed as an anomaly or a sign of immaturity (the sign of maturity being the desire to settle and to have a family), the female fighter within this world is viewed as almost a common occurrence – if she can prove her ability to be one. This sets *Game of Thrones* apart from other fantasy creations, including *The Lord of the Rings* (both the books and the films) in which the females are presented either as beautiful objects or as enemies – and both these incarnations are part of the typical male quest. As Charlotte Runcie notes in *The Telegraph*:

> Before I watched *Game of Thrones*, I had come to accept that most women in fantasy fiction were just that – a fantasy. . . . How many women do you actually know who are immortal, beautiful and have a range of specific sexual needs that can be fulfilled only by a navel-gazing wandering hero?
>
> (Runcie, *The Telegraph*, 15 April 2014)

Importantly, the behaviour of the female characters of *Game of Thrones* is not limited to a specific type of quest: male or female, a lone warrior or a passive beauty, a poisonous queen or a fragile wallflower. They are all different and portrayed with depth typical of multiple focalisation: each of them is shown as a human, breathing character with her own complexities and conflicts, and choosing a unique and difficult path in the brutal world. This is true equality: equality in action; not everyone is fit to become a fighter, be it man or woman, but if you have enough pluck to take up your sword and put on your armour, your gender stops being a concern. Ultimately, what matters is your courage and your skill – such are the rules of the ruthless medieval world. Gender inequality is something only 'civilised' societies can afford.

Chapter 8

The body

Phenomenology and cinema

Luke Hockley

Introduction

Bringing together the Jungian approach with that of phenomenology is, on the face of it, a rather curious undertaking. The way that Jung conceives of the psyche, and actually the world in general, is that it is imbued with unconscious activities that are purposeful and which have agency. For Jung the unconscious is structured in relationship to and with the world, as they exist in a reciprocal relationship. Much like the famous conundrum of which came first, the chicken or the egg, it is not clear whether for Jung meaning in the world is inscribed by the unconscious or whether the material world creates the conditions through which the unconscious may express itself. These two aspects of the conscious world, and the unconscious structures that enable psychological meaning to take place, are dependent one on the other. This type of relationship is a very long way indeed from the phenomenological approach, which has no need of the unconscious as an idea at all.

In phenomenology something that is unconscious quite simply refers to something that is as yet not known or something we are not yet aware of. It certainly does not give a sense of purpose to that unknown aspect, and it is certainly not teleological, at least not in the way that Jung understands the psychology of human development. However, it is the contention of this chapter that actually there are ways in which some of the central tenets of the phenomenological orientation towards film in particular can both inform and enhance a Jungian view of the cinema. Such a combination is of particular assistance in examining just how it is that viewers find deep personal meanings in what they know to be fiction films – and that has been one of the themes of this book. Before we get to the issue of how to undertake this enmeshing of the depth psychological with the ultra-conscious phenomenological we need to map out a few of the core concerns of phenomenology itself, and in particular the ways it has been applied to films.

It is by no means self-evident that phenomenology will be of any use when it comes to understanding the cinema psychologically. Daniel Frampton makes the point in his book *Filmosophy* (2006), where he suggests that phenomenology is not likely to be of much help when it comes to questions of 'being' in the cinema. This is largely because phenomenology is a philosophy of consciousness and as such it aims to understand the 'lived experience' that is the human condition. By contrast, the Jungian view of being, and hence being in the cinema, is that it does have an unconscious component. However, just as psychoanalytic film theory found similarities between cinema and the structure of the human psyche, so too, using the approach offered by phenomenology, it becomes possible to find a parallel between our experience of the world, and the 'behaviour' and/or being of films.

One of the keys to this is Merleau-Ponty's claim that the act of looking is an act of gathering the world to oneself. As we look, so too we possess; a point not missed by psychoanalytic theory either, though there it has different repercussions. From a phenomenological perspective, to look is to possess, even if this possession takes place at a distance. Just as the act of looking turns the world into our personal possessions, so too the camera lens possesses the actors, the set, the lighting and so forth as they are turned into its world. In so doing each film becomes a type of being that has similar anatomical qualities to those of the human body: cinema hears (microphone), it sees (the lens), it talks (the loudspeaker), it touches (the sense of surface). In this regard, cinema films possess a body – of sorts.

Alternatively we might say that each film is situated in the world in a way that is distinctive. Each film gathers the world to itself in a way that is unique to itself but which is also aligned with the perceptual preconditions that contribute to our sense of lived experience. The cinematic experience is then composed of two aligned looks – the look of the camera and the look of the eye, and together they combine to form what I conceive of as the 'cinematic vision' – it is this that we experience in the cinema and which is central to our being in the cinema.

Yet, of course, the experience of film as it looks and creates the world is of necessity phenomenologically different to the act of human perception. Hence the problem that Frampton alluded to, namely that 'being' for film and 'being' for humans are rather different categories. In this respect, film does not make human being or thinking available to its spectators – such illumination comes only in the combined experience of the cinematic vision, not from the film *per se*. Yet it is precisely because there is a clear distinction between our human perception and a mechanical filmic perception that Merleau-Ponty suggests we find pleasure in art. For him, pleasure comes from difference, or more technically, in the space that exists between the two different types of perception. There would be little pleasure in merely finding the world replicated as it is; it would be a pointless exercise in reproduction. Instead, what matters are the ways that art can offer back to us differing versions of our world in such a manner that is rearranged so that we may see the world, and the art, differently. In order for this arrangement to have meaning it is necessary to establish the existence and the meeting of the two bodies that are implied, or indexed, through the two looks – the human and the filmic. (The question of the third body in the cinematic vision is something we will return to later.) For Merleau-Ponty what matters then is the meeting of two bodies in the act of making meaning – the human body and the film body – engaged in the act of mutual perception.

> The meaning of a film is incorporated into its rhythm just as the meaning of a gesture may immediately be read in that gesture: the film does not mean anything but itself. The idea is presented in a nascent state and emerges from the temporal structure of the film as it does from the coexistence of the parts of a painting. The joy of art lies in its showing how something takes on meaning – not by referring to already established and acquired ideas but by the temporal or spatial arrangement of elements. As we saw above, a movie has meaning in the same way that a thing does: neither of them speaks to an isolated understanding; rather, both appeal to our power tacitly to decipher the world or men and to coexist with them. It is true that in our ordinary lives we lose sight of this aesthetic value of the tiniest perceived thing. It is also true that the perceived form is never perfect in real life, that it always has blurs, smudges, and superfluous matter, as it were. Cinematographic drama is, so to speak, finer-grained than real-life dramas: it takes place in a world that is more exact than the real world. But in the last analysis perception permits us to understand the meaning of the cinema. A movie is not thought; it is perceived.
>
> (Merleau-Ponty, 1964: 57–58)

As Merleau-Ponty makes clear in the above quotation, the value of cinema lies in the way that it observes the world in exacting detail – it is phenomenological in the way it records what it sees. It might at first seem that such a forensic approach to life would be overly scientific in how it captures the details of experience. However, it turns out that it is this very detail that allows us not to think but to perceive, and hence to be. Here, a clinical example is instructive. A father described in therapy how he always read his son a bedtime story. A touching scene, until it became clear that his son hated him sitting on the bed, or even being in the bedroom. Instead, he resorted to sitting on the stairs outside the bedroom, which annoyed the other family members as in so doing he blocked the way to the bathroom. In this vignette, a happy story becomes transformed. It becomes evident that the acts of detailed reconstruction and recording change the psychological affect and meaning of the situation. It is the perceptual veracity of the film that allows the two looks of the eye and the lens to coalesce, and in so doing form the cinematic vision as reconstruction and also to record change, understanding and affect. It is the perspicacity of that vision, and not the thought of viewers, that allows us to comprehend what it is to 'be' and the result is to enter into an awareness of how we are in the world, and to gain a fuller understanding through experience of what it means to be.

The film body

There are numerous theorists who have set out to reflect on film through the use of a phenomenological framework. Among the first was Casebier with his 1991 work *Film and Phenomenology*. Other important contributions have been made by Marks (2000), Shaviro (1993) and Barker (2009). But without doubt one of the most significant theorists to have worked in this field is Vivian Sobchack with her two major interventions: *The Address of the Eye* (1992) and *Carnal Thoughts* (2004). Sobchack argues that the lived existence of film's body is a fact. Here she does not mean to suggest that films have an actual corporal, fleshy body. Nor according to her should the film-body be though of as a metaphor. Rather, the film's body is the location of the consciousness of film – it is where its sense of the world is located. This seemingly abstract way of positioning film derives from Sobchack's desire to understand how it is that something that is clearly mechanical and constructed can come to embody a particular way of seeing the world that viewers can relate to emotionally and viscerally. For her, film is an incarnation of Renaissance perspective. In this mode of representation the world is rearranged in a painting in such a way that the elements of the image coalesce around an imagined individual perspective. When transposed from painting to the cinema the result is the viewer comes to regard each film as having a purpose that is predicated on a subjective point of view. Sobchack's is an ocular-centric view of the world that places at its centre the viewer's subjectivity around which the world is re-arranged.

To momentarily divert, it is worth noting how different this is from the Jungian conception of image. Image for Jung is embodied and, importantly, it is not just something that is seen. Rather, image, or more particularly the psychological image, is felt. Jung's clearest formulation of the psychological qualities of the image is what he terms the *fantasy-image*. By this he means to refer to an image that is a psychological fantasy but one that also encapsulates our sense of a situation and what it is that we feel about it. If the ocular-centric approach to perception suggests a split between body and world, then the Jungian view of perception locates image as a site of psychological meaning that is internalised within the body and where the body expresses and encodes the psychological situation. Such meanings often have strong unconscious components and, gradually, some branches of psychotherapy are coming to see how complexes, and emotional responses to the world more generally, are encoded by and in our bodies. For example: a father complex (sic image) can become encoded in visceral felt sensations; unexpressed anger might be expressed in back pain and so forth.

This is at odds with the phenomenological position which argues that film is similar to human vision because it is both something to be looked at and it is also something that itself looks. In the act of looking, and to-be-looked-at-ness, the film is at the same time a voyeur and the object of voyeurism: through its representations it looks, while through its screen it presents itself to be looked at. Frampton puts it neatly, noting:

> For Vivian Sobchack, following on from Merleau-Ponty, film is understood to be itself a 'subject', and 'object-subject' that sees and is seen. For her film is both presentational and representational, both viewing subject and a visible object for the film-goer – film is existentially embodied (mechanical) perception.
>
> (Frampton, 2006: 41)

The claim that film is 'existentially embodied . . . perception' is something that will be returned to momentarily, though as already suggested this is difficult to reconcile with a Jungian view of the situation. Before we explore this further, it is important to be clear about what Sobchack is arguing. Her position is that film does not just present an image to be seen by the viewer. Rather, she argues that film has a purpose or intention in the way it embodies its view of the world. Just as we as viewers have bodies and look with intention, so too film presents a framed view of the world, framed by choice in a meaningful and purposeful manner. (Here we have hints of Jung's concept of the purposive qualities of the unconscious – even if Sobchack's argument has a different focus.) There is a sense in which this is self-evident. Narrative films are of course constructed and made in a particular way, with the explicit intention of conveying a particular set of meanings – the narrative of the film. However, Sobchack is getting at something rather different to this view of film as constructed narrative and narration. For her film has a type of existence outside its narrative function. It is as though the film itself, not its creators, looks with intention, as if once created the film takes on a life of its own as it views and presents the world in its particular and individual way. Sobchack terms this act of looking with purpose the 'viewing view'. To return to Frampton:

> In both seeing and expressing its seeing, film is not just a view (an image or a scene) for Sobchack, it is a 'viewing view'. The viewing view *presents* (the body-subject of vision). Film's viewing view is its meaningful choice-making gaze, and thus a new organisation of the whole, a new *mode of attention*. This viewing view thus consists in having and expressing perception: that is, film simultaneously has vision and intention, it sees objects and expresses its intention about those objects.
>
> (Frampton, 2006: 41)

However, film does not make human thinking visible to us and it is quite clear that both the perception of film and its representation of the world are different to human perception and thinking. For example, dream sequences in films do not bear much resemblance to actual dreams. Nor does the act of calling to mind a particular memory resemble a flashback in a film. However, it is of course the case that the nature of our bodies partly determines our understanding of the world. Our physical characteristics directly shape how we see the world, how we experience the world and the way we can 'be' in the world. Someone who is colour blind experiences the world differently to some who is not. So too the individual characteristics of the film body shape its representation of the world. As Sobchack points out, when filming a man running a film can either follow him, let him run past the camera, or let him run towards the camera, keeping him the same size (through the use of a telephoto lens with a narrow depth of field that compresses perspective) or as he approaches the camera letting his image grow in size, with a deep focus wide angle lens. Again, the very argument that asserts that film has body requires that same body to be rather different to our own. While Sobchack does not want such devices to be expressive, they are. Indeed, the meaning of films in no small part depends exactly on the use of such expressive devices. While it is important to be clear about the techniques of film making and the difference between say, a shot that tracks in to its subject and one that zooms in, what matters most is not the description of the technique itself but rather it is the meaning of such devices within the narrative of the film. Sobchack terms the observations of these types of filmic mechanisms and techniques the 'film's attention', the movement of a lived body. However, it is actually much more than attention – as the formal properties of cinema encode its narrative and emotional intentions. It is not entirely clear why Sobchack wants to restrict the movement of film to the film's attention. It seems to be an attempt to see the film-body as without agency in the way it acts as viewer and viewed. Yet to assert that looking is meaning making, would actually in some ways strengthen her argument, namely that film possesses a consciousness – a particular type of consciousness to be sure, but a consciousness nonetheless.

What is still more problematic from the phenomenological position that Sobchack adopts is the very idea of a film-body itself, regardless of whatever its attributes and qualities might turn out to possess. Her idea is an anthropomorphic one in which our human qualities are projected onto something that is quite clearly not human. It is, if you will, a fantasy that we can animate the material world in ways that reflect our subjectivity. It raises some thorny questions: If film does indeed have a body, then where exactly is this body? If that body possesses a consciousness then what is the nature of the consciousness that film is supposed to have? Further, what is it possible to know about such a consciousness? The issue is that conceptualising film as body separates it from the filmic world, as the filmic body is to some extent situated outside the world of the film – in much the same way that the viewer is positioned outside the film. However, this is a problem as phenomenologically the film is its world and it cannot somehow be separated from it. As we have our own unique way of being in the world, mediated through the experience of our senses, so too film is situated in its own mediated view of the world. We cannot be in the world in any other way, and nor can film.

Another interesting aspect to Sobchack's argument is the way that she sees film as having an existence outside the perception of the viewer and this is something she refers to as 'other'. That film is constituted independently of the viewer is in one sense obvious. Films exist as digital data streams, as DVDs, as rolls of celluloid, as collections of still images and so forth. The materiality of film, irrespective of whether it is electronic or optical, is not what is at stake here. What is important is establishing if film constitutes a subject within its own terms and also where its meaning exists independently of the viewer. To put this another way: can film be the subject of its own vision? Certainly from Sobchack's position it can. Film embodies a set of cultural representations that are encoded within the film itself. Questions of *mise-en-scène*, representation, narrative theme, i.e. the formation of the look and the subject of the look, strongly suggest a certain type of identity for a film. Lens quality, film stocks, lighting techniques, digital enhancements and so forth all evidence how the apparatus of cinema constitutes a certain sense of identity One only has to look at a Technicolor film of the 1950s to see how its materiality is historically located – the film's body belongs to another era.

To amplify the point, currently film studies is particularly concerned with uncovering the production of both individual films and groups of films. This is of course an interesting undertaking that provides great opportunities for scholarship and the enhancement of the academic project. To be clear, the current argument is not intended to undercut or critique such an enterprise but equally the historical project is one that is markedly and significantly different to both phenomenological enquiry and Jungian psychology where the focus of attention is not on creation but on the volatile and ever-changing qualities of the site of reception. In this sense the historically orientated undertaking will only ever be partial and limited. It is a reductive approach. Just as psychoanalysis encouraged a return to the repressed life of childhood as a means to better understand adult life, so too historical materialist approaches refuse to let films grow up. Instead what comes to dominate is the site and context of production – the conception and birth of the film, if you will. The historical process involves a stripping back of our current ideological perspective as a means to understand more fully what has been hidden in the film. Much as Freud made a distinction between the manifest and latent content of a dream so too these historical undertakings peel away the audio-visual surface of films to uncover their latent cultural meanings. As such, the undertaking is both materialist and ideological. But it also robs film of its own bodily subjectivity as it attempts to attribute to film a series of somewhat fixed and stable meanings. However, as we are coming to see, film as a body changes – there is a way in which it matures and grows old. What seemed fresh and exciting at the time of its creation comes with the passage of time to seem either tired and clichéd or warmly nostalgic and comforting. Both the film itself and its viewers are no longer the same. The black and white movie from the 1940s we watch on a Sunday afternoon is different to that same movie as it was originally released.

The preceding illustration serves to mount a critique both on Sobchack and also on the historical approach as the example demonstrates how it is that is that film comes into being only when watched. The implication is that each time a movie is watched, a different film comes into being. The meaning of a film is composed of more than just its narrative, as it also needs all that the viewer can bring to that narrative. Film needs the consciousness and unconscious of the viewer in order for it to have meaning. Meaning, in this sense, is constantly negotiated between viewer and film, and it arises from, and in, a state of interplay between conscious forces and unconscious expectations. Established film theory has touched on this area, though here we are going considerably further in destabilising inscribed narrative meanings and asserting the primacy of the viewer–film relationship as the container which holds the meaning of the 'cinematic vision'. For example, as explored in a previous chapter, genre films are predicated on the previous film-going experiences of their viewers and, as we will see, this also holds good, albeit in a more general psychological sense, for other films too.

> Film is its own reality, its own world, and the *attention* of any possible, conceptual film-being, must be theorised as being part of that world, not separate and observational. We are subjective beings, but film seems more fluid in its place of intent.
>
> (Frampton, 2006: 46)

Film does not mirror or replicate our human perception of the world in its own mechanical and audio-visual terms. Actually, film exceeds the human. In some regards at least it is super-human in the ways that it can do so much more than we can – we cannot zoom, shift our depth of field, have a split screen. Film can do that, with ease, and so much more. Yet at the same time, and this is what Sobchack is rightly driving at, in its cinematic devices film reveals how it sees the world. It does not replicate how we see the world. Rather, to use a visual metaphor, film exposes itself. It is in this lack of concealment, in this act of overexposure, that film provides viewers with the basis on which to reflect on their own experiences of the world. Films have no option as to what they reveal about themselves – it is there on the screen to for us to make of what we will. By contrast, as humans we constantly 'screen' the extent to which we reveal ourselves in the world. If the world is a surface onto which we project ourselves, then we regularly consider the degree to which we want to make ourselves public. Of course, the unconscious part of ourselves adjusts, shifts and compensates for our conscious decisions. But here it is clearly evident that the human body and the film body behave in quite different ways, for a central part of our human somatic existence involves the enactment of unconscious processes and fantasies.

From a depth psychological perspective, the person who is not at the whim of unconscious processes has become a robot – they have, as it were, become a film of their own lives in which they live out an overly rational fantasy about human existence. Film is different as it is a mechanistic and rationalistic fantasy, and it needs to be so if its voice is to be heard in the post-modern condition. It is a dialogue that talks to where we are right now. It meets us at the point at which we experience our own being, as prescribed by the conditions of post-modernity and post-modernist culture. Yet film somehow is also more than that and to understand why this is the case it is necessary to add to a phenomenological understanding a psychological point of view to clarify why it is that the designation of 'image' implies much more than the physical image.

Psychologically, while it is quite possible for us to empathise with a view of the world because it is similar to our own, it is also the case that we have intense emotional reactions to views of the world because they are different to our own. It is not difficult to think of people we might dislike because we believe them to be different to ourselves, or because they are actually rather like a part of ourselves that we dislike – which admittedly is a slightly different type of difference, but it remains a difference nonetheless. In Jungian psychology, such reactions take the form of psychological images – these are the fantasy-images that were explored earlier in this section, which, as noted, are thought, felt, and embodied and laden with affect. While not necessarily actual images, they represent an image that contains the psychological reality of the situation. It follows that the emotional and psychological meanings of images do not require something to be similar to us. Instead, images require that the context provide sufficient familiarity for us to recognise the image as a depiction of our world. The unconscious structures and beliefs that we hold about others, and about ourselves, will fill in the representational gaps in often surprisingly inaccurate ways. Curiously, it is actually these inaccuracies that can reveal a great deal about the psychological reality of what is happening when we watch a film. Put another way, 'misreading' a film has the potential to be psychologically more instructive than accurately understanding its narrative.

It is not necessary to see a film as constituting, and constituted of, a body as we can find meaning in a view of the world that does not in and of itself consider itself to be either viewer or viewed. It is hard to see how abstract art demonstrates an awareness of a body, for example. It does not offer a changing view of the world as its gaze moves around its landscape. Yet, such art is quite capable of evoking strong psychological and emotional reactions. An image does not need to be representational for us to relate to it – what we do need is our expectation that the image in some way pertains to our world, and that it provides a type of commentary on it. Film does not need to have a 'body' – material or otherwise, in order for it to communicate to us psychologically.

The third image

Notwithstanding the above commentary, it is still possible to adopt a broadly phenomenological stance towards the viewing of films. To do so requires shifting the critical attention away from the construction of the film itself towards the reception of films by their viewers. To help in this investigation a Jungian understanding of the psyche can usefully be supplemented with some insights derived from phenomenology.

The Jungian model of the psyche is predicated on the assumption that there are large tracts of the psyche of which we are unaware. Despite this lack of awareness the unconscious part of the psyche still effects and affects our daily lives. As we come to understand these subterranean forces we become increasingly conscious of them and in due course our intellect is increasingly able to comprehend what it is that is happening for us. However, in the Jungian version of the psyche it is important to move past this point of intellectual comprehension because a thinking and solely conscious understanding of our ourselves can only be partial. In its place what comes to matter is an awareness of our felt self in relationship in the world. As we saw in the discussion about Merleau-Ponty and cinema, consciousness is an awareness of how we are in the world and it is composed of much more than thinking. It is these insights concerning the depth of the psyche and the limitations of thinking as means to psychological understanding that underpin a Jungian conception of image and specifically the fantasy-image.

In order to explicate the Jungian understanding of image Hockley (2014) devised a tripartite structure of the psychological image in the cinematic experience – the first image, the second image and the third image. This was an attempt to reconcile a Jungian view of image with a phenomenological account of the viewing experience. This is not without its problems because, as already noted, phenomenology does not see the need for any form of unconscious structuring agency. In its place phenomenology uses a more straightforward construction of what there is in experience, and what we are either aware of or unaware of. Yet the idea of an unconscious with purpose and intent is a pillar of Jungian psychology.

Why then bring these two rather different theories together in the first place? The strength of phenomenology in this context rests in its focus on the experience of watching a film. The emphasis is not on the narrative of the film itself, though of course that does play a role, but is instead on the reception of the film. This is significant as one of the curious aspects about watching a film is the very different response that two people can have to the same film and it is commonplace for people to watch a film together and to have opposing views about it. A possible explanation is that one person might be more insightful or knowledgeable about films and has therefore seen something, good or bad, that has been missed by the other viewer. But what if both viewers are equally knowledgeable and still their views are polarised? In such a situation there is the possibility that the film itself has triggered something personal in one of the viewers – for example, someone who has just been in a car accident might well react negatively to such scenes in a film which would be less troubling to the other viewer. This takes us to the nub of the issue.

It is highly probable that our individual life experiences and our personal psychology interact with films in ways that are deeply unconscious – i.e. finding psychological meanings is a purposive activity – the function of the cinematic vision is to open up previously repressed areas of experience with a view to engaging in psychological insight and growth. In so doing we create and negotiate meanings with films that reflect our individual qualities. Many of these will be unconscious, and we might well find ourselves reacting to films in ways that we had not expected and also in ways that are unlooked for and which seem quite puzzling to us. Wherever there is a strong outpouring of affect, and whenever a film evokes a strong emotional reaction, that provides the cue to look for unconscious processes. If we find a film boring, distasteful, excessive, dull, the most amazing film we have ever seen, hilarious, deeply sad, then all these are pointers for us to take time to reflect on what might be going on underneath these emotions. It is possible that such reactions might be an appropriate and proportionate response to the narrative of the film. But it is also possible for our emotional responses to be overwhelming and out of control and for them to invade our consciousness, even when the intellectual and thinking part of ourselves knows that such responses are disproportionate.

Here then we have the conditions for deploying a Jungian phenomenological approach to understanding the personal meanings that a particular film might hold for us: we are deeply attached to the film in ways that cannot be explained by our rational mind alone; when thinking is not enough and when our feelings seem to evade our control. It is then that it is likely that we have been experiencing something that has deep psychological qualities. This is an experience of the fantasy-image, with its personal and archetypal aspect that cinema evokes. To draw on Don Fredericksen's (1979) terminology, this is to experience the liminal both in the cinematic experience itself and also in our own psyche – indeed, in an experience of the fantasy-image the cinematic and the psyche are inextricable.

In the tripartite taxonomy of the image the three categories that are proposed are in turn derived from the idea of the intersubjective field. According to psychodynamic theory the intersubjective field is something that constellates between client and therapist in the consulting room. The field consists of an 'image' that is co-created and 'felt' to exist in the space between client and therapist. The image encapsulates what is happening for the client and is brought into being as a result of the therapeutic relationship – as such it approximates to the fantasy-image. It therefore is not really descriptive at all but instead it contains an interpretative quality as it provides a type of poetic commentary, or insight, into the client's interior world. The suggestion is that something similar happens in the cinematic experience, particularly when viewers experience strong emotional responses that are unexpected and not proportionate to the narrative of the film itself. The three images I identify can be either treated separately or, as is more likely, seen as operating at the same time, perhaps with different degrees of emphasis – it is as though the viewer looks through these images to the cinema screen but the intensity varies as the relative strength of each image changes.

The first image is the most straightforward and is concerned with the image on screen itself. This is the most conscious of the three images, and here intellect and aesthetic sensibility are of the utmost help in coming to understand the effectiveness of how a film communicates. Focusing on this image, the viewer's understanding of the film comes from a detailed reading of its images, both visual and aural. This is appreciating the film at the level of description. Noting, for example, such elements as the effectiveness of the lighting, camerawork, *mise-en-scène*, acting and so forth. In so doing, an aesthetic orientation to the film is cultivated in which it becomes possible to become aware of what might otherwise go unnoticed in the technical and artistic rendering of the film's narrative.

The second image involves the activity of seeking to interpret and understand films. While this is largely a conscious activity it also has a substantial unconscious component. The activity of interpretation is both intellectual and intuitive in as much as it incorporates an aesthetic sensibility. It follows that the interpretation of a film is something that requires the activity of both consciousness and the unconscious. Here, the viewer engages with the film conceptually yet is also sensitive to what it is that is being felt when the film is being watched. In so doing an understanding of the film is formed concerning its narrative and the way meaning is encoded in its structure – shooting, editing, lighting etc. The object of understanding is the film and the approach is one of conscious hermeneutic activity that deconstructs the film's diegetic and representational aspects. This constitutes the second image as it is the image that we create in our mind of what the film is about, of what the film is trying to explore and how we understand it. Here we draw on our own subjectivity, our intuitive capacity and our ability to empathise with the on-screen characters to help in understanding the film. In the creation of the second image we pay particular attention to use of formal narrative devices such as metaphor, symbol and allegory in the film. We interpret the meaning behind the editing, the framing and lighting etc. For example we might notice how music in the film reinforces the emotions of the scene, or subverts them, or how it alludes to emotions and characters other than those on the screen, to other genres or how it makes extra-textual references.

This brings us to the third image, but first a note of caution. It would be a mistake to see these three images in a hierarchical relationship as each image has an important role to play in appreciating and understanding the psychology of the cinematic experience, as each image needs the other. For example, without an appreciation of description it is hard to unpick what is happening in an experience of the third image, or in some particular, partial and personal interpretation based on the second image. Equally, a second image interpretation might point the way to something that is latent in the interpretation that has within it a more unconscious aspect. The metaphor of the three images makes it possible to shift register between the aesthetic, the interpretive and the experiential while allowing for the simultaneous experience of all three. In some ways the idea of a third image might seem like a curious one, but the proposition is that the psychological meaning of an image lies not in its denotative qualities but arises from the interaction between an individual psyche and the image itself. It is, if you will, a type of psychological connotation that grows from the original image. To explain this idea it is helpful to draw on a piece of psychotherapy thinking that is concerned with the clinical setting, namely transference and countertransference.

There is a vast clinical literature on this complicated subject. In its simplest form transference involves the transferring of the client's previous feelings and beliefs onto the figure of the therapist. It is as though the therapist comes to stand for someone significant from an earlier period in the client's life – typically, though not always, a parental figure. In one sense, this is a fairly unproblematic idea and it is quite possible to see how such a situation might arise. However, the theory goes a couple of steps further in suggesting that the emotions that related to the previous relationship are transferred onto and into the therapist. The work of the therapist is to attend to these feelings and to offer them back to the client in a meaningful form. What is odd about this is that while it is a cornerstone of psychodynamic work, very little is known about how such feelings leave the client and find their way into the therapist. Putting this problem to one side for the moment, it is clearly important that the therapist is able to distinguish between his or her feelings and those that belong to the client.

When some personal psychological disturbance happens to the therapist as a result of the client's material this is termed 'countertransference'.

When client and therapist are working particularly well, or to use a more psychodynamic language, when they are attuned, there can be a strong sense that the meaning of what the client is talking about, as mutually understood, constellates as a fantasy-image in the space between client and therapist. It is as though something momentarily comes to fill the inter-subjective space. These images are hard to understand, momentary and yet palpable too – they seem to encapsulate a shared understanding through a powerful, affect-laden bond.

The suggestion is that something similar can also happen in the cinema. To transpose the clinical setting to the cinema, the inter-subjective space is now the distance between the screen and the viewer and the third image comes to fill this gap. If this is so it would give one explanation of those moments when we find ourselves powerfully moved by a film, without knowing why. Such an understanding gives a different perspective on why it is that one person can be obsessed by a movie while it leaves others cold – at an unconscious level the viewer and the film become attuned. The contention is that personal psychological relationships with films are much more significant and prevalent than is often recognised.

It might seem that the third image is analogous to the process of suture, in which the unconscious of the viewer is stitched into the diegetic reality of the film. However, that is not the case, as the viewer forms an individual relationship with the film that might or might not have much to do with the actual narrative or technical construction of the film. This is not a process of being stitched into an imaginary world, rather the third image involves the creation of a new and personalised understanding of the film. In this way, phenomenologically, no two people have the same relationship or understanding of a film, and every screening of film is a fresh and potentially revelatory experience. It is important to also remember that in this taxonomy the three images work in consort with each other. Additionally, it is also worth underscoring such personal relationships and experiences of the third image do not alter the actual narrative meaning of the film, which belongs, primarily, in the first and second images. What the third image helps to explain are those powerful emotional reactions we can have to films, which appear to be a complete mystery to others.

In summary, Jung's conception of the psychological or fantasy-image is instructive in demonstrating how it is possible to adopt a fresh approach to understanding the cinematic experience. When the look of the eye and look of the camera are combined in the cinematic vision, it opens up the sense of difference and space between the two looks. Put another way, a new meaning arises from the space between viewer and screen – a meaning that is not predicated on similarity and representation but on difference and personal experience. Here, the personal meanings that arise from watching a film are quite often related to psychological difference – we are moved by seeing a life on screen that is quite unlike our own. Sometimes it offers a vision of a better and more contented life, while at other times there is relief and solace is being grateful that our life is not as tragic as the one being shown. However, more pertinent are those unlooked for and unexpected outpourings of affect that suggest the existence of some forgotten trauma or psychological complex that has been bought back to life through the passage of a film's images and sounds.

Both the phenomenological perspective and the Jungian regard meaning as a complicated process in which relationship is central. While the phenomenological position as outlined and explored particularly by Sobchack, but also others, remains interesting, it nonetheless possesses a level of complexity that seems to add little to aid in understanding what it is that happens when we watch films. Instead, the much more straightforward taxonomy of the first, second and third image suggests a different way to understand the emotional and psychological aspects of the cinematic experience. In particular it is third image moments that provide a useful example of just what Jung had in mind when he described how images encapsulate a fantasy that expresses the psychological reality of an individual's situation. The unconscious finds in films a way to express itself and in so doing to find individualised meanings with the collective commercial products that are fiction films. Adopting such an approach allows viewers and film theorists alike to attend to their emotional reactions to films with a degree of fidelity and veracity that is not offered by other approaches. In seeing how the two looks of cinema constellate unconscious psychological meanings we allow ourselves to find profound psychological meanings in the seemingly mundane activity of watching a film – we only need to watch with care and attention, and to watch closely, to see what we have never seen before – that psychologically the film lives in us, as much as we in it.

Bibliography

Altman, Rick (1984) 'A Semantic/Syntactic Approach to Genre', *The Cinema Journal*, 23, 3 (Spring): 6–18.

Altman, Rick (1999) *Film/Genre*, London: British Film Institute.

Apperson, Virginia and Beebe, John (2008) *The Presence of the Feminine in Film*, Newcastle upon Tyne, UK: Cambridge Scholars Publishing.

Ashton, Paul and Bloch, Stephen (eds) (2010) *Music and Psyche: Contemporary Psychoanalytic Explorations*, New Orleans, LA: Spring Journal Books.

Babcock-Abrahams, B. (1975) 'A Tolerated Margin of the Mess: The Trickster and His Tales Reconsidered', *Journal of the Folklore Institute*, 11: 147–186.

Barker, Jennifer (2009) *The Tactile Eye: Touch and the Cinematic Experience*, Berkeley, CA: University of California Press.

Barthes, Roland (1977) *Image, Music, Text*, trans. S. Heath, London: Fontana.

Bassil-Morozow, Helena (2010) *Tim Burton: The Monster and the Crowd*, London: Routledge.

Bassil-Morozow, Helena (2012) *The Trickster in Contemporary Film*, Hove, UK: Routledge.

Bassil-Morozow, Helena (2014) *The Trickster and the System: Identity and Agency in Contemporary Society*, Hove, UK: Routledge.

Bateson, Gregory (1936) *Naven: A Survey of the Problems Suggested by a Composite Picture of the Culture of a New Guinea Tribe Drawn from Three Points of View*, Chicago, IL: Stanford University Press.

Baudrillard, Jean (1968; 2005) *The System of Objects*, London and New York: Verso.

Baudrillard, Jean (1981; 2000) *Simulacra and Simulation*, London: Routledge.

Baudry, Jean-Louis (1986) 'Ideological Effects of the Basic Cinematographic Apparatus', in P. Rosen (ed.), *Narrative, Apparatus, Ideology: A Film Theory Reader*, New York: Columbia University Press, pp. 286–299.

Baumlin, James S., Baumlin, Tita French and Jensen, George H. (2004) *Post-Jungian Criticism: Theory and Practice*, New York: State University of New York Press.

Beebe, John (2011) '*The Wizard of Oz*: A Vision of Development in the American Political Psyche', in Christopher Hauke and Luke Hockley (eds), *Jung and Film II: The Return*, Hove UK: Routledge, pp. 302–327.

Berger, John (1977) *Ways of Seeing*, Harmondsworth, UK: Penguin.

Berry, Sarah (1999) 'Genre', in Toby Miller and Robert Stam (eds), *A Companion to Film Theory*, London: Blackwell, pp. 25–44.

Bishop, Paul (2009) *Analytical Psychology and German Classical Aesthetics: Goethe, Schiller and Jung*, Hove, UK: Routledge.

Bordwell, David and Thompson, Kristen (2003) *Film Art: An Introduction*, New York: McGraw-Hill.

Botting, Fred (1995; 2013) *Gothic*, Hove, UK: Routledge.

Bourdieu, Pierre (1977; 2002) *Outline of a Theory of Practice*, London: Cambridge University Press.

Bourdieu, Pierre (1992; 2003) *The Logic of Practice*, Cambridge, UK: Polity Press.

Branson, Clark (1987) *Howard Hawks: A Jungian Study*, Santa Barbara, CA: Capra Press.

Bravin, Jess (2015) 'George Miller Returns to His Personal Wasteland in "Mad Max: Fury Road"', *Wall Street Journal Blog*, http://blogs.wsj.com/speakeasy/2015/05/14/george-miller-returns-to-his-personal-wasteland-in-mad-max-fury-road/ [accessed May 2015].

Brook, Heather (2015) 'Engaging Marriage: Rom Coms and Fairy Tale Endings', in Luke Hockley and Nadi Fadina (eds), *The Happiness Illusion: How the Media Sold Us a Fairytale*, Hove, UK: Routledge, pp. 145–161.

Buscombe, Edward (1977) 'The Idea of Genre in American Cinema', in Barry Grant (ed.), *Film Genre: Theory and Criticism*, Metuchen, NJ: Scarecrow Press, pp. 24–38.

Campbell, Joseph (1959) *The Masks of Gods: Primitive Mythology*, New York: Viking.

Campbell, Joseph (1968; 2008) *The Hero with a Thousand Faces*, Novato, CA: New World Library.

Carter, Angela (1995; 2012) *The Bloody Chamber and Other Stories*, London: Random House.

Carter, Matthew (2014) *Myth of the Western: New Perspectives on Hollywood's Frontier Narrative*, Edinburgh, UK: Edinburgh University Press.

Casebier, Allan (1991) *Film and Phenomenology*, Cambridge, UK: Cambridge University Press.

Caughie, John (ed.) (1981) *Theories of Authorship: A Reader*, London: British Film Institute.

Cawelti, John (1999) *The Six Gun Mystique Sequel*, Bowling Green, OH: Popular Press.

Chapman, Brenda (2012) 'Stand up for Yourself, and Mentor Others', *The New York Times*, 14 August, http://www.nytimes.com/roomfordebate/2012/08/14/how-can-women-gain-influence-in-hollywood/stand-up-for-yourself-and-mentor-others [accessed October 2016].

Chopra-Grant, Mike (2006) *Hollywood Genres and Postwar America: Masculinity, Family and Nation in Popular Movies and Film Noir*, London: I. B. Tauris.

Copjec, Joan (1988) '*India Song/Son Nom de Venise dans Calcutta Desert*: The Compulsion to Repeat', in Constance Penley (ed.), *Feminism and Film Theory*, London and New York: BFI and Routledge, pp. 229–243.

Davies, Oliver (2004) 'Theorizing Writerly Creativity: Jung with Lacan?', in James S. Baumlin, Tita French Baumlin and George H. Jensen (eds), *Post-Jungian Criticism: Theory and Practice*, New York: State University of New York Press, pp. 55–75.

Deleuze, Gilles (2005) *Cinema 2*, London: Continuum.

Deleuze, Gilles and Guattari, Felix (1984) *Anti-Oedipus*, London: Continuum.

Doane, Mary Ann (1988) 'Woman's Stake: Filming the Female Body', in Constance Penley (ed.), *Feminism and Film Theory*, London and New York: BFI and Routledge, pp. 216–228.

Dorje, Rinjing (1997) *Tales of Uncle Tompa*, Barrytown, NY: Station Hill Arts.

Doty, W. (1993) 'A Lifetime of Trouble-Making: Hermes as a Trickster', in W. J. Hynes and W. Doty (eds), *Mythical Trickster Figures: Contours, Contexts and Criticisms*, Tuscaloosa, AL and London: University of Alabama Press, pp. 46–65.

Eagleton, Terry (1996; 1997) *The Illusions of Postmodernism*, Oxford, UK: Blackwell.
Eagleton, Terry (2003) *After Theory*, London: Allen Lane and Penguin.
Easterling, P. E and Hall, Edith (2002) *Greek and Roman Actors: Aspects of the Ancient Profession*, Cambridge, UK: Cambridge University Press.
Ellis, Jack (2000) *John Grierson: Life, Contributions, Influence*, Carbondale and Edwardsville, IL: Southern Illinois University Press.
Fellini, Frederick (2007) *The Book of Dreams*, Milan: RCS, Libri Spa.
Fireman, G., McVay, T., Flanagan, O. and Duke, J. (2003) *Narrative and Consciousness: Literature, Psychology and the Brain*, Oxford, UK: Oxford University Press.
Foley, Malcolm and O'Donnell, Hugh (eds) (2009) *Treat or Trick?: Halloween in a Globalising World*, Cambridge, UK: Cambridge Scholars Publishing.
Frampton, Daniel (2006) *Filmosophy*, New York: Columbia University Press.
Fredericksen, Don (1979) 'Jung/Sign/Symbol/Film, Part One', *Quarterly Review of Film Studies*, 4, 2: 167–192.
Fredericksen, Don (1980) 'Jung/Sign/Symbol/Film, Part Two', *Quarterly Review of Film Studies*, 5, 4: 459–479.
Fredericksen, Don (2001) 'Jung/Sign/Symbol/Film', in Ian Alister and Christopher Hauke (eds), *Jung and Film: Post-Jungian Takes on the Moving Image*, London: Routledge, pp. 17–55. [Originally published as two essays in the *Quarterly Review of Film Studies* (1979, 1980).]
Fredericksen, Don (2005; 2012) *Bergman's Persona*, Poznan, Poland: Wydawnictwo Naukowe UAM.
Fredericksen, Don (2011) 'Jungian Film Studies: The Corruption of Consciousness and the Nurturing of Psychological Life', in Christopher Hauke and Luke Hockley (eds), *Jung and Film II: The Return*, Hove UK: Routledge, pp. 99–108.
Freud, Sigmund (1960; 2001) 'On Narcissism: An Introduction', in J. Strachey (ed. and trans.), *The Standard Edition of the Complete Psychological Works of Sigmund Freud*, Vol. 14, London: Vintage, pp. 67–102.
Freud, Sigmund (1960; 2001) 'Leonardo da Vinci and a Memory of His Childhood', in J. Strachey (ed. and trans.), *The Standard Edition of the Complete Psychological Works of Sigmund Freud*, Vol. 11, London: Vintage, pp. 59–139.
Freud, Sigmund (1976) *The Interpretation of Dreams*, The Pelican Freud Library, Vol. 4, Harmondsworth: Penguin Books.
Fuchs, Thomas (2012) 'Body Memory and the Unconscious', in D. Lohmar and J. Brudzińska (eds), *Founding Psychoanalysis Phenomenologically: Phenomenological Theory of Subjectivity and the Psychoanalytic Experience*, London: Springer, pp. 69–82.
Gane, Mike (1993) *Baudrillard Live: Selected Interviews*, London: Routledge.
Gardner, Leslie and Hockley, Luke (2011) *House: The Wounded Healer on Television*, London: Routledge.
Geertz, Clifford (1964) 'Ideology as a Cultural System', in D. Apter (ed.), *Ideology and Discontent*, New York: The Free Press of Glencoe, pp. 47–76.
Geertz, Clifford (1973) *The Interpretation of Cultures*, London: Hutchinson.
Genette, Gérard (1982) *Palimpsestes: La Littérature au second degré*, Paris: Seuil.
Gilbert, Gerard (2011) '*The Killing*: When Celibacy and Sleuthing Make for a Fatal Attraction', *The Independent*, 23 November.
Grant, Barry (ed.) (1986) *Film Genre Reader*, Austin, TX: University of Texas Press.
Hauke, Christopher (2000) *Jung and the Postmodern: The Interpretation of Realities*, London and Philadelphia, PA: Routledge.

Hauke, Christopher (2001) '"Let's Go Back to Finding Out Who We Are": Men, *Unheimlich* and Returning Home in the Films of Steven Spielberg', in Christopher Hauke and Ian Alister (eds), *Jung and Film: Post-Jungian Takes on the Moving Image*, Hove, UK: Brunner-Routledge, pp. 151–174.

Hauke, Christopher (2005) *Human Being Human: Culture and the Soul*, Hove, UK: Routledge.

Hauke, Christopher (2014) *Visible Mind: Movies, Modernity and the Unconscious*, Hove, UK: Routledge.

Hauke, Christopher and Alister, Ian (eds) (2001) *Jung and Film: Post-Jungian Takes on the Moving Image*, Hove, UK: Brunner-Routledge.

Hauke, Christopher and Hockley, Luke (eds) (2011) *Jung and Film II: The Return*, Hove UK: Routledge.

Hillman, James (1975; 1992) *Re-Visioning Psychology*, New York: Harper Perennial.

Hillman, James (1990a) 'Imaginal Practice: Greeting the Angel', in *The Essential James Hillman: A Blue Fire*, Hove, UK: Brunner-Routledge, pp. 50–69.

Hillman, James (1990b) 'Therapy: Fictions and Epiphanies', in *The Essential James Hillman: A Blue Fire*, Hove, UK: Brunner-Routledge, pp. 71–92.

Hillman, James (1998) *The Myth of Analysis: Three Essays in Archetypal Psychology*, Evanston, IL: Northwestern University Press.

Hockley, Luke (2001a) '*Film Noir*: Archetypes or Stereotypes', in Christopher Hauke and Ian Alister (eds), *Jung and Film: Post-Jungian Takes on the Moving Image*, Hove, UK: Brunner-Routledge, pp. 177–193.

Hockley, Luke (2001b) *Cinematic Projections: The Analytical Psychology of C. G. Jung and Film Theory*, London: University of Luton Press.

Hockley, Luke (2007) *Frames of Mind: A Post-Jungian Look at Cinema, Television and Technology*, Bristol, UK and Chicago, IL: Intellect.

Hockley, Luke (2014) *Somatic Cinema: The Relationship between the Body and Screen*, Hove, UK: Routledge.

Hockley, Luke and Fadina, Nadi (eds) (2015) *The Happiness Illusion: How the Media Sold Us a Fairytale*, Hove, UK: Routledge.

Homer, Sean (2004) *Jacques Lacan*, Hove, UK: Routledge.

Izod, John (1992) *The Films of Nicolas Roeg: Myth and Mind*, London: Palgrave Macmillan.

Izod, John (2001) *Myth, Mind and the Screen: Understanding the Heroes of Our Time*, Cambridge, UK: Cambridge University Press.

Izod, John (2006) *Screen, Culture, Psyche: A Post-Jungian Approach to Working with the Audience*, Hove, UK: Routledge.

Izod, John and Dovalis, Joanna (2015) *Cinema as Therapy: Grief and Transformational Film*, London: Routledge.

Jacobi, Jolande (1942; 1973) *The Psychology of C. G. Jung*, 8th edition, trans. Ralph Manheim, New Haven, CT and London: Yale University Press.

Jacobi, Jolande (ed.) (1953) *Psychological Reflections: An Anthology of the Writings of C. G. Jung*, London: Routledge and Kegan Paul.

Jacobi, Jolande (1964) 'Symbols in an Individual Analysis', in Carl Gustav Jung and Marie-Louise von Franz (eds), *Man and His Symbols*, London: Picador, pp. 323–374.

Jacoby, Mario (1994; 1996) *Shame and the Origins of Self-Esteem*, London: Routledge.

Jacoby, Mario (2010) *Individuation and Narcissism*, Hove, UK: Routledge.

Jameson, Frederic (2009) *The Cultural Turn: Selected Writings on the Postmodern, 1983–1998*, London: Verso.

Jung, Carl Gustav (1963; 1995) *Memories, Dreams, Reflections*, London: Fontana.

Jung, Carl Gustav and von Franz, M.-L. (eds) (1964; 1978) *Man and His Symbols*, London: Picador.

Kerényi, Karl (1956; 1972) 'The Trickster in Relation to Greek Mythology', in Paul Radin, *The Trickster: A Study in American Indian Mythology*, New York: Schocken Books, pp. 171–192.

Kitses, J. (2007) *Horizons West: The Western from John Ford to Clint Eastwood*, London: British Film Institute.

Kitses, Jim and Rickman, Gregg (1998) *The Western Reader*, New York: Limelight Editions.

Lacan, Jacques (1977) *Écrits: A Selection*, trans. Alan Sheridan, London: Routledge.

Lacan, Jacques (1998) *The Seminar of Jacques Lacan. Book XX: On Feminine Sexuality: The Limits of Love and Knowledge*, New York: W. W. Norton and Company.

Laplanche, Jean and Pontalis, Jean-Bertrand (1988) *The Language of Psychoanalysis*, London: Karnac Books.

Latham, Michaela, 'Quentin Tarantino. *Kill Bill: Volume 1.* Interview', *BBC Website*, 6 October 2003.

Llewellyn Smith, Julia (2014) 'Michael Bond: "I Was Worried That I'd Let Paddington down. . ."', *The Telegraph*, 23 November.

Luciano, Patrik (1987) *Them or Us: Archetypal Interpretation of Fifties Alien Invasion Films*, Bloomington, IN: Indiana University Press.

McArthur, Colin (1992) *The Casablanca File*, London: John Libbey.

McWhirter, Andrew (2014) 'Film Review: *The Matrix*', *International Journal of Jungian Studies*, 6, 3: 268–274.

Marks, Laura (2000) *The Skin of Film: Intercultural Cinema, Embodiment and the Senses*, Durham, NC and London: Duke University Press.

Merleau-Ponty, Maurice (1964) 'The Film and the New Psychology', in *Sense and Non-Sense*, trans. H. L. Dreyfus and P. A. Dreyfus, Evanston, IL: Northwestern University Press, pp. 48–60.

Metz, Christian (1974) *Film Language: A Semiotics of the Cinema*, New York: Oxford University Press.

Metz, Christian (1977; 1982) *The Imaginary Signifier: Psychoanalysis and Cinema*, Bloomington, IN: Indiana University Press.

Miller, Catriona (2009) 'Dracula Was a Woman', in Hugh O'Donnell and Malcolm Foley (eds), *Treat or Trick?: Halloween in a Globalising World*, Cambridge, UK: Cambridge Scholars Publishing, pp. 227–237.

Miller, Catriona (2011a) '"I Feel Like a Failure": In-House Feminism', in Leslie Gardner and Luke Hockley (eds), *House: The Wounded Healer on Television*, London: Routledge, pp. 188–203.

Miller, Catriona (2011b) '*Twilight*: Discourse Theory and Jung', in Christopher Hauke and Luke Hockley (eds), *Jung and Film II: The Return*, London: Routledge, 185–205.

Miller, Toby and Stam, Robert (1999) *A Companion to Film Theory*, London: Blackwell.

Moore, Thomas (ed.) (1990) *The Essential James Hillman: A Blue Fire*, Hove, UK: Brunner-Routledge.

Morris, Colin (1972; 2004) *The Discovery of the Individual*, Toronto, ON and London: University of Toronto Press.

Mulvey, Laura (1975) 'Visual Pleasure and Narrative Cinema', *Screen*, 16, 3 (Autumn): 6–18.

Mulvey, Laura (1995) 'The Myth of Pandora: A Psychoanalytic Approach', in Laura Pietropaolo and Ada Testaferri (eds), *Feminisms in the Cinema*, Bloomington and Indianapolis, IN: Indiana University Press, pp. 3–19.

Mulvey, Laura (2013) 'Visual Pleasure and Narrative Cinema', in Constance Penley (ed.), *Feminism and Film Theory*, London and New York: BFI and Routledge, pp. 57–68.

Murdock, Maureen (1990; 2013) *The Heroine's Journey: Woman's Quest for Wholeness*, Boston, MA: Shambhala.

Nagari, Benjamin (2016) *Music as Image: Analytical Psychology and Music in Film*, Hove, UK: Routledge.

Neale, Steve (1990) 'Questions of Genre', *Screen*, 31, 1: 45–66.

Neumann, Erich (1949; 1969) *Depth Psychology and a New Ethics*, trans. Eugene Rolfe, London: Hodder & Stoughton.

Neumann, Erich (1949; 1989) *The Origins and History of Consciousness*, London: Karnac Books.

Neumann, Erich (1959; 1974) *Art and the Creative Unconscious: Four Essays*, Princeton, NJ: Princeton University Press.

Neumann, Erich (2002) *The Child: Structure and Dynamics of the Nascent Personality*, London: Karnac Books.

NRSV (New Revised Standard Version) (1995) *The Holy Bible with Apocrypha: Anglicized Edition*, Oxford, UK: Oxford University Press.

Nünning, V., Rupp, J. and Ahn, G. (2013) *Ritual and Narrative: Theoretical Explorations and Historical Case Studies*, Berlin: Transcript Verlag.

Penley, Constance (1988) *Feminism and Film Theory*, London and New York: Routledge.

Philipson, Morris (1963) *An Outline of Jungian Aesthetics*, Boston, MA: Sigo Press.

Radin, Paul (1956; 1972) *The Trickster: A Study in American Indian Mythology*, New York: Schocken Books.

Rich, Katey (2015) '*Mad Max: Fury Road* Director George Miller: "I Can't Help but Be a Feminist"', *Vanity Fair*, 14 May.

Ronnberg, Ami (ed. in chief) and Martin, K. (ed.) (2010) *The Book of Symbols: Reflections on Archetypal Images*, Cologne: Taschen.

Rosen, P. (ed.) (1986) *Narrative, Apparatus, Ideology: A Film Theory Reader*, New York: Columbia University Press.

Rowland, Susan (2011) 'The Nature of Adaptation: Myth and the Feminine Gaze in Ang Lee's *Sense and Sensibility*', in Christopher Hauke and Luke Hockley (eds), *Jung and Film II: The Return*, London: Routledge, pp. 148–163.

Runcie, Charlotte (2014) '*Game of Thrones*: Nowhere Else on TV Do You Get Women This Good', *The Telegraph*, 15 April.

Salter, Jessica (2013) 'Game of Thrones: Interview with George RR Martin', *The Telegraph*, 25 March.

Salter, Jessica (2013) '*Game of Thrones*'s George RR Martin: "I'm a Feminist at Heart"', *The Telegraph*, 1 April.

Samuels, Andrew (1985) *Jung and the Post-Jungians*, London: Routledge.

Samuels, Andrew (1993) *The Political Psyche*, London: Routledge.

Samuels, Andrew (2001) *Politics on the Couch: Citizenship and the Internal Life*, London: Karnac Books.

Samuels, Andrew (2015) *Passions, Persons, Psychotherapy, Politics: The Selected Works of Andrew Samuels*, London: Routledge.

Sarris, Andrew (1968) *The American Cinema: Directors and Directions 1929–1968*, London: Da Capo Press.

Segrave, Kerry (1997) *American Films Abroad: Hollywood's Domination of the World's Movie Screens*, Jefferson, NC: McFarland.

Shaviro, Steven (1993) *The Cinematic Body*, Minneapolis, MN: University of Minnesota Press.

Shoard, Catherine (2015) 'Charlize Theron on Mad Max: "We Live in a Very Toxic World"', *The Guardian*, 14 May.

Silver, Alain and Ursini, James (eds) (1999) *Film Noir Reader*, New York: Limelight Editions.

Silverman, Kaja (1988) *The Acoustic Mirror: The Female Voice in Psychoanalysis and Cinema*, Bloomington, IN: Indiana University Press.

Singh, G. (2014a) 'Recognition and the Image of Mastery as Themes in *Black Mirror* (Channel 4, 2011–present): An Eco-Jungian Approach to "Always-on" Culture', *International Journal of Jungian Studies*, 6, 2: 120–132.

Singh, G. (2014b) *Feeling Film: Affect and Authenticity in Popular Cinema*. Hove, UK: Routledge.

Skal, David (1993) *The Monster Show: A Cultural History of Horror*, London: Plexus.

Sobchack, Vivian (1992) *The Address of the Eye: A Phenomenology of Film Experience*, Princeton, NJ: Princeton University Press.

Sobchack, Vivian (2004) *Carnal Thoughts: Embodiment and Moving Image Culture*, Berkeley, CA: University of California Press.

Stam, Robert (2000) 'Introduction', in Robert Stam and Toby Miller (eds), *Film and Theory: An Anthology*, London: Blackwell, pp. 1–6.

Stam, Robert and Flitterman-Lewis, Burgoyne (1992) *New Vocabularies in Film Semiotics: Structuralism, Post-Structuralism and Beyond*, London: Routledge.

Stam, Robert and Miller, Toby (eds) (2000) *Film and Theory: An Anthology*, London: Blackwell.

Stevens, Anthony (1990) *On Jung*, London: Routledge.

Strachey, J. (ed. and trans.) (1960; 2001) *The Standard Edition of the Complete Psychological Works of Sigmund Freud*, London: Vintage.

Tannen, Ricki Stefanie (2007) *The Female Trickster: The Mask That Reveals*, London: Routledge.

Tarkovsky, Andrey (2008) *Sculpting in Time: Reflections on the Cinema*, Austin, TX: University of Texas Press.

Tomashevsky, B. (1925) *Teoriya literatury. Poetika*, Moscow and Leningrad: Krug. [Reprint: Letchworth, 1971].

Turner, Victor (1969; 2009) *The Ritual Process*, New Brunswick, NJ and London: Aldine Transaction.

Turner, Victor (1974) *Dramas, Fields, and Metaphors: Symbolic Action in Human Society*, Ithaca, NY: Cornell University Press.

Turner, Victor (1975) *Revelation and Divination in Ndemby Ritual*, Ithaca, NY: Cornell University Press.

Turner, Victor (1979) *Process, Performance and Pilgrimage*, New Delhi: Naurang Rai.

Turner, Victor (1992) *Blazing the Trail: Way Marks in the Exploration of Symbols*, Tucson, AZ and London: The University of Arizona Press.

Van Gennep, Arnold (1909; 2004) *The Rites of Passage*, London: Routledge.

Vogler, Christopher (1998; 2007) *The Writer's Journey: Mythic Structure for Writers*, London: Pan.

Von Franz, Marie-Louise (1964) 'The Process of Individuation', in Carl Gustav Jung and Marie-Louise von Franz (eds), *Man and His Symbols*, London: Picador, pp. 159–254.
Von Franz, Marie-Louise (1970; 1973) *An Introduction to the Interpretation of Fairytales*, Zurich: Spring Publications.
Waddell, Terrie (2006) *Mis/takes: Archetype, Myth and Identity in Screen Fiction*, Hove, UK and New York: Routledge.
Waddell, Terrie (2009) *Wild/Lives: Trickster, Place and Liminality on Screen*, Hove, UK: Routledge.
Walker, Stephen F. (2002) *Jung and the Jungians on Myth*, New York and Hove, UK: Routledge.
Welsford, Enid (1936) *The Fool: His Social and Literary History*, London: Faber and Faber.
Willeford, William (1969) *The Fool and His Sceptre: A Study in Clowns and Jesters and Their Audience*, Evanston, IL: Northwestern University Press.
Wright, Basil (1948) *The Use of the Film*, Oxford: Bodley Head.
Wright, Basil (1976) *The Long View: An International History of Cinema*, London: Paladin.
Wright, Will (1977) *Six-Guns and Society: A Structural Study*, Berkeley, CA: University of California Press.
Wu, Cheng'en (1590; 1993) *Journey to the West*, Beijing: Foreign Languages Press.
Young-Eisendrath, Polly and Dawson, Terence (eds) (1997) *The Cambridge Companion to Jung*, Cambridge, UK: Cambridge University Press.

Television programmes

BBC Newsnight, 1 November 2011.

List of names

Index